MW01688040

FIND YOUR NEXT PROFESSIONAL JOB

Tamara Pinkas & Scott Weighart

FIND YOUR NEXT PROFESSIONAL JOB

First Edition

ISBN 978-0-9621264-8-2

Printed in the United States of America

TAMARA'S DEDICATION

It is with profound respect that I honor my mentors Nan Poppe, Bob Way and Andrea Newton. Through them I learned how to be a professional, that it is better to ask forgiveness than permission and what a joy a community of colleagues can be.

TAMARA'S ACKNOWLEDGEMENTS

My dream of someday writing a cooperative education textbook specifically for community college students became real after meeting Scott Weighart, the author of *Find Your First Professional Job*, at a Cooperative Education and Internship Association conference a few years ago. I am deeply grateful to Scott who welcomed the opportunity to collaborate with me on a community college version of his book and thank him for his vision, confidence, and patience.

I am indebted to Lane Community College's Faculty Professional Development for granting me a one-term sabbatical which provided me with time away from teaching to meet with Scott, interview faculty and students and write.

Sincere and deepest thanks go to my dear friend, colleague and technical adviser Jim Bailey for his support and advice as well as for connecting me with one of his successful students Katie Van Meter whose insights are included in this book. Many thanks to my Lane Community College colleagues Chuck Fike, Jean Harcleroad, Jamie Kelsch, Gary Oldham, Joe McCully, Margaret Robertson and Merrill Watrous who all contributed their thoughts and comments for the book. Additional thanks to colleague Teresa Hughes whose student McKenzie Baldwin allowed us to include his experiences. I offer my genuine appreciation to past and present Lane colleagues Joe Freeman, Carol Woodman, Al King, Phoebe Anderson and Marv Clemons. I am especially thankful to all of my students, from whom I have learned so much, especially Alan Ayers, Jord Nelsen, and Matt Ray for their thoughtful comments and stories which have been included.

I'd also like to recognize the artistry of Connie Huston who created the book's black and white illustrations and Steve Kuhn, our talented book designer. And finally, I give my thanks to my sister Debora and son Aaron for their love and support during the creation of this book as well as in memory of my parents Leo and Evelyn Pinkas.

SCOTT'S DEDICATION

I dedicate this book to Charlie Bognanni and Nancy Johnston for their many years of support, friendship, and inspiration, professionally and personally.

SCOTT'S ACKNOWLEDGEMENTS

First and foremost, I am so grateful to Tamara Pinkas for her vision in seeing how my *Find Your First Professional Job* book could be transformed to meet the needs of community college students. This book would not exist without her persistence and drive to make it happen, and she taught me so much about what would resonate with this audience.

From my days at Northeastern University, I would like to thank Charlie Bognanni, Susan Bacher, Danielle Dicoscia, Erin Doyon, Theresa Harrigan, Deb Hunt, Mary Jane Miller, Bill Munze, and Bill Sloane for their years of unwavering support and friendship. Nancy Johnston of Simon Fraser University continues to inspire my understanding of experiential learning and has become a trusted friend as well. I'm also grateful to Vicki Arico for her many years of work in designing book covers, including this one. Thanks to all other contributors to this book, particularly Linnea Basu. And, thanks to Melissa Morse for her excellent 11th-hour efforts in copyediting this book.

Most of all, thanks to my wife, Ellie, who has really done the heavy lifting for years when it comes to the logistics of making the many versions of this book into a reality—an ever-evolving one!

Contents

Introduction

Being successful in your next professional job is not magic: It requires a positive attitude and the willingness to keep taking small steps toward self-improvement in your career. Whether you are planning for your first co-op or internship job or changing careers, this guide book was written to show you exactly what separates the extraordinary new professional from those who are ordinary or mediocre. Follow these steps carefully, and you can transform yourself into a great job candidate and performer…a little at a time.

Find Your Next Professional Job was written to be a key resource for community college students, from first time job seekers to experienced workers, who are gaining skills for a new career. Thousands of students have used the reliable and time-tested information offered in earlier versions of this book to successfully update their resumes, interview with confidence and deal with multiple job offers. The aim of this guidebook is to provide useful support to co-ops, interns, and job seekers in all majors.

Colleges across the country are embracing multiple forms of practice-oriented education, including co-op, internships, practicum assignments, volunteer work/community service learning, work abroad, and clinical rotations to name a few. The rising cost of higher education has students asking "What return will I get on my investment in higher education?" As a result, schools ranging from small community colleges to big-name Ivy League institutions are offering students more opportunities to get real-world experience.

In addition, how people find jobs, especially in difficult economic times, has changed. Gone are the days when all it took to get a job was to show up at the gate of the local manufacturing plant, go to the union hall or get a referral from the state employment department. In our current world co-ops, internships, and practicums are often the best and only way to get a foot in the door.

You, the 21st century student, now have the opportunity to work in your field through co-ops and internships, giving you a chance to test a career, build a resume and references, make connections between the classroom and the real world, create connections with post-graduation employers and–often but not always–earn money.

While this represents a great opportunity, it also creates challenges for students. Some of these challenges relate to planning your co-op or internship. What can you do right now to increase your chances of getting the best possible internship? How will the job market affect your co-op options? The first chapter of this guidebook, "Planning For Your Next Professional Job," tackles these questions.

Other challenges arise during the preparations stage—the weeks and months immediately preceding your co-op job, internship or other work-related endeavor. How can you write an effective resume when you don't have related work experience, just skills gained in school course work? What should you include and emphasize on your resume and what is best to leave off? How can you overcome your jitters about interviewing and present yourself positively but honestly? How can you deal with fuzzy open-ended questions that may be asked? What do you do if you get an offer from Company A when you're waiting for Company B to get back to you? Chapter 2 ("Writing An Effective Resume") and Chapter 3 ("Strategic Interviewing") of the guidebook cover this terrain and much more.

Once you have lined up your work experience, the real work begins. What is at stake when you are working as a co-op? How can you live up to your interview and make the most of your co-op opportunity? How can you balance a part-time internship with full-time classes? What should you do if problems arise? How can you get the best possible evaluation and reference? Chapter 4 reviews "Keys To On-The-Job Success" in handling these concerns among others. Plus, this edition features comprehensive information on e-mail and IM etiquette, as these forms of communication have become more critical in today's workplaces.

You also may wonder about how to make sense out of what happened during your co-op or internship. What might you need to do to get credit for your work experience? What are some options to consider as you process the experience? Chapter 5 goes over "Making Sense Of Your Experience" and considers the reflection steps that are required at different educational institutions.

The appendices include many other materials that are useful to co-op students and that co-op professionals may want to incorporate into their courses. Appendix A explains the Co-op/Internship process in detail with great recommendations for working with college systems. Appendix B features our Skills Identification Worksheet. This is a useful confidence builder for many first-time job seekers who have a hard time believing that they actually already have many soft skills that are attractive to employers. Appendix C covers how to write effective cover letters, whether you are looking for a co-op job or pursuing a full-time job after graduation. Appendix D is a list of additional interview questions we recommend you use when practicing for a co-op job interview.

Appendix E is a brief "bridging" exercise, geared to help you make connections between your resume and actual job descriptions. Appendix F covers behavior-based interviewing, which is an increasingly common feature of employer interviews. In this appendix, you will learn how to develop impressive stories for behavioral-based interviews and also how to use these stories in a conventional interview. New to this book edition is Appendix G which is a resume evaluation guide called a rubric. You can easily use this rubric to see if your resume is as exemplary as you think it is with tips for making it the best it can be.

This book has been through numerous editions and the content has been used by thousands of students around the United States, including Northeastern University and Case Western Reserve University as well as LaGuardia Community College in New York City and Lane Community College in Eugene, Oregon. As such the material is tested by experience—just as you will be as you go through your next professional job experiences. While this is certainly serious business, we have tried to write the book in a light conversational way, including many real-life anecdotes and quotes to make the book as fun to read as it is informative. It's really exciting for us to have the voices of some of our best co-op students included in the guidebook. You'll find these thoughtful perspectives in sidebar boxes.

Here's an example.

A STUDENT'S PERSPECTIVE ON THIS GUIDEBOOK

By Keith Laughman

The co-op guidebook is a student's Bible to landing that great job during co-op semesters and even upon graduation. It's the only book that I've used for all five years of college! The information contained in this guidebook may be overwhelming at first, but believe me when I say that it will greatly influence your resume skills, interview skills, and job searching skills.

***Keith Laughman** was an MIS/Marketing student at Northeastern University, Class of 2002*

This guidebook includes the perspectives of experienced co-op faculty from Lane Community College, LaGuardia Community College, Lone Star College-Tomball, and Northeastern University. In addition, insightful comments from employers offer advice useful to students everywhere. You might be surprised at how much a student in any major can learn by reading and reflecting on the recommendations from various perspectives. There is a considerable amount of wisdom in this field that proves to be universal.

Like most aspects of being a new professional in the workplace, what you get out of this guidebook will depend heavily on the amount of effort you spend in truly understanding the material that we present to you here. If you just skim through the chapters, you will find that this text is no more useful than giving a menu to starving man.

If, however, you really put some energy into thinking about how this material applies to you and incorporating these concepts into how you approach resume writing, interviewing, and your actual co-op job, you will find that these principles will help you in your career long after you have graduated.

We hope that this book inspires you and helps you gain confidence as you approach your co-op job, internship, clinical experience, practicum or full-time job after graduation. Good luck in your preparation activities and in all of your efforts to professionalize yourself in the weeks and months to come. You might just amaze yourself with the results!

Tamara Pinkas and Scott Weighart
March 2012

CHAPTER ONE

Planning For Your Next Professional Job

Whether you opt for a co-op or internship, a clinical assignment or simply your next full-time job after graduation, you have a great deal at stake. Many students realize how important some form of practical job experience is these days, yet not all students really understand everything that they're going to get out of the experience. Additionally, many students fail to realize that there is a great deal that can be done to get ready for a co-op or internship—even if this experience is months and months away.

This chapter is intended to get you thinking about your next work-based learning experience now so you will have a better understanding of the benefits of getting practical experience and what you can do to give yourself a head start on the process.

BENEFITS OF PROFESSIONAL EXPERIENCE

For all college students getting real-world experience, there are still many common themes when we consider the benefits of doing a co-op job, internship, clinical assignment, or practicum before graduation.

Career Testing

Getting practical work experience as part of your academic preparation helps you determine whether you are on the right career path. It's one thing to be in a finance class for three or four hours per week: It's a whole different ballgame to do a finance job for hours on end amidst all the complexities of a corporate environment. You really wouldn't want to devote your time and energy to learning an occupation only to find out six months into your first job in your new career that you actually dislike working in that field as a full-time professional. What do you do then? Go back to school?

Occasionally one of our students will experience the following scenario: John Schlobotnik goes to see his co-op coordinator during his first co-op job experience in accounting (or psychology or physical therapy or any other major). The co-op coordinator welcomes John and asks how the job is going. "What are you learning on your job, John?" John looks at the ground, and sheepishly says, "Uhhh, I think I learned that I don't want to be in accounting."

It's almost as if John thinks that his co-op coordinator will criticize or condemn him for such thinking! Hardly. We remind the student that this is a primary purpose of internships and co-ops, and then we can begin a dialogue about what other concentration or major may be more appropriate.

Scott has worked with a few physical therapy students who absolutely loved the subject in the classroom. During their first field experience, however, a few found out that they felt amazingly uncomfortable having to touch people in their role as a physical therapist in training. For most, this was a startling and upsetting realization—but also an absolutely critical discovery that led them to make a necessary change in their career plans.

CAREER TESTING – A CO-OP PROFESSIONAL'S PERSPECTIVE

by Chuck Fike

Doing a co-op can really help a student decide if a career is right for them. I had a student who wanted to be in the veterinary field thinking there would be a lot of cuddly, fuzzy, positive interactions with animals. After being on the job for a couple of weeks, the student learned that the job had blood, animals crying in pain, animals that didn't make it plus all the worried and grieving pet owners. This experience made the student realize there was a whole other side to the career choice she was making and allowed her to see the big picture, not just the idealized job she had created in her mind.

Chuck Fike, *faculty Cooperative Education Coordinator in Career Skills at Lane Community College*

Experience Building

You may not begin your first internship or co-op with much directly relevant job experience on your resume. However, you will mostly likely find that after completing even one term of co-op or internship, you will have gained both skill and confidence. Depending upon your career field and the opportunities at your college, you may have the chance to obtain a significant amount of experience before you graduate.

If you began college with a very clear sense of your career goals—and if your real-world experience through your co-op confirms those goals for you—you may be able to graduate with a great deal of experience. For example, Tamara works with drafting students at Lane Community College. Student A takes the appropriate courses during her first year of college and chooses to do a co-op in the summer. During this first term, she primarily corrects existing drawings for a mechanical engineer, thus helping her hone her computer skills and learn about the company products. If she finds this co-op a good fit and her work site wants to keep her, she may continue doing co-op every term during her second year of school where her duties diversify and increase into preparing shop drawings, bills of material, being a liaison with the shop floor and contributing to the product design team. She will graduate with over a year of part-time experience with one company and a well developed understanding of mechanical drafting to add to her resume.

Meanwhile, Student B doesn't really know what type of drafting he wants to do. Maybe he starts out with that same mechanical drafting job but finds the tasks too repetitive. The next term he accepts a second co-op doing architectural-related drafting but finds it frustrating to deal with the designers who keep changing their minds. The following term, for his third co-op, he is connected with a machine job shop where he regularly draws new and different parts and also learns to program the wire electric discharge machine to cut highly precise parts. This student graduates with greater breadth of experience. He does not have the depth of experience as student A; however, he may have more options available to him now and more doors open to him later. So there are positives either way.

Additionally, any professional experience that you obtain will do more than improve your technical skills in a given field—the experience will provide you with great opportunities to professionalize yourself. While most students come into internships and co-ops focusing on what technical skills they may be able to acquire, many come away from their co-op rather surprised at how much they learn about working that has nothing to do with learning technical skills and responsibilities. Every workplace has its own written and unwritten rules about performance and behavior. Organizational politics can have a dramatic impact on your ability to function effectively in a position. Supervisors can vary dramatically in terms of their managerial skills, expectations, and pet peeves. Developing the adaptability to handle different work environments and to obtain great evaluations in situations that require radically different behavior can be a big challenge. Learning the changing rules of the game and making sure that you succeed regardless of varying expectations is a characteristic of the best future professionals.

Most students—especially those working full-time hours in their work experience—find that they feel more confident about their professionalism after each

CONFIRMING CAREER PLANS AT LAGUARDIA COMMUNITY COLLEGE

by Marie Sacino

An internship can provide an opportunity to discover your passion, to make a solid contribution to your employer, and to grow. Zoe Cornielle, a liberal arts student in our social science and humanities curriculum, explored her interest in the field of social work during her first internship at the Hospital for Special Surgery. Zoe was assigned to work in the Department of Patient Care and Quality Management. Under the supervision of a program coordinator and a managed care associate, Zoe worked as part of a health care team to provide education, advocacy, and assistance to outpatients in both rheumatology and orthopedic clinics.

With training, support and supervision from social work professionals, Zoe began to provide outreach services to patients in various patient waiting areas. Zoe listened to patients' concerns and questions, provided information on education and support groups, made referrals to community based agencies, and kept records of patient activity.

On my visit to HSS, I got a first-hand opportunity to see Zoe at work. I was so impressed by her professionalism, her ability to engage patients, her understanding and sensitivity of the impact of barriers to health care as well as her dedication to the patients with whom she worked. HSS was also quite impressed: Zoe was invited back for her second full-time internship this past summer. She discovered her passion—helping people—and confirmed her career plans: social work. Zoe expanded her role greatly as she took on the new role of "first" lead volunteer. She had an opportunity to participate in developing training materials and in leading group discussions. Zoe also provided support and supervision to new interns and trainees as they began to work with patients. She eventually transferred to Hunter College to pursue a degree in social work.

Marie Sacino *is an Associate Professor of Cooperative Education at LaGuardia Community College* job experience. The discipline required to make it to work on time every day and to get your work done well and on time seems to develop good habits that become more automatic over time in most cases. It's often exciting for a co-op or internship coordinator to see a student after one job experience: Both of us are often amazed to see big changes in professional etiquette when these students return to our offices and interact with us. Frequently, going to work in a professional setting helps you develop a greater sense of purpose both in the classroom and in your professional relationships.

Building a Great Resume and Getting Valuable References

If you're building your experience, then you obviously are also building an impressive resume detailing all of that experience. Just as importantly, if you perform well, you can end up with a long list of respected professionals who will recommend you to future employers. Developing a network of people who are able and willing to assist your future job searches can make a big difference—many jobs are filled through personal connections rather than simply pulling in a bunch of anonymous candidates through online advertisements on LinkedIn, Monster, or www.craigslist.com.

Enjoying a Trial Period with Potential Full-Time Employers

Many organizations who hire students for co-op jobs, internships, and other forms of practice-oriented learning are looking for more than a person to do a job for three to six months—they are using the co-op period to "test out" someone that they may or may not wish to make a job offer to upon graduation.

As one Fortune 500 co-op employer told Scott: "If we hire ten co-op students, we figure that at least nine of them will work out well and get productive work done in a cost-effective manner. If three of those nine are such stars that we want to hire them after graduation, then that's really the ultimate goal for us. After all, at our company, we can't just fire someone—we have to coach them to death!"

Indeed, this organization doesn't allow managers to fire employees who are clearly poor performers. Instead, the manager must hold regular "coaching meetings" and document them heavily. In the end, the employee still ends up being terminated. As you might imagine, this employer really doesn't want to hire the wrong people—that's a mistake that costs thousands of dollars in addition to causing numerous headaches! Hiring co-ops helps them know what they're getting and makes it less likely that they will have to go down that costly and time-consuming path with a wayward employee.

Integrating Classroom Learning with Workplace

Certainly one of the greatest payoffs for students who immerse themselves in a relevant real-world setting is the opportunity to make meaningful connections between theory and practice. Better still, it's a two-way street: Concepts that are hard to really understand in the classroom can come alive for you when you see how they apply to real-world situations. At other times, you will learn how to do something while on co-op but perhaps not really understand the underlying concepts until you learn about them in a class after completing your work experience.

Better still, co-op, clinicals, and internships can bring home the importance of classroom concepts, sometimes in dramatic and unexpected ways. Students who don't get meaningful, career-related job experiences sometimes have a harder time believing that some required courses are all that important. Even if you have a gifted professor, it may be hard for a student to believe that coursework in finance or accounting has any relevance to them if they "know" that their future is in MIS or Human Resources.

Getting that professional experience as an undergrad can reveal that this way of thinking is an illusion. One of Scott's students who completed a PC support position with senior management at The Gillette Company had to provide computer and audiovisual assistance to some of the most powerful people in the organization. His coursework in accounting took on a newfound urgency for him as he ended up assisting during several heavy number-crunching meetings, in which the executives spoke with great passion about balance sheets, income statements, and other concepts that the student had found only mildly interesting before the job began.

Tamara frequently has drafting students who favor mechanical or architectural drafting and comment that they just don't see any reason to take the required drafting courses outside their desired area. Quite frequently, these same students contact her a year or two later, thankful that they were well prepared for both types of drafting because it helped them land a great professional job.

Coursework outside of your major also can have a dramatic impact on your career, and vice-versa. One of the biggest mistakes students make when picking electives is to just pick something that sounds relatively painless without considering the possible benefits of liberal arts courses. A marketing student might be well advised to take a communications course that helps build public speaking skills; a civil engineering student with lofty aspirations might be wise to take classes in corporate finance. Scott knew a student who felt that her self-confidence and interpersonal skills improved dramatically by taking a class in acting.

In the community college setting, many two-year degrees include few if any electives outside the discipline. If this is true for you, we still encourage you to find a way to add an extra class or two if at all possible. Recently Tamara has had several drafting students take the introductory GIS (Geographic Information Science) course in addition to their required drafting classes. All of them beat out other candidates for jobs—even though GIS skills were not required for their co-op jobs. Their hiring supervisors were impressed with the added skills they gained as well as their ability to take on extra coursework.

One of the funniest stories along these lines came from one of Scott's students who absolutely had to add a social science course to meet a liberal arts requirement for business students. He signed up for Introduction to Psychological Counseling, basically because the class hadn't filled up yet and it fit the requirement. When his next co-op ended up being a PC support job, he couldn't believe his dumb luck: He was shocked to find himself using techniques he had learned in class—such as active listening—when trying to calm down and help computer users who were frequently angry, embittered, and impatient due to their PC problems. You just never know what coursework might eventually prove to be valuable!

Earning Money (including Part-Time Work)

While co-op or internship earnings will not pay all the costs of education for most students, they can make a nice dent in your expenses. Many internships are unpaid, but some offer stipends or at least modest salaries. How much money you make will depend mainly on your field and your experience. For example, even an outstanding intern in early childhood education will make much less than the average student in accounting, engineering, or computer science. Also, it makes sense that a multimedia student with no job experience and little coursework in the field will have much less earning power than a second-year student with classroom knowledge and co-op experience. As for part-time internships, it makes sense that someone doing a computer-related job is more likely to get a paid position than someone who wants to work in an aquarium, a TV station, or a social service agency.

Your earnings as a co-op or intern also can be affected heavily by your flexibility. Having a car obviously will open up numerous opportunities for you versus the student who is stuck on public transportation. While this is true in all fields, it can be especially dramatic for some majors depending on where they are seeking a job. For welding/fabrication students at Lane, most of the good quality jobs are not incredibly far away with a car—but they are almost completely inaccessible by public transportation.

Other factors affecting earnings may include the economy, your grades, the time of year that you choose to work, your effort in the job search (including effort in teaching yourself relevant skills), and soft skills such as communication skills, interpersonal skills, and attitude.

Return on Your Investment in Education

Above all, real-world experience gives you a chance to get a nice return on the investment of time, money, and energy that you have put into your collegiate career. Studies have shown that full-time co-op students get a nice head start in terms of post-graduate earnings and quality of job opportunities. The more you strive to accomplish, the bigger the payoff at the end.

GETTING READY FOR A FUTURE REAL-WORLD EXPERIENCE

Maybe your first or next professional job experience is still a long way off. For some people reading this book, their first clinical or co-op or internship may be more than a year away. That's a long time, and there's no point in beginning a job search when your availability is in the distant future. Still, there are plenty of things that you can do right now to improve your chances of getting a better job when the time comes. But first, it's important to understand a critical question: What do employers want when they are looking to hire an intern, co-op candidate, or even a full-time hire coming right of college?

Common Fears

In addition to being excited about beginning work, many students experience a good degree of fear and anxiety about finding a professional job, whether it's a co-op, internship, practicum, or full-time role after completing their two-year degree. This is natural: Most students recognize the value and importance of practical experience but begin the program with limited knowledge about the job market and the job search process as well as significant concerns about their lack of work experience in the field and beginning a new career.

Very frequently, students meeting with their career educator for the first time express concerns about what their next job may hold: "No one will ever want to hire me—I have absolutely no related experience!" Believe me, we hear that one often. Students also worry about the negative impact of poor grades, lack of a car, a sagging economy, and competition from other (presumably better) candidates.

The first thing to remember is that we want you to limit your fears and concerns to the things that you can control. You can worry about the economy, the job market, and how good other job candidates are—but in the end, worrying about these things won't change them at all.

Fortunately, there are quite a few things that you can control. You also may have more going for you than you realize, as you'll soon see.

What Are Employers Seeking When Hiring Co-ops and Interns?

Amazingly, both Scott and Tamara began their careers as co-op coordinators in similar ways. Upon advice from experienced colleagues, we first began our jobs by going out and meeting as many employers as possible in order to understand the needs of our programs. It was great advice, and it yielded surprising information. We thought we knew what employers were seeking when they hired co-op students: job specific skills, naturally! We expected employers to list skills such as software experience, equipment operations, or how to take blood pressure: "Well, we want someone who can use Novell NetWare and who knows Visual Basic or another programming language…."

We did hear some employers say those kinds of things—but only about one-third of the time. Two times out of three, the manager would say something like

HIRING CO-OP STUDENTS – AN EMPLOYER'S PERSPECTIVE

by Mike Naclerio

Energy and passion: You can teach a student or an employee the skills that are necessary for a position, but you cannot teach someone dedication and enthusiasm. If you build an organization based on quality people, you will get quality results.

***Mike Naclerio** is the Director of Relationship Management at the workplace HELPLINE*

this: "Technical skills and experience are great—the more the better. But more than anything, we want someone who wants to be here every day, someone who thinks it's fun to learn new things, a hard worker who communicates well and gets along with people.... Someone who can work independently and show initiative but also work in a team... Someone who doesn't complain and moan and whine when something has to be done that's a little less fun. We'd much rather have a student who is weak on technical skills and strong in terms of these other qualities than to have it the other way around."

After hearing this several times, Scott asked a few managers to explain why they felt this way. "In six months, I can teach someone a lot about UNIX or Windows NT, assuming that they're smart and motivated," a manager said. "But I can't teach a person to want to come in to work every day."

Another manager flipped it around the other way. "If you haven't learned how to take pride in what you do, how to respect other people, and have a positive attitude in the first 18 years of your life," she mused, "then how am I going to change all of that in just six months?!"

Even Microsoft—an employer that obviously features an extremely technical environment—basically follows this rule. Look at the sidebar box on this page, and consider the emphasis.

For most students, this is extremely encouraging news: Students who want to be in a practice-oriented program requiring work generally have a strong work ethic. Most students we've met have at least some of those desirable soft skills. We have found—just as those managers had told us—that it is indeed very hard to change who a person is as opposed to changing their skill set.

Of course, there are a few catches here. If possible, most typical managers would prefer to hire someone who has the soft skills AND some relevant technical

HIRING CO-OPS AND INTERNS – AN EMPLOYER'S PERSPECTIVE

by Steve Sim

From a Microsoft perspective, it's difficult to specify anything in particular, but we look for the core competencies we wish all MS employees to possess:

- Passion for Technology
- Big Bold Goal Mentality
- Honest and Self-Critical
- Accountability
- Intelligence
- Team & Individual Achievement

***Steve Sim** was a Technical Recruiter at the Microsoft Corporation*

skills—especially in a tough economy in which jobs are less plentiful. An inexperienced student who is a great person will not get a position if they're competing with great people who also have experience. Additionally, can't any con artist walk into an interview and claim to have a great attitude, excellent ability to work independently, and a terrific work ethic?? Possibly. But there are steps you can take to change your skill set NOW that will serve the double-dip benefit of helping to prove that you really have those soft skills. Let's consider those next.

Ways to Improve Your Marketability

This has to be one of the most underutilized steps that you can take, and there's nothing to keep you from starting to do this right away—even if your next job search is not on the immediate horizon. Here's the key: start devoting some time toward improving your knowledge and skills related to your field. A criminal justice student could go out and do informational interviews with professionals in law enforcement and security. A veterinary science student would gain valuable experience and demonstrate a great deal about her interest in her field by volunteering at an animal shelter. For a finance student, this could mean reading The *Wall Street Journal* or *Smart Money* or any number of other periodicals or books that will help you understand stocks and bonds, mutual funds, investment philosophy, and concepts such as risk versus reward and the present value versus the future value of money. Entering a stock-buying competition would be another good idea. Just about any information technology student (whether majoring in computer science, engineering, or business) would benefit by picking up computer skills on their own—whether through using online tutorials, reading books such as HTML for Dummies, or attending on-campus workshops on specific computer skills.

Several years ago, Scott worked with a student who had earned about five computer certifications on her own. This absolutely raised the eyebrows of potential employers, and she managed to get her first internship at Microsoft. As a paid hobby of sorts, Scott writes for www.uscho.com, also known as US College Hockey Online. Whenever he meets someone who is interested in building a career in sports management, he urges them to start on that path immediately by writing for an online sports publication such as USCHO, blogging, getting involved with the student newspaper, becoming a team manager, and so forth. Likewise, there are online blogs that often will pay a modest amount of money for people who will write about any number of areas of interest. A good resource to learn about such jobs is: http://www.online-writing-jobs.com/

IMPROVING YOUR MARKETABILITY – AN EMPLOYER'S PERSPECTIVE

by Joe McCully

The best way to improve your marketability, especially if you don't have any paid work experience in your field, is to volunteer for community events that give you relevant experience. In the culinary field, there are many opportunities to help out like working at the local food bank or Thanksgiving dinner for the homeless. If I'm considering two candidates who seem about equal, I'll give preference to the one who worked in the community… It shows his or her character and that's the kind of person I want to have working for me.

***Joe McCully** owned McCully's Rooftop Restaurant for 17 years and is currently faculty Cooperative Education Coordinator in Culinary at Lane Community College*

Making Connections with Professional Associations

Joining a professional association in your field is another way to make yourself more marketable… but that's not the only reason to do so. If you attend professional association meetings and events, you'll have an opportunity to rub shoulders with professionals in your field. This is a great way to do some networking that eventually could lead to an interview, a co-op job, an internship, or even a full-time job after graduation. Also, your conversation with these professionals can be informal informational interviews: What do professionals in your field actually do? What do they like most and least about their jobs? This may help you figure out if you're in the right field or not.

Another great thing to know is that while some professional associations can be expensive to join, they may offer substantially discounted student membership rates. For example, as of April 2010, the Council of Supply Chain Management Professionals (SCSMP) charged professionals $295 for an annual membership, but students only had to pay $35 to join and have the opportunity to receive career-related newsletters, attend conferences at reduced rates, and many other benefits. Ask your co-op, internship, or career services coordinator—or an academic faculty member—for information about professional associations in your field and whether they would be worthwhile for you.

UTILIZING ON-CAMPUS RESOURCES – A CO-OP PROFESSIONAL'S PERSPECTIVE

By Chuck Fike

I tell students that they would be amazed at what is available to them here on campus. For students who want to do career research on their own, I send them to our library, which has a great collection of career materials. I also send them to our Career and Employment Services center that offers free help researching careers, free employment services and some free or low-cost tests that can help students get lists of possible careers that fit their preferences and values. I encourage students to take a credit career life planning class if they don't really know what they want to do and want some guidance. And, once they've picked a career, they can talk with the faculty co-op coordinator in that field who has current information about co-op and employment opportunities.

***Chuck Fike** is a faculty Cooperative Education Coordinator in Career Skills at Lane Community College*

Making the Most of All On-Campus Resources

Most colleges have tons of student resources, whether or not you take advantage of them. Most community colleges have Departments of Career Services—featuring numerous resources that you may find valuable. You can research jobs in different fields, take tests that help you build self-awareness about how you might match up with different careers, and perhaps even have a practice interview videotaped and critiqued. In particular, you may want to look into whether a campus professional can administer the Myers-Briggs Type Indicator, Myers-Briggs Career Report, the Campbell Interest and Skill Survey, or the Strong Interest Inventory. The Myers-Briggs tests are often useful in understanding your personality, which can translate into a better sense of what elements you should seek in a job. The various interest inventories are great for seeing how your preferences and dislikes match up with professionals who are happy and successful in a great variety of fields.

As you can see in the sidebar on this page, your college or public library is a good source for information relating to different fields, careers, and organizations.

Most community colleges also have counseling centers—good places to go if personal problems are causing you difficulties, whether school, job-related or otherwise. Another little-known fact is that many counseling centers can also help with issues such as time management and test-taking anxiety.

Taking Advantage of Online Resources

Even if you aren't able or willing to get assistance from professionals on campus, there are some online options that may prove helpful. If you Google terms such as "Myers-Briggs" or "Campbell Interest Inventory," you'll get links to sites that offer online testing for a fee. Some sites offer free testing as well—try Googling "Free Myers-Briggs test," for example—but you may be surprised to fill out a 70-item test and then be told very little... unless you THEN shell out some amount of money.

Taking Career-Related Courses

Increasingly, many colleges are offering and even requiring career-related courses. Some—such as the excellent Gateway To The Workplace course at LaGuardia Community College in New York—are mandatory prerequisites to obtaining an internship or co-op job through the program. Given that these courses are often one-credit, pass-fail courses, some students might be tempted to go through the motions in these courses, doing just enough to get by. However, that would be a missed opportunity. These classes give you a chance to get questions answered, undergo some career counseling, learn the fundamentals of resume writing and interviewing, and start to understand the logistics of how the co-op process works for you. It also can help you develop a good relationship with a co-op coordinator who can be a resource for you during all of your college years.

Start Owning the Responsibility for Your Success

One characteristic of interns and co-op students who are highly successful is that they own the responsibility for their success. In other words, a great co-op student is one who doesn't wait for things to happen but instead makes things happen for themselves. Just recently, a student came to see Scott ONE FULL MONTH after the official start date for his first co-op. Why did he blow off working with the co-op department? Well, a couple of friends had told him that the job market was tough and that he probably wouldn't be able to get a professional job. In talking to him, Scott quickly learned that he had good communication skills and a car. Scott had to tell him that basically 100 percent of his students with cars had been able to find related jobs in their majors—even in the bad economy. What a shame that he listened to people who knew little about the situation: Based on gossip and speculation from uninformed classmates, he went out on his own and got a job as a cashier in a restaurant. He looked absolutely sick when I told him that people with less going for them than him were making as much as $16/hour doing work directly related to their major!

Show some initiative as you plan ahead for your future co-op. When you interview for a psychology job and are asked about some aspect of the field, you don't

CAREER EXPLORATION—A PROFESSIONAL'S PERSPECTIVE

By Dr. Sarah David

"As a faculty member teaching a Human Development - Career Exploration course, I have found that students that put in the effort have a tremendous advantage at exploring and confirming their career choice. Many students upon completing the course have identified their major. One of my assignments is to have students write letters to themselves at the beginning of the class about what they hope to accomplish and visualize their dream career. I then mail those letters to them upon completion of the course. They are so excited upon discovering their career path they plan to take which is a direct result of the time and effort they put into taking advantage of the career exploration course. This newly defined career decision results in better focus, retention and success in college. There are a number of other courses students can take to "test" out their career choice. Grab a campus catalog and explore career options that are right at your fingertips."

***Dr. Sarah David** is a Certified Personal Branding Strategist, National Certified Counselor and Certified Career Management Coach. She teaches a Career Exploration class in Human Development where she serves as a Counselor and Professor at Lone Star College - Tomball*

want to say "I don't know anything about that because we haven't covered it in class yet." Maybe you can talk about reading Irvin Yalom's excellent book *Love's Executioner*, which features remarkable tales of psychotherapy. Likewise, journalism students should be able to cite *New York Times* articles that they thought to be excellent; political science students should be able to speak—very diplomatically, of course—about pressing political issues in their city, state, or in the nation. Hiring managers look for results-oriented self-starters who don't sit back and wait for someone to force them to learn a new skill set or about relevant developments in the field.

A great deal will depend on your outlook. If you have negative expectations about your co-op or internship, you are more likely to focus on the negatives in your job. If you take the attitude that hard work, good performance, and a cheerful tone can overcome the negatives in most jobs, you probably will find that to be true. The key is to start taking small steps toward success.

OWNING YOUR SUCCESS – AN EMPLOYER'S PERSPECTIVE

By Margaret Robertson

When I hire, I hire for attitude; it is what I value most. For me a positive attitude is more important than skills because it means that the individual will be positive about the workplace, about their own ability to learn and about working effectively with fellow workers. I look for individuals who care about doing a good job and who are conscientious. I also look for people who recognize that they don't know everything and are willing to put effort toward continuous improvement of their skills. And, I look for people who will be at work when expected and who are ready to work when it is time to start, even if they don't feel like it.

***Margaret Robertson** was the Engineering Manager for Mobius and is currently a faculty member in Drafting at Lane Community College*

UNDERSTANDING THE JOB MARKET

As stated in the last section, you cannot control the nature of the economy, the job market, or cyclical factors that affect the quantity and quality of jobs available in your field. Yet although it does little good to fret about what you can't control, you still need to be aware of these elements and the impact they may have on your job search.

The Economy

The United States economy is large, complex, hard to understand, and certainly impossible to change. Yet you should realize how this can affect you as an individual. Historically our economy undergoes cycles from prosperous booms to deep crises and all phases in between.

During 2001 and 2002—and again from 2008 to at least 2010—students found out the hard way that this is the case. Some employers went bankrupt or laid off the majority of their workers; others cut back their co-op/internship headcount due to economic uncertainty or lack of work.

The upshot has been that many students have struggled to get jobs during these years, especially if they a) started their job search late, b) were inflexible about what type of job they were able and/or willing to do and where they would or could work, or c) were inconsistent in their job-search efforts. Doing everything on time and to the best of your ability is no guarantee of getting a job in a challenging economy, but expending energy on the controllable part of your job search will help you fare better when grappling with something as uncontrollable as the US economy. The amount of effort expended on the job search is the single biggest factor in determining whether or not an individual student is meaningfully employed or not—a much bigger factor than skills and job experience! Most co-op and internship programs are NOT placement agencies—they don't simply assign you to a job; you have to earn it.

Here's an analogy to consider. Working with a career office is not like going to Burger King to get fed. Think of it as if you instead decided to attend a culinary institute. In other words, it might seem convenient if you were able to go to your career office and be handed a job. However, what you really need to get out of your career office is much more than that. After all, jobs seldom last more than a few years, and then you need to obtain another position. As such, you really need to learn what it takes to find a job as well as how to manage your career. This book can be a tool in this philosophy of "lifelong learning."

Along those lines, remember this Chinese proverb: "Give a man a fish and you feed him for a day. Teach a man to fish and you feed him for a lifetime." Your career educator is well equipped to assist you with your job search activities, but you don't want that person to do everything for you. Learn how to write a resume, look for a job, and interview, and you will be confident in these critical areas for the rest of your life.

The Job Market in Your Field

Your chosen field will have a big impact on the quality and quantity of job options available to you. Although the economy also affects job markets—for example, architectural drafting students in the Pacific Northwest, had incredible options until around 2007 but now struggle with home construction at a virtual standstill—you will always be affected by the simple laws of supply and demand. 2002 and 2003 were great years for health science students in the Northeast—even though they were lean years for many other fields. If the demand in the job market for professionals in your field is greater than the supply of workers available, you may have some amazing options, even as an entry-level co-op student. But if you're in a field that is very popular with college students who are competing for a limited number of jobs, then it's a very different story.

A great resource for understanding how your choice of major affects your future earnings potential as a full time professional is a book called T*he College Majors Handbook, With Real Career Paths And Payoffs* (Jist Publishing). This 2004 publication is especially helpful if you are considering a career that requires a bachelors degree or higher.

In the co-op realm, though, let's consider a few specific examples. Several years ago, the dot-com bust and media attention on jobs going overseas resulted in a substantial drop in the number of students pursuing majors in computer science, computer engineering, and management information systems. As a result, students in these majors continued to find good co-op jobs and internships even after the economy tanked in Fall 2008. At Northeastern, Scott went from having perhaps 130 jobs for 60-70 MIS concentrators to having about 60-70 jobs for 25-30 job seekers. This leads him to believe that there will be an astonishing shortage of information technology professionals once the economy rebounds completely.

On the other side of the coin, there are always students who want to get into what we often call "sexy" jobs. A "sexy" job involves working in a field that individuals often consider glamorous. Imagine how many aspiring professionals want to work in the music industry, fashion, television, professional sports management, publishing, and advertising. Likewise, how many co-op students would want to work for organizations such as Nike or the FBI or in the White House?

Given that so many students want to work in these fields or with these organizations, the result is that these employers often opt for students who will work as unpaid interns instead of hiring paid co-ops. If you really, really want to work in a "sexy" field or with a high profile employer, be prepared to work for little or nothing.... Or be creative about how you break into the field.

Scott had a student a few years ago who wanted to have a career in baseball. He was the third-string catcher on his collegiate team, and he had a specific goal in mind: He thought he could make it as a professional bullpen coach and/or bullpen catcher. Scott asked him if he was willing to do an incredible amount of legwork and unpaid jobs to make it happen. He was game for it. Over the next few years, he picked up unpaid gigs as a bullpen catcher for various amateur and minor leagues. He wrote letters to all 26 major league general managers, and he received a couple of replies. Finally, he got a temporary scouting job with a major league team. After months and months of work and networking, he landed a fabulous job after graduation: a job combining scouting and his old baseball position as a catcher. His new employer? The New York Yankees. In addition to checking out young talent, they put him to work by having him help pitchers bounce back from injuries by throwing to him at their Tampa baseball complex.

So you can break into glamorous fields if you're willing to pay the price in terms of time and money. The other way to do it is to acquire hot skills and use those skills as a way to differentiate yourself from other candidates. Years ago, Scott did a presentation on interviewing at a national co-op conference. Afterwards, two gentlemen from the CIA introduced themselves. Without any prompting from Scott, they said, "Tell your students that if they want to work for the FBI and CIA, the way to do it is to major in computer science, MIS, or computer engineering. You have no idea how many criminal justice students contact us, and we're not interested in them!"

You always have to think about whom you're competing with for jobs and how you're going to be able to say, "I'm different!" We'll talk about that more in the interviewing chapter.

Time of Year

Your ability to get the position of your choice also can be influenced by the time of year during which you hope to land that co-op, internship or practicum. An obvious example is students preparing to become public school teachers who want regular classroom experience. In general, summer education practicums tend to be in summer enrichment programs or assisting in a remedial setting, both great experiences and good preparation for an educational career but, nevertheless, not traditional classrooms.

For community college students, your certificate or degree program may dictate exactly when you are allowed do your work experience. If, on the other hand, your program lets you choose what time of year you do your co-op or internship, there are tradeoffs no matter when you elect to do it.

If you start work during the late spring or early summer, you're competing with everyone else in the collegiate world who is seeking a summer job. If your program allows you to work more than the three months that a typical summer-only worker can promise, this may give you an edge over students from conventional programs.

As we saw when considering "sexy" jobs, what you want to avoid is doing what everyone else does. Scott talks to students frequently about "zigging when everyone else is zagging." In other words, how can you differentiate yourself from other candidates? What jobs are out there that may be less obvious options for the usual horde of job seekers? For example, it can be really hard for a student to look for a summer-only job: Depending on your region, you might be competing with every other college student PLUS some co-op students who may be able to work for six months. Not recommended. Likewise, a student interested in accounting might find less competition when pursuing accounting jobs at a university or in a non-profit organization rather than a big-name accounting firm.

Your chosen field also may have a different supply of jobs at different times of the year. Hospitality students have many more opportunities if they choose to do their co-op during late spring, summer and in some areas early fall due to the increase in tourism. This is a win-win situation because organizations can get help for their busy season and not have to pay for year-round people who won't be necessary during the winter. Meanwhile, students get to work in action-packed jobs, which are always preferable to slow-paced work environments.

You and your co-op coordinator may consider a couple of other issues when choosing the timing of your work experience. First, the skills and knowledge you bring with you from prior work experience and how they fit with your field of study in college may have an impact on when a co-op is right for you. You'll also want to consider how quickly you have completed program courses and how well you have developed the skills needed for an internship. For example, if one of Tamara's drafting students completes two terms of Computer Aided Design coursework (CAD 1 & 2) and has an extensive construction background, he or she may be ready to begin co-op a term or two sooner than a student with no knowledge of construction.

In addition to the valuable experiences you'll gain from a job, you may also have other hopes and/or expectations that impact the timing of your work term. Many career/technical students want to do their co-op or internship during the term immediately prior to graduation with the hopes it will turn into regular full-time employment. And, sometimes it does! The advantage of waiting is that you'll have completed most of the courses in your discipline and will have developed significant skills. This makes you very attractive to an employer. Plus employers like to hire students at this phase of their education because they know they'll soon be available for full time employment.

Some students hope to do their co-op as early as possible in their college career in hopes that it will transition into a solid part-time job to help support them for the duration of their education. Other students, as described before, prefer to use co-op to explore careers or experience different aspects of their chosen field.

Tamara had a writing student who couldn't decide which direction to proceed with her education and career. During the spring quarter of her first year she interned with the award winning journal of art and literature, *CALYX*, where she assisted with a poetry contest. Thinking publication may not be right for her, the next fall quarter she did a co-op at a homeless youth shelter offering drop in writing projects. Through this experience she discovered teaching in this type of setting was not the right direction for her either. She decided to take as many additional creative writing courses as she could and then did a third co-op during her last quarter at Lane as the editor of our student literary arts journal, *Denali*. As a result of these three co-ops and her coursework, she was accepted into a prestigious creative writing BA program. As you can see, the timing of her co-ops helped her make important decisions about her college classes and her future.

Having Realistic Expectations

This is especially true for first-time co-op students. We sometimes meet with nursing students who think that their first job as a nursing co-op will entail providing direct care for patients—even though their background is limited to prerequisite courses in anatomy and physiology. Then there is the culinary student who wants to own a restaurant some day and thus gets a job in a restaurant, believing that she will be making decisions about the menu. Or the computer science student who believes he will be a key member of a software development team, taking the lead in designing a new software application for the company. Wrong, wrong, and wrong!

No company in their right mind is going to hand major decision-making power to an inexperienced intern or co-op student! Legally, health care providers have to be very careful about what they allow co-ops, interns, and clinical students to do. For American Sign Language students, most job opportunities require fully trained professionals with degrees. As a result, the best that an ASL co-op or intern may be able to hope for is a position that provides them with opportunities to practice their ASL skills with deaf people, rather than a role in which he or she is an "official translator."

More than anything, your first co-op is a great opportunity to gain initial exposure to the professional world in the field of your choice—just "being around" in that kind of environment can be a good learning experience, even if your job duties entail somewhat monotonous Quality Assurance software testing to find and document programming bugs or chopping vegetables up at a restaurant or being a "sitter" in a hospital: basically sitting by a patient in an Intensive Care Unit for hours to make sure that they don't pull any of their tubes out (all possible duties for the students mentioned in the previous paragraphs).

Co-op students need to work their way up the ladder by proving themselves in whatever role they are given. Repeatedly in this book, you will hear about how co-op success—versus mere survival or outright failure—is all about momentum. Co-ops and interns are often given low-level tasks when starting a new position. Why? Employers want to see what you can do, and they often want to give you tasks that you can handle to build confidence and start off successfully.

If you take on these low-level tasks cheerfully and efficiently, you may find that you are suddenly being asked to take on more and better projects. Fail to do them with the right attitude or without success, and you are less likely to get more advanced work to do. Having realistic expectations about your first job will enable you to approach the job with a good attitude—an understanding that you may need to work your way up in the organizational world.

UNDERSTANDING YOUR JOB SEARCH

To conduct an effective job search, it is helpful to think about why employers hire new employees. It may seem obvious; employers hire a regular employee, a co-op, or an intern because they have something that needs to be done, usually in the least expensive and most efficient way possible. Your task as a job seeker is to do everything you can to show how you are the best person to meet their need. A job search is about providing evidence to the employer through your resume, cover letter, interview and other documents (like a portfolio) that you will not merely be able to do the job but that you can do it effectively.

Job Search as Sales

It is fairly common knowledge that job search is about "selling" your skills and abilities to a prospective employer. It doesn't matter if you are applying for a part-time, non-paid internship or a full-time job, the principle is the same. Everything you do related to seeking a job—from a casual conversation with your best friend's father who might have an opportunity for you at his company to filling out an application with a cover letter and resume—is a chance to tell someone why they should hire you. Don't let the idea of selling yourself scare you. Being able to clearly and concisely explain what you bring to an organization and how they will benefit by hiring you isn't hard; it just takes some focused attention and practice.

Preparation Is the Key to an Effective Job Search

You'll want to begin by analyzing your skills and abilities so that you can refer to them in your job search (see Appendix B). Once you've identified your skills, you'll want to prepare your resume (Chapter 2) and prepare for your interviews (Chapter 3). It is crucial to invest considerable energy upfront on these elements. Once you have a strong resume and a strong sense of how to "marry" your skills and experiences to a specific job description, you can concentrate on applying for jobs with confidence that you'll be able to pull together a specific interviewing strategy quickly. If you put off doing any one of these activities, you may find yourself missing out on the co-op of your dreams because you couldn't respond quickly enough with a polished resume or because you performed poorly in the interview due to lack of preparation.

Job Searches in the Digital Age

After leaving his job at Northeastern University at the end of the 2009-2010 academic year, Scott spent a busy summer as a consultant. Among his various projects, he handled all of the recruiting efforts for a start-up company in Cambridge, Massachusetts. He also began looking into some new full-time jobs on his own behalf. As a result, he quickly developed an appreciation for how job search processes have changed over the last decade or so.

The Internet has changed job search processes substantially. This is both a blessing and a curse. It's now incredibly easy for job seekers to find jobs online and apply to them. As a result, though, employers now get inundated with resumes—particularly in a bad economy. So while it's easier to apply for a job, it has become more difficult to get the attention of a potential employer and stand out in a crowded field of candidates.

How do you overcome this? We'll be talking about that throughout this book, but there are some steps that fit perfectly into this chapter. Let's review those now.

Start Networking Now. Unless you're a cookie-cutter fit for a posted job—or unless the economy is much better than it is in September 2011—even an experienced job candidate may find it difficult to get noticed when applying to jobs online. Think about it: Often, some HR person may have to sift through 100+ resumes to find, perhaps, eight or so to contact. However, there are ways to overcome that. If your career educator knows someone at the company, see if they can encourage the organization to give you a closer look. If not, you should see if someone in your own personal network can help by giving a hiring manager a nudge.

No doubt that some of you are now saying, "But I don't have a personal network of contacts!" That's a problem. However, it's one that you can solve... but you need to start working on it now. Do you have a LinkedIn account? If so, have you completed your profile? How many contacts do you have? This is something you really need to work on regularly. Think of it as a garden: You might not need to work on it every day, but you don't want to let it go for weeks at a time.

LinkedIn is the top social media site for job seekers. It's a way for you to advertise your background with a professional profile listing your job experiences, but it's also a way to connect with people who may be able to help you with job searches in months and years to come.

Here's how it works: Let's say you have a terrific relationship with a professor, so you ask her to become a connection on LinkedIn. Maybe you write a LinkedIn recommendation for that professor. If you do, LinkedIn's interface encourages the other person to return a favor. So now you have a nice recommendation on your profile. Time goes by, and you repeat this process with employers, professors, and friends in the professional world.

Now let's fast forward a few years. You are now in the market for a new job. Suddenly you see a terrific new job posted, but you don't know anyone at that company. What can you do to make sure your resume gets noticed? LinkedIn makes it easy for you to find out if any of your connections have a link to someone at that organization. Maybe you'll discover that a primary connection is actually working at that company now. More likely, you'll learn that one of your primary connections knows someone at that organization. Then you ask your contact if they're willing to reach out to the appropriate party on your behalf.

Scott had this work to his advantage when looking for consulting work as well as full-time positions. When targeting one employer, he realized he knew no one who worked there. Fortunately, a former student of his worked at another branch of that large organization. Scott reached out to him, and his contact put him in touch with someone who knew who would be making the hiring decisions. He also had some insight into what issues would be facing someone in this role. All of a sudden, people in that group were e-mailing Scott, mentioning the introduction and commenting favorably on his resume.

The point, though, is that all of this networking does not happen instantly or magically. You can't usually ask someone to connect with you on LinkedIn today and then recommend you for a job tomorrow. Therefore, try to build your online network little by little each week. Lastly, make sure that you only try to connect with people who you know AND respect and who will be inclined to say positive things about you if asked.

JOB SEARCH OPTIONS

The way students find co-op jobs or internships varies widely not only from one community college to the next community college but also from one co-op coordinator or career services coordinator to the next. In some colleges, each co-op coordinator posts openings for students, who apply for jobs from these postings. In other colleges, all internship opportunities are listed and applied for via a website. In many institutions, you'll be expected to develop your own co-op or internship through an extensive job search. Some colleges offer plenty of help, and some provide very little. Students at Lane work directly with a co-op coordinator who will refer them to known openings but who also will encourage them to seek additional opportunities on their own.

If possible, we recommend a "best of both worlds" approach. By all means, you should take a long look at any jobs that your college makes available. That said, no college has the market cornered when it comes to possible co-op jobs or internships. Sometimes a personal connection combined with some informal networking can lead to a great position. We'll talk more about how to do this shortly.

When it comes to capitalizing on your college's resources during a job search, though, bear in mind the following. Generally speaking, the students who get the most help are the ones who plan ahead, demonstrate a high level of commitment to their college work, and actively seek our guidance and direction. However—given the size of our student loads—we just don't have enough hours in the day to call up individuals regularly to ask why they haven't finalized a resume or checked in regarding next steps. It's really up to you to be on top of what you need to get done and when you have to do it in terms of the process.

CO-OP JOB SEARCH – A STUDENT'S PERSPECTIVE

by Mark Moccia

Students should be active as soon as their college career begins. The key to landing the job you want is not throwing pennies into a fountain, hoping for the Gods of Co-op to "bestow the perfect job upon thee." Students must work hard to improve grades, add skills, participate in clubs, and take on other activities to show they are hard working and potential leaders.

Equally as important, students must first decide their priorities before looking for a job. Some students might be looking to make money, gain valuable experience, work for a large company, small company, etc. Once this is decided, the student then can begin to search for particular jobs.

Mark Moccia *was an Accounting/MIS student at Northeastern University, Class of 2002*

WORKING WITH CAREER SERVICES—A PROFESSIONAL'S PERSPECTIVE

By Dr. Sarah David

"I have discovered in my twelve years of working as a career counselor in college and university career service offices, many times students mistake Career Services as "staffing or placement agencies." In most cases Career Services offer career development, job search resources, co-op and internship listings. Unfortunately, many of these offices particularly at the community college level are "one woman or one man" shows. Staffing resources are normally not available for these offices to serve in a staffing or placement capacity. Many career service offices offered at the community college provide resources in order to connect students with employers. Students are under the impression that all they have to do is register with the office and wait for the office staff to call with a job offer. Unfortunately, this is not the case in most circumstances. Career service offices provide a more holistic approach and educate students on how to identify a major or career field, prepare for a job search, provide resume writing resources, share job search techniques and provide career assessments. Career Services provides a platform to connect job seekers and employers. The students who get the job opportunities are those that take a proactive approach and look for opportunities instead of waiting for opportunities to find them."

***Dr. Sarah David** is a Certified Personal Branding Strategist, National Certified Counselor and Certified Career Management Coach. She teaches a Career Exploration class in Human Development where she serves as a Counselor and Professor at Lone Star College – Tomball*

Working with a Co-op or Internship Coordinator and/or Career Services Department

If your college has a co-op/internship coordinator or career services department, by all means take advantage of these resources. At schools with established programs, these career professionals are the liaison to hundreds, even thousands, of work-based learning opportunities. The co-op/internship or career services coordinator should have a good understanding of the specifics of the job market in your field and region. Plus, he or she talks to hundreds of employers about their employment needs. If you don't work with a coordinator, you won't have access to all kinds of information!

The best advice we can give you regarding working successfully with your co-op or career services coordinator is to treat this individual in the same way that you would treat your supervisor in the workplace. Use your interactions with co-op coordinators as opportunities to hone your professionalism.

What does this mean in practical terms?

- When meeting a coordinator for the first time, introduce yourself, shake hands, and clearly state your reasons for the office visit.
- Be on time to appointments with these professionals. If you

absolutely cannot make an appointment, call in advance to cancel instead of just being a no-show.

- Be sensitive to the coordinator's need to juggle multiple priorities on a tight time schedule.
- When faced with uncertainty, assume the best: For example, if your coordinator asks you to change your resume, assume that it's with your best interests in mind, not to inconvenience you!
- If you need to state concerns or air conflicts, try to do so in an upbeat, solution-oriented way rather than simply blowing off steam or complaining.
- When in doubt about what you should do in any situation—before, during, or after you obtain your job—ask your coordinator.

It's definitely in your best interest to develop a good working relationship with your coordinator. Inevitably, when great new jobs come in, we think first about the students whom we know well and who are in touch with us regularly. With large student loads, students can easily fall off our radar screens. Stay in touch regularly to make sure that doesn't happen, and you likely will be the beneficiary of a wealth of good advice and assistance. "I just haven't had time" or "You're not available at times that are convenient to me" just don't cut it as excuses—it only takes a minute or two to write an e-mail or leave a voice mail with an update. More often than not, your coordinator also can make accommodations to meet with you if the posted appointment times or walk-in hours don't correspond well with your availability.

Finding a Job on Your Own

Some students may find it useful or even absolutely necessary to find a job without much help from their college or university. Some schools don't have formal co-op or internship coordinators or programs. Even if you go to a big co-op school, you may want to look for your own job for various reasons. You also may need to or want to find your own job if you are seeking work in a field that your co-op department typically doesn't work with. Examples might be some of those "sexy" fields that were mentioned earlier in this chapter: music industry, fashion, and sports management come to mind.

Although your job search falls outside of the conventional paths available through your school, you still have options. However, there are a few things to bear in mind before striking out on your own:

1. *Always check with your co-op or internship coordinator before approaching any companies.* If you have a connection with IBM, for example—even one through a classmate, friend, or family member—it would be a mistake to approach the company without getting clearance from your co-op coordinator first. The reason is that your school may have already established a co-op relationship with them, and both IBM and

the co-op department may perceive you as trying to "beat the system" or do an "end run" instead of legitimately following the process as other students do. In some cases, you may need to discuss your job lead with the appropriate co-op coordinator before making contact to avoid any misunderstandings.

2. *You must get your co-op coordinator's approval before accepting any job found on your own, and you must get that approval BEFORE the beginning of the work experience.* Not all jobs qualify as co-op positions. For nearly all students at Lane, the co-op site must provide a minimum of 10 hours a week for a full term and the learning experience must be appropriate to the student's career or major; other programs may be more flexible or more strict about what qualifies as a co-op, but you need to be sure. Also, your coordinator is responsible for knowing your whereabouts on co-op and for submitting data about your employment status (paid or unpaid) and wages to the college administration. In most programs, coordinators simply will not give a student credit for a work experience if they fail to discuss the position with her or him beforehand—even if the student obtained a fantastic position on his or her own.

3. *Even though you are pursuing your own job, don't forget that your co-op coordinator can be very helpful to you in your job search.* Sometimes coordinators can give students job leads depending on their circumstances, and most coordinators can help with resumes, cover letters, networking tips, and advice on how to sell the idea of co-op to an organization. Take advantage of this resource. Also note that Appendix C in the back of this book has information on how to write a cover letter. You would be amazed at how many long-time professionals really have no idea how to write cover letters effectively. Learn now!

4. *Be sure to complete the appropriate paperwork with your co-op coordinator.* Find out about and follow your college's procedures for filling out the agreement form (or any other paperwork required by your school) upon locating a suitable position. This is especially true for international students, who absolutely must receive work authorization before beginning any job.

Coming Up with Job Options on Your Own

For most students, one of the most challenging parts of finding their own co-op job is managing to get in the door for interviews. After all, co-op employers don't usually put co-op job listings in the newspaper or on a job board. The trick is becoming more creative about how you come up with options. Here are some suggestions:

1. *Network through family and friends.* As stated earlier, don't use family and friends to get to employers that already work with your school's co-op or internship program—discuss this step with your co-op

coordinator first. After clearing that hurdle, you'll find that networking is the single most effective way of finding your own job. We described how to do this online with LinkedIn earlier in the chapter, but face-to-face networking has been around much longer and is still very valuable.

An entrepreneurship/small business management student of Scott's a few years ago came to see him and announced that she wanted to find a job in Denver. She had a cousin who lived there but otherwise knew no one in Colorado. Together, they worked hard on how to network. Armed with that knowledge, she began grilling her cousin: Whom do you know who works in a small business? Where do they work? What's their phone number? When she found people who worked in small businesses, she tried to get them thinking about her situation: Could your company use someone to work on marketing projects? Someone to help with computers? An individual who could crunch numbers, work as a good team player, and serve as a Jill-of-all-trades?

Even though she experienced a lot of rejection, the student stayed positive, upbeat, and persistent—to the point where people really wanted to help her find a job. Plus she tried to avoid any dead ends: Anyone she talked to was an opportunity to get more names and phone numbers. Finally, she got a fantastic job, working for a small business that helped other businesses put together IPOs and go public. How many people did she have to go through to make this happen? The job was obtained through her cousin's boyfriend's father's friend's friend!!! It just shows what you can do if you are willing to expend some energy in an intelligent, directed search for your own job.

2. *Check out job boards and newspaper listings.* Many community colleges host free job boards for students and alumni in their Career Services area. Frequently this is a web-based service making it very easy to access once you've set up an account. Find out if your school offers this service, which is usually free; it is definitely worth checking. Some employers are purely interested in hiring full-time employees who have completed their degrees (or who will do so very soon), while others can be approached about co-ops or internships and are interested in forging bonds with the college. You'll also find listings of temporary or hourly positions that are appropriate for a student seeking a co-op job.

Beyond that, there are numerous job boards out there. A few include www.monster.com, www.vault.com, and www.USJobBoard.com. Another fast-growing site is www.careers.msn.com. More recently, our students are telling us that they've found opportunities through going to www.craigslist.com to review job possibilities. Many of these sites also have timely career advice and industry updates. Some sites are extremely national and general, while others focus more on specific fields and regions: For example, www.dice.com features high tech jobs. The Princeton Review's website (www.review.com) lists numerous internships around the country. Just go the bottom of the home page and click on "Internship Search" under Academic Programs. Another intriguing site is idealist.org, which lists over 46,000 nonprofit and community organizations in 165 countries. They list paid internships and volunteer opportunities spanning the globe for those interested in civic-minded ways to gain experience and broaden your exposure to the world. Journalism students can go to asne.org (American Society of Newspaper Editors) to see dozens of paid internships with newspapers. There are dozens of other possibilities broken out by region or field—ask your co-op, internship, or career services professional for other ideas.

Bear in mind that most employers list full-time jobs on some of these boards—not co-op jobs or internships. Therefore, students may not be successful at targeting specific listed jobs. Instead, the job boards will give you some indication of who is looking to hire in your field. Chances are that an employer hiring significant numbers of full-time employees may view a co-op program as another good (if longer-term) recruiting option.

Of course, sometimes organizations listing multiple jobs on the boards are actually employment agencies, which generally are not interested in placing co-op students. While these may be useful for those of you seeking your first full-time job after graduation, co-op and internship seekers probably should steer clear of them at this point in their careers.

Most of the same rules apply for newspaper listings. One good thing to know, though, is that many newspapers also have their classified jobs online. Given that the days of thousands of ads in the Sunday paper are now long gone, be sure to take your search online!

3. *Making Cold Calls.* Telephoning, e-mailing, or stopping in at an employer is a last resort because you will put in a lot of energy without much return in many cases. You can improve your chances by targeting larger employers, checking whether there is information about co-op jobs on their website, and then getting in touch to express your interest.

Selling a Company on the Value of a Co-op Employee or Intern

One of the best things about finding your own job is that it is a great way to test your ability to be entrepreneurial. You have to not only sell yourself in the interview as you ordinarily would: Often you will need to be able to articulate how cooperative education works and why it benefits potential employers. Here are some key points to hit:

1. *Co-op employees and interns represent cost-effective labor.* In many cases—especially with corporate jobs—these employees are a less expensive resource than the alternatives, such as contractors or temps.

2. *Co-ops/interns do not need to receive benefits.* Health care benefits and paid vacation time are expensive to employers; many companies are under pressure to keep their "headcount" (full-time employees who are eligible for benefits) at a minimum. Co-ops and interns are one way

to help achieve this goal. Note that in most situations co-ops are NOT contractors: state and federal taxes DO need to be withdrawn from your pay. With rare exceptions, the Internal Revenue Service does not view co-ops or interns as being sufficiently experienced to be considered "consultants," as is implied by the status of contractor.

3. *Co-ops/interns can provide long-term help but are not a permanent commitment.* If you can make yourself available for at least four to six months, that's a long time—long enough for you to provide a return on the investment the company may need to make in training you. However, the company need not make any commitment beyond the six months to you or other co-op students or interns. This may be important to start-up companies, which may need help now but are unsure about what their future needs may be. Likewise, even large employers may be reluctant to commit to a permanent hire during times of economic uncertainty. Hiring a co-op or intern for three to six months is far preferable to hiring a full-time employee without knowing if they will need to lay off the person in the next year.
4. *Co-op and internship programs help the organization to maintain a recruiting pipeline.* From the organization's perspective, it's nice to be able to get cost-effective help for several months. However, many employers tell us that they especially love co-op and internship programs because they are a great way to source future full-timer hires. Maybe the economy is down right now, but it will bounce back eventually. When it does, an employer can reach out to the best performers over the last few years and try to bring them on board in a full-time job. You can be much more confident when hiring someone who has already performed well for you versus someone who has merely interviewed well.
5. *Interns and co-op students have much at stake and are therefore more motivated than other temporary workers usually are.* People who work as temps usually do so simply to make money. Co-op student workers usually focus on learning as much as they can and securing a good reference for future employment. Those co-op students who are earning college credit and a grade have even more at stake because their grade point average is also on the line. As a result, co-ops often show more interest and effort in their jobs.

Your coordinator may be able to provide you with an introductory brochure about co-ops and interns for potential employers and other materials that may be useful to you in marketing yourself as a temporary student/employee.

Now that you have a good understanding of how to plan ahead for your first professional job, you are ready to tackle the nuts and bolts of the preparation stage: writing a resume, learning how to interview, and generally ramping up for your job search.

CHAPTER 1 REVIEW QUESTIONS

1. Name at least four of the benefits of working as a co-op or intern.

2. List three things that you could do now to make yourself more marketable for a future position in your field.

3. Explain why many hiring managers consider soft skills more important than technical skills when hiring co-ops, interns, or graduates?

4. Describe the process at your college for getting a co-op, internship, or practicum. Include the criteria for eligibility and any difference between the programs if any exist.

5. Name at least three ways in which co-ops and internships are beneficial to employers.

CHAPTER TWO

Writing An Effective Resume

Your resume is a vital component of an effective job search. It is a personal statement and advertisement of who you are. You may have more talent, knowledge, and skills than any other applicant for a particular job. However, if you don't get an opportunity to communicate those qualities to an employer, you may never get the chance to demonstrate your abilities. A good resume will provide you with that opportunity. It WILL NOT get you a job but it CAN get you an interview.

As you will see in this chapter, there are different schools of thought on how resumes should be written. This creates some degree of confusion, as you may come across contradictory advice when you talk to employers, look at resume tips online, or consult your professors. Some co-op and internship coordinators or career services professionals believe that resume writers should go beyond describing simply what they did to weave in soft skills demonstrated in previous work experience. Alternatively, your co-op coordinator may encourage you to put some "spin" on your job descriptions—encouraging you to describe how you did a given job or what made you a good or great employee in a given position. That will help a potential employer infer what soft skills you have. However, other co-op coordinators believe that it's best to emphasize what you did and not force the potential employer to wade through a long-winded job description—especially given that a prospective employer may only look at your resume for 60 to 90 seconds! From this perspective, the idea is to use the interview to convey your soft skills and anything more qualitative that the interviewer may want to know about your previous positions. Some employers believe that resumes are somewhat overrated (see box).

Conversely, some employers believe resumes are critically important. This type of employer may not call a student in because of a careless typo or a poorly organized resume. There is definitely no one "right" way to prepare resumes. For example, some people believe that an INTERESTS section doesn't belong on a resume;

RESUME WRITING – AN EMPLOYER'S PERSPECTIVE
by Mike Naclerio

Not much impresses me on resumes. I don't spend much time reviewing them and view them as a mere formality. The personal interview is what counts, and where you can truly determine whether an individual will fit into your unique working environment.

***Mike Naclerio** is the Director of Relationship Management at the workplace HELPLINE* job search is serious business and interests are too personal. We've heard employers express indifference to the inclusion of an INTERESTS section on a resume, but we've also had employers tell us that they are amazed when someone omits that section. We'll explain why later in the chapter.

Opinions also vary dramatically when it comes to what elements should appear on a resume. Some recommend an OBJECTIVE or SUMMARY OF ACCOMPLISHMENTS on the top of a resume, while others are opposed to those devices. We'll explain why later in the chapter.

Your best bet is to find out what your co-op or career services professional believes would work best for you, given your work history as well as your field. After all, this individual has direct communication with the employers who will receive your resume, so they generally have the best idea of what will resonate with interviewers. You also need to think about what feels right and comfortable for YOU. Maybe your brother's girlfriend thinks you should do your resume a different way—the approach that she used in getting some fantastic job—or your mom is an HR manager who sees hundreds of resumes per year and believes she knows what is best for you. In the end, though, your co-op coordinator is the one who has co-op jobs available, whereas your brother's girlfriend probably doesn't have any! Make sure your coordinator understands your goals and values: Are you comfortable, for example, with a resume that really sells your skills? Once your coordinator knows you, trusting that person's judgment is usually the best move. Of course, you also need to feel comfortable that your resume truly reflects the real you. Even if you were urged to have a resume that features a "hard sell" of your skills, you shouldn't do so unless you're comfortable with that.

Just about any professional would agree on many factors that differentiate a strong resume from a poor one. An effective, competitive resume is one that highlights your best achievements, accomplishments, and contributions at work, at school, and in the community. It also can reflect your hobbies, interests, and background, making you into a three-dimensional person instead of a name on a page. A strong resume also must be flawless in terms of typos or errors—after all, if you can't get things right on your resume, why would anyone expect you to have excellent attention to detail as an employee?

In contrast, a mediocre resume will provide minimal work and academic history plus extremely basic job descriptions. Also, a poor resume is unattractive to look at—maybe it's hard to read due to small type or poor alignment, perhaps it is just very inconsistent in terms of formatting. A weak resume also will have poor grammar or outright errors on it: failure to abbreviate properly, misspelled or misused words, or significant omissions.

You would be amazed at how many job seekers have truly poor resumes. During July 2010, Scott had a consulting job as a recruiter for a start-up company, and he reviewed a few hundred resumes in two weeks. Repeatedly, he was amazed to find people had submitted resumes that looked awful. Many were filled with glaring typos. Quite a few were ugly due to poor and inconsistent formatting. One was about five pages long… but not even 500 words! Believe us: By simply having a resume that is nicely formatted, clear, and error-free, you will be way ahead of many job seekers!

Obviously, a bad resume makes it easy to move your resume into the "reject" pile—especially in a tough economy. So why do so many job seekers shoot themselves in the foot in this way? Our guess is that it takes a little more time and effort to write a great resume and to then ensure it's perfect by getting many pairs of eyes on it. It's all too easy to apply online on a company's website these days, and job seekers sometimes race to that step before making very sure that they have a great product.

If you want your resume to stand out positively from the rest of the pile, you need to invest considerable time and thought. Therefore, to learn how to write a winning, professional resume, read on!

WRITING YOUR RESUME

The first step in writing your resume is easy. It has to do with the way your resume will look when it is finished. Remember, appearance does create a strong first impression. Just as you would not go to an interview dressed in a t-shirt and shorts, your resume also needs to look professional. The following five tips will help you to have a "good-looking" resume.

Five Resume Tips

1. Create a resume appropriate for your years of work experience. Less experienced students need only one page; more experienced students may need two. Scott's general rule is to ask whether forcing the resume to be only one page will effectively penalize the job candidate. For example, if a student can get her resume down to one page by only listing two secretarial jobs instead of all three that she has held, then he would recommend omitting the redundant job. However, if creating a one-page resume forces the student to leave out compelling experience or important job-related skills, then by all means go with two pages.

2. Use neutral colors when selecting paper (white, ivory, off-white, cream, gray) and, unless you are a student in a creative field like graphic design, in most situations it should be on 8 ½ x 11 paper. Use heavier paper like 60# text; 20# bond is too flimsy and won't stand out as professional. If you put your resume in a portfolio where it is inside of a plastic page

RESUME WRITING – A STUDENT'S PERSPECTIVE

by Jord Nelsen

Your resume is the important first impression an employer has of you. It is essential for getting that coveted interview.

To create a good resume use words that animate your skills and job descriptions. Use dynamic language like action words and adjectives because they give it flow and capture the attention of the reader. Interesting wording helps the potential employer imagine you doing the task and shows you have the right amount of confidence in yourself and your skills. When deciding what to put on your resume, remember you are selling yourself, with integrity, so don't be too modest or oversell yourself either.

You also need to pay a lot of attention to the layout of your resume. Your resume is a reflection of who you are and a well-organized, error-free resume helps you come across as a thorough, detail-oriented person, no matter what field you go into.

Jord Nelsen *is a Drafting student at Lane Community College, Class of 2011* protector, avoid white paper because it looks like ordinary 20# printer paper, even if it isn't.

3. Type your own resume on a word processor and save it where you'll have easy access to it. Be sure to have your file backed up, perhaps on a flash drive or thumb drive. This will enable you to make changes and corrections at any time. Also, most students will need to upload their resume onto the school's computer system and/or give an electronic copy of their resume to their coordinator.

4. Almost everyone uses Microsoft Word when writing their resume, and 90 percent of resumes seem to use Word's default font—Times New Roman—as a result. Dare to be different! Experiment with other fonts. Garamond is one reliable alternative… and there are many others such as Calibri and Helvetica. Just don't go too wild—unusual fonts may cause you problems when submitting a resume online or converting it to a PDF format. Some fonts are also very difficult to read.

RESUME WRITING – A STUDENT'S PERSPECTIVE

by Alan Ayers

My first experience making a resume was a year ago when I moved to a new area and wanted to apply for a CNC (computer numerical control) job with a temp service. I created the resume with a template, and it was unattractive. The information was really congested on the page. The agency's representative gave it one glance and put it aside. I never heard from her. I think I came across as unprofessional even though I had many years of continual employment in the field.

I decided to change careers and took classes at Lane Community College. In Tamara's pre-co-op seminar, I created a completely new resume from scratch in Word. During my first job interview, I could tell the difference between the impact of my old and new resume. The interview was very casual; all three of the interviewers were leaning back in their chairs, legs crossed. As they started asking me questions, I offered them my resume and gave one to each of them from a nice black portfolio. Their eyes got big; they all leaned forward and stayed that way for the rest of the interview. I felt like they took me more seriously. The resume gave them a good opportunity to look at my skills and ask me direct questions about my experience rather than general questions. One interviewer saw that I had been on the safety committee at my previous job and asked me about it. Preparing my resume helped me be really prepared for my interview.

***Alan Ayers** is a Drafting student at Lane Community College, class of 2011*

5. Your resume should reflect you as a professional and as an individual—do not directly copy from the sample resumes in this chapter or any other source. Employers have commented on how too many resumes look exactly alike. Write your own!

SECTIONS/HEADINGS

Your resume will be broken down into a number of separate sections, which will be used to describe aspects of your life and qualifications. Every co-op resume should include sections on:

EDUCATION
EXPERIENCE
SKILLS

These sections will become the headings on your resume. Depending on your background, you also might include several other possible sections, such as OBJECTIVE, INTERESTS, MILITARY EXPERIENCE, VOLUNTEER EXPERIENCE, MEMBERSHIPS, MAJOR ACCOMPLISHMENTS, and PROFESSIONAL CERTIFICATES or LICENSES.

HOW TO START

Every resume should start with an introduction. When you meet someone for the first time, you always tell them your name. Your resume is the same. Your name should be at the top, either centered, left, or right—whichever you think fits best. Address, telephone numbers (cell number and home land line if you have both), and e-mail address are critical. Employers need to reach you should they want to interview you or make you an offer! Therefore, include a permanent (family) and temporary (local) address if they are different. Remember, your resume may stay on file for over a year with an employer while you move in the meantime. Your permanent address and telephone number will ensure that you can always be reached for a job offer. Likewise, you always want to include a reliable e-mail address that you check regularly.

If you're always having trouble with your GMail or Yahoo account because you exceed the storage limit for messages, you need to do something to make sure that that won't make it difficult for a potential employer to reach you. And, make sure your e-mail account is professional enough for job search. Scott and Tamara have both had students with e-mail address like "greeneyedtigress" or "frozen&faceless" which, although memorable, don't give the right impression to an employer. Keep those fun addresses for your friends and family and create a more appropriate one just for job search. An e-mail address that includes your name is often best and makes it easier for an employer to recognize that an e-mail is from you rather than junk mail that gets deleted without being viewed.

When listing more than one address, it's advisable to make sure that the number and address you want employers to contact first is on the left-hand side, as they are most likely to use that one.

For example:

JANE SMITH

Janesmith89@hotmail.com

CURRENT ADDRESS	**PERMANENT ADDRESS**
7 Bognanni Hall, Box 10	89 Fifth Avenue
Boston, MA 02115	Natick, MA 01760
(617) 377-0000	(508) 555-0001

International students who use an Americanized nickname can include that on their resume. It could look like this:

WAI MAN "ANDY" LAM

What if you have an extremely difficult to pronounce name and are afraid that an employer may be reluctant to call you as a result? Recently, we heard of one enterprising student who included the pronunciation of his name right below it. You could do that like so:

OLUMIDE NGUNDIRI

(first name pronounced "oh-LOO-mee-day")

olumide@yahoo.com

EDUCATION

While you are still a college student, the EDUCATION section is usually listed first. For community college students who are changing careers, it is especially important to feature your new skills gained in school at the top of your resume. This will ensure that those elements will be the first thing an employer sees when looking at your resume. Once you gain experience in your new career though your internship, co-op, or practicum, the EDUCATION section often moves below the EXPERIENCE section. When writing the EDUCATION section, you should use the following guidelines:

- Format: reverse chronological order (current college listed first, other universities and colleges second, high school last if at all. You do not need to list high school if you attended over 10 years ago or if you already have a college degree)
- Include anticipated degree (e.g., Associate of Applied Science, Multimedia; Certificate of Completion, Drafting) and expected month and year of graduation or certificate of completion (e.g., May 2013)
- Include program name, concentrations and dual concentrations or minors, if applicable
- Honors: include GPA if 3.0 or above and any honors lists you have earned such as "President's List" as well as scholarships received (Compute your GPA to no more than two decimal places: 3.45 is fine; 3.4495 does not indicate greater honesty or make any significant difference to an employer)

- Include activities related to your education, especially leadership roles such as student government and Phi Theta Kappa
- Include the above information for other schools you have attended
- If you are financing a significant portion of your education yourself, you could opt to include that fact. Many employers put themselves through school and look very favorably upon students who also do so. Plus, if you are earning good grades, it is a terrific way to demonstrate time management skills. For example:

  Financing 80% of college tuition and expenses through cooperative education internship and part-time job earnings.

  Or:

  100% self-supporting college education

Here's how the section might look:

EDUCATION
Lane Community College, Eugene, OR

Associate of Applied Science Degree: Nursing
Expected Graduation: May 2012
GPA: 3.2

Honors and Activities:
Vice President's List, Joe Smith Memorial Scholarship, Intramural Basketball

Financing 75% of tuition and living expenses through part-time job income.

Students with degrees from other institutions should list them after their current education. If you have a masters degree or PHD in a field unrelated to your current area of study, you may elect not to list it. Your goal is to paint a picture of yourself as a qualified person in your current field of study. Some employers may consider you overqualified for an entry-level position if you have an advanced degree—even if it is in another field. It is important to remember that a resume is not a list of everything you've ever done in your life; rather, it is a carefully selected list of information about your skills, abilities, education and experiences that qualify you for a particular type of job and career.

Many students who have not yet had significant work experience will find it helpful to include their high school education in this section. Because your resume is written in reverse chronological order, the recording of your high school experience would come after your college notation(s).

EXPERIENCE

This is the most vital section of your resume. This is the time not only to list where you worked and what you did, but to list your accomplishments and achievements! Take time to think about what you want to say—it's worth doing right! Here are some key points:

- *Include company name (the official name), location (meaning city & state, not street address), job title, and dates of employment.* Employers want to see this information in order to determine exactly what you have done and how long you spent doing it. They might use this information to contact your present or previous employer in order to find out more about the relevance of your experience and the accuracy of your statements. Note that you probably shouldn't bother listing a job if you only did it for a month or two: Fairly or unfairly, it may raise questions about your ability and willingness to keep a job.

  When listing your dates of employment, consider listing the year only, not the month (and never the exact day). This works best when you have held one job for several years as opposed to working in numerous jobs for less than two years apiece. Given that most people who look at resumes spend a very short amount of time looking at each one, this strategy helps focus the viewer on your content rather than having them spend time calculating exactly how many months you worked somewhere. When you list your employment dates in this manner, you are not lying or being misleading. You will usually be asked to fill out an application in addition to submitting a resume where you will need to provide exact dates of employment.

  Some experts suggest you avoid listing dates of employment as well as dates of your education altogether. Unfortunately, when you do this it may be assumed that you are trying to hide something. Including dates for your employment is highly recommended.

- *Jobs should be listed chronologically from present position, then backwards.* List your present or most recent position first, then your second most recent and so on. If your most recent experience related to your field of study is a non-paid co-op, list it first even if you are also working another job to pay your bills while attending classes. You might want to split up your job listing into two sections with one section called "RELEVANT EXPERIENCE" or "RELATED EXPERIENCE" first, followed by another section called "OTHER EXPERIENCE" or "OTHER EMPLOYMENT."

  List your jobs going back ten years, not more, typically. By listing jobs from over ten years ago, you may increase the chances that you will be discriminated against due to your age. If you choose to list employment older than ten years, consider using the heading "EARLY CAREER" above a short summary statement of your work experience during that time, especially if it is related to your new career. For example, if you worked in construction and are now studying architectural drafting, be sure to list it because it shows you have valuable knowledge beyond what is taught in the classroom.

- *Sentences should always begin with an action verb.* Avoid starting sentences with weak linking verbs such as had, got, did, etc. Use verbs that convey confidence, such as handled, improved, managed, designed, etc.

There is a long list of great action verbs toward the end of this chapter. An alternative is to start with a compelling adverb: "Effectively handled," "Successfully managed," etc. There is a helpful list of action verbs on page 65.

- *Use present tense verbs for your current job and past tense for all other jobs.* For example, if you currently work as a night custodian for the local elementary school, you would say in your first sentence "Clean five school buildings nightly including 40 classrooms." If you no longer have this job you would write "Cleaned five school buildings. . . ."
- *Do not underestimate the power of word choice: Use power words, not passive words.* For example, don't say "Got information on orders for people who asked for it." Instead, say "Responded effectively to customer and colleague requests by tracking order status on computer and over the telephone."
- *Do not use personal pronouns such as "I," "me," "we," or "them."* On a resume, this amounts to stating the obvious. If your name is on the top of the resume, the reader knows that the statements refer to you unless you state otherwise.

- *If possible, include accomplishments as opposed to just listing responsibilities.* Never begin a sentence with "Responsibilities included..." or "Duties include...". This type of beginning may capture what you did, but

TAILORING YOUR RESUME – A CO-OP PROFESSIONAL'S PERSPECTIVE

by Rose Dimarco

A resume initially gives you a script. When you think about what you're willing to put on paper about yourself, it typically reflects how you're going to explain yourself. So are we talking about a resume that's going to introduce you, or is it going to be a leave-behind that is going to help an employer remember you and differentiate you from someone else? It might introduce you and that may be the only decision-maker that they have to determine whether they call you for an interview, and that might adjust your resume somewhat. I'm just concerned that you're not boastful; that it's factual, but you also give yourself credit for what you've done.

If transferable skills are things that you feel are of value, that's what I would help you put on a resume in such a way that the interviewer reading it would conclude those things that you know about yourself: That you're a hard worker; that you're flexible—you don't necessarily want to use those terms on a resume, but you want them to conclude that from reading it. That's the art of resume writing in general, but in health care those are the things that we want to bring to the surface.

Rose Dimarco *is a cooperative education faculty coordinator in Physical Therapy at Northeastern University*

you need to go further than that. Starting with action verbs helps you capture what you did and how you did it. Were you good at your job? If so, tell us why. If not, well, then stick with your responsibilities, simply stated.

The order in which you list your job duties also matters. List the most complex, highly skilled, and most frequently done parts of your job first and end the list with the least skilled, infrequently done tasks. There is no need to list every single thing you did at your job especially things like "swept floors." Instead create broader statements that demonstrate responsibility, such as "efficiently cleaned restaurant kitchen at closing, meeting the highest level of cleanliness standards."

- *Quantify and qualify whenever possible.* For example: "Increased sales by 15%," or "Increased sales significantly by using suggestive-selling techniques." Either of these statements tells the reader much more about precisely how well you did or how you went about accomplishing this task. This is far preferable to simply writing "Sold products." Notice how much more powerful the following descriptions are when the large, bold-type descriptive part of the sentence is added:
    - » Owned and operated snowplowing business **grossing $3,500 a winter**
    - » As member of three-person team, consistently **exceeded shift production goals by 5%.**
    - » Hired and supervised **five** employees
    - » **Using Adobe InDesign,** created a **150-page color** presentation for the annual sales meeting
- *Highlight transferable skills.* As stated earlier, professionals disagree as to whether so-called "soft skills" or transferable skills—such as interpersonal skills or attention to detail—should be included in a resume. However, most professionals agree that job seekers who have NO experience in their chosen field should consider including at least one or two specific soft skills in each job description. Think of it this way: Let's say you're a former welder studying to become a drafter who has only worked on the shop floor and never worked in an office environment. You will want to describe how the interpersonal skills gained on the shop floor have prepared you to be part of the office team. Therefore, most co-op coordinators—but not all—believe that it's helpful for inexperienced candidates to include some transferable skills on your resume.

  How can you identify what your transferable skills are? Ask yourself two questions: Were you good at the job you did? If so, why? Was it because you managed to figure out how to do the job well in a short time (ability to learn quickly)? Your ability to keep customers happy (customer-service skills or maybe interpersonal skills)? Was it that you never missed work or showed up late (dependability or strong work ethic or positive attitude)?

The transferable skills that you choose to highlight will depend heavily on your concentration and the type of co-op job that is being sought. As Scott's colleague Rose Dimarco points out in the sidebar box, it also depends very much on what purpose the resume needs to serve. If you're in a co-op or internship program in which the coordinator arranges the interview schedule for the employer, this calls for a very different resume compared to a situation in which the resume alone must get you in the door! She also emphasizes that sometimes it's enough to imply that you have a specific transferable skill. For example, why bother saying "demonstrated ability to multi-task" when you could have a bullet as follows: "Simultaneously handled telephone calls, in-person customer service, data entry, and invoice processing." We think that the reader will figure out that you are a bona fide multi-tasker!

Look at the list at the end of this chapter for a more complete list of transferable skills.

The use of certain verbs will help you capture transferable skills. Some good examples are: displayed, demonstrated, utilized, exhibited, showed, and used. Often you can start out a job description sentence using one of these verbs and an appropriate adjective in front of a transferable skill. For example:

- Demonstrated excellent interpersonal skills when....
- Utilized solid communication skills when....
- Displayed outstanding ability to learn quickly while....

A "transferable skill cheat sheet" toward the end of this chapter has lists of these verbs and a summary of this transferable skill formula.

Note that you need to be a little careful about throwing transferable skills around. The worst thing you can do is to just mention these skills and leave out anything about what you actually did on the job. Employers need to know what you actually did—even if it was simply operating a piece of equipment. Also, be careful not to overuse the transferable skills—weaving one or two of them into each job description may be adequate. Above all, NEVER claim that you have a certain transferable skill unless you are confident that you really have that skill—and that your former employer would agree. At worst, overemphasizing the transferable skills may come off as "BS" to some employers—especially if they believe that you're using them as a smokescreen to hide the low level of what you really did. Calling a garbage collector a "sanitation engineer" doesn't change the nature of that smelly job. Likewise, it can come off as insincere overkill if you say "Demonstrated outstanding ability to learn quickly when maintaining lawns." How hard is it, really, to learn how to mow a lawn? In that case, it might be better to keep it simple: "Efficiently mowed lawns for neighborhood customers."

RESUMES – AN EMPLOYER'S PERSPECTIVE

by Myretta Robens

In a co-op resume, we mostly just look to see that it is neat and grammatically correct. Experience is not essential. In fact, one of my favorite resumes included the line, "Demonstrated a positive attitude while cleaning out horse stalls." I figured that if Sara could do that, she could handle anything our users threw at her. And that turned out to be the case.

Myretta Robens *was the Director of Technology Operations at Harvard Business School Publishing. She is now the published author of two romance novels*

- *Take time to think about how your job/contribution fits into the "big picture."* When capturing your job experience on a resume, don't just think about what tasks you did each day. Instead, consider the importance of these tasks with relation to what helped the organization accomplish its goals. For example: Don't just say, "Created window displays." Instead, show how your work made a small but important difference for your employer: "Generated customer interest by creating innovative window displays."

- *Either the bullet/outline format or the paragraph format is acceptable.* When writing up your job description, use which works best for you. If your job experience is complex and relatively hard to explain, the paragraph format may work best. If you had numerous and highly varied job responsibilities, you might find the bulleted format easier to use. It's up to you. One caution about bullets—five is probably about the most you'll want to list per job. If your job was highly complex, combine two and possibility three related items into one bullet and consider using some of the details in your cover letter rather than on the resume. When using the paragraph format, use five to seven sentences; anything longer probably won't be read.

- *Volunteer experience can be included under* EXPERIENCE *or in a separate section.* Although you can be flexible about where to include volunteer experience, just make sure that you don't fail to include it somewhere on your resume. Working as a volunteer can show concern for others as well as a desire to learn through unpaid experience. If your volunteer experience was a non-paid co-op, practicum, or internship, it is best to list it as experience rather than under a "volunteer" heading. Most college-related experiences are more rigorous and have clear learning outcomes; volunteering a few hours per week exercising dogs for the local animal shelter is not as substantial. When listing your non-paid experience, use a job title for the work you did, such as "Teacher Aide." Do not list the experience as "Volunteer" or "Volunteer Teacher Aide." If you feel compelled to mention that it was non-paid and for credit, the last sentence of your job description or the last bullet could read "Earned college credit for work experience."

- *In most cases, write out numbers below 11.* Unless you're writing about percentages (e.g., 5%), you generally should write out numbers from one through ten (e.g., "Utilized two database programs"); higher numbers are written numerically (e.g., "Generated 75 leads for potential sales").

- *Identify accomplishments to demonstrate what kind of worker you are.* If you, either alone or as part of a team, did something that helped the company save money, make money, or contributed to more efficient or effective operations, you can describe your role in one or two sentences.

Some resume experts recommend calling out your accomplishment in a separate paragraph under the job description. Here are multiple examples:

Accomplishment: Created jig that increased production speed by 30%.

Accomplishment: Redesigned a frequently used form, resulting in decreased printing costs and faster data entry time.

Accomplishment: As member of three-person team, reviewed product parts and found less expensive substitute, decreasing manufacturing cost by 7%.

Accomplishment: Reviewed manufacturing process and identified two redundant steps, resulting in a streamlined assembly process that reduced manufacturing time by 2%.

Accomplishment: Reorganized office furniture to better utilize natural light, reducing the need for electric lighting several hours of each day.

Remember, the EXPERIENCE section usually is what a potential employer studies to make a preliminary decision about whether you can do the job. An ordinary description means you are an ordinary person. Now is the time to show an employer that you are extraordinary. The following are some helpful hints on how to do that.

A STEP-BY-STEP APPROACH TO WRITING UP YOUR JOB EXPERIENCE

Writing job descriptions takes time, effort, and practice. But once you learn how to do this effectively, you will have mastered a skill that will help you for the rest of your career. Let's look at a step-by-step formula to writing effective job descriptions. Note that the changes in each step are indicated by having the text underlined: You would not underline any job description text on a real resume.

In the interest of giving equal time to two different perspectives, the first example will incorporate transferable skill phrases; the second will show how to write a job description without touting your soft skills.

Step 1

Write down the organization's name and location, then the job title and dates of employment on the second line:

SANTA'S TREE FARM Kent, CT
Laborer 2009 – Present

Step 2

Write down in simple terms the various duties you have or had in a given job:

SANTA'S TREE FARM Kent, CT
Laborer 2009 – Present

- <u>Plant trees and help them grow.</u>
- <u>Mow property.</u>
- <u>Cut down trees for customers, accept payments, and tie trees to customers' cars.</u>

Step 3

Unless you worked for an organization that almost everyone knows (such as Pizza Hut), consider adding details about the nature of the employer and the purpose of the job:

SANTA'S TREE FARM Kent, CT
Laborer 2009 – Present

- Working as only hired employee for small family-owned business, plant trees and help them grow to ensure that adequate supply of Christmas trees is available each winter.
- Mow property regularly to make sure that trees have adequate exposure to sunlight and room to grow.
- Cut down trees for customers, accept payments, and tie trees to cars.

Step 4

Add quantitative details and professional terms when possible to bring the experience to life:

SANTA'S TREE FARM Kent, CT
Laborer 2009 – Present

- Working as only hired employee for small family-owned business, plant over 300 trees annually and help them grow to ensure that adequate supply of Christmas trees is available each winter.
- Mow property regularly to make sure that all four varieties of evergreen trees have adequate exposure to sunlight and room to grow.
- Cut down approximately 200 trees per year for customers, accept payments, and safely tie trees to cars for transportation.

Step 5 (Optional)

Add a phrase or two containing transferable skills in order to capture how well you did the job and what you might be able to provide to a co-op employer in a more professional setting:

SANTA'S TREE FARM Kent, CT
Laborer 2009 – Present

- Working as only hired employee for small family-owned business, exhibited an outstanding work ethic when planting over 300 trees annually and helping them grow to ensure that adequate supply of Christmas trees is available each winter.
- Demonstrated strong attention to detail when mowing property regularly to make sure that all four varieties of evergreen trees have adequate exposure to sunlight and room to grow.
- Cut down approximately 200 trees per year for customers, accepting payments, and safely tying trees to cars for transportation.

Step 6 (Optional)

Add an accomplishment that exemplifies how you contributed to the company's success:

SANTA'S TREE FARM Kent, CT
Laborer 2009 – Present

- Working as only hired employee for small family-owned business, exhibited an outstanding work ethic when planting over 300 trees annually and helping them grow to ensure that adequate supply of Christmas trees is available each winter.
- Demonstrated strong attention to detail when mowing property regularly to make sure that all four varieties of evergreen trees have adequate exposure to sunlight and room to grow.
- Cut down approximately 200 trees per year for customers, accepting payments, and safely tying trees to cars for transportation.

Accomplishment: Initiated relationship with a high school service club, which sold wreathes at farm, resulting in an 18% increase in tree sales.

By crafting this type of job description, a student shows a potential employer that they have many qualities that might be desirable in an employee. Including transferable skills tends to matter less as you gain direct experience in your field, but it can be a helpful tactic for those looking for their first experience in a new career area.

ANOTHER EXAMPLE OF THIS STEP-BY-STEP APPROACH

One of the great advantages of using this step-by-step approach is that it will make your interview easier. If you take the time to nail down an excellent description of your job and employer, then that becomes one less thing that you will need to worry about accomplishing during the interview itself... when you won't have much time to think about what to say! Instead of having to explain the basics of your previous experience, you can build on the resume by diving into specific examples of the points made on your resume.

Let's consider another step-by-step example, leaving out the transferable skill formula this time around:

Step 1

Write down the organization's name and location, then the job title and dates of employment on the second line:

FENWAY PROJECT ADMINISTRATIVE OFFICE Boston, MA
Office Assistant 2010-Present

Step 2

Write down in simple terms the various duties you had in a given job, like this:

FENWAY PROJECT ADMINISTRATIVE OFFICE Boston, MA
Office Assistant 2010-Present

- Schedule and organize events.
- Perform research and administrative tasks.
- Supervise students in after-school program.

Step 3

Add details describing the nature of the employer in question and the purpose of the job:

FENWAY PROJECT ADMINISTRATIVE OFFICE Boston, MA
Office Assistant 2010-Present

- Schedule and organize events and community services for needy socioeconomic groups in inner-city Boston.
- Perform research on corporate and nonprofit organizations to identify strategic methods for getting donations of resources.
- Supervise elementary school students in after-school program.

Step 4

Add quantitative details and professional terms when possible to bring the experience to life:

FENWAY PROJECT ADMINISTRATIVE OFFICE Boston, MA
Office Assistant 2010-Present

- In a timely manner, schedule and organize events and community services for over 50 inner-city Boston teenagers in needy socioeconomic groups.
- Research roughly 250 corporate and non-profit organizations to identify strategic methods for soliciting donations of resources.
- Manage conflicts effectively when supervising elementary school students in after-school program.

From this job description, we get a much better sense of who this student really is. We get a sense of her research experience, altruistic motives, and ability to juggle tasks—without directly mentioning these soft skills. A hiring employer could infer that the student was responsible and motivated. As you will see when you read the chapter on interviewing, these qualities are probably the most important that any potential supervisor wants to see in a new hire.

Passive versus Active Verbs

If, after all this, your resume is still lacking something, try to review your use of verbs. Remember: never use passive verbs where you can use active verbs instead. The following is a list of POWER words for inclusion in your resume.

PASSIVE VERBS	ACTIVE/POWER VERBS
Maintained	Enhanced
Assisted	Contributed (to)
Answered	Directed
Spoke to...	Resolved problems
Sold	Increased sales by...
Taught	Instructed
Processed	Expedited
Received	Earned
Coordinated	Negotiated

As mentioned earlier, a more comprehensive list of action verbs in various categories is available toward the back of this chapter.

SKILLS

This can be a very important section, and we strongly urge you to include it on your resume. Most careers have a special set of knowledge, skills, and abilities that students gain from coursework when preparing for their career. The SKILLS section provides you with a way to identify which of these special skills you possess. In other words, the SKILLS section helps the employer quickly see if you have the skills they are seeking in a job candidate. Always include relevant computer skills in this section. For instance, graphic students would indicate their knowledge of desktop publishing software such as InDesign. Naming your SKILLS section with a career title is highly recommended for more specialized careers; two examples are NURSING SKILLS or VETERINARY TECHNICIAN SKILLS.

Where to place your skills is a bit of a judgment call. If your skills are very strong, you may list them either at the top of your resume or between your EDUCATION and EXPERIENCE sections. If your skills are less impressive, putting them below your EXPERIENCE section is usually the most sensible idea.

Every college student will have at least some basic computer skills. Thus, if you don't choose to list other skills, you can at least have a section entitled COMPUTER SKILLS. Do not overstate your abilities, but don't be modest either. You need to state your abilities clearly. Are you proficient with, familiar with, or do you just have exposure to a particular software program? Can you work with IBM PCs, Macs, or both? As mentioned, if your career requires extensive computer skills such as multimedia, desktop publishing, drafting, and any other computer-related career, you'll want to make sure they are listed in your SKILLS section. In this technological age, stating your computer skills can be the edge you need to get an interview—even when pursuing jobs in supposedly non-technical fields such as the humanities and social sciences!

With this in mind, let's take a closer look at how to capture your computer skills on this section of a resume. Sometimes people either will forget about what PC skills they have or—incredibly—feel that they can't put a given skill down because they learned it on their own, outside of the classroom or workplace. Did you know that some employers are actually more impressed with candidates who taught themselves how to use software applications? Even if you taught yourself "just for fun," that says a great deal about your ability and enthusiasm to learn on the computer. With this in mind, here's a quick checklist you can use to determine whether you have included all of your relevant computer experience.

Do you have experience with:

- *Word processing* (Microsoft Word, WordPerfect, etc.)
- *Spreadsheets* (Microsoft Excel, QuickBooks, Peachtree, Dynamics, Lotus 1-2-3)
- *Databases* (Microsoft Access, dBase, Oracle, MySQL, etc.)

- *Operating systems* (Windows NT/2000/XP/Vista, UNIX, MacOS, Linux, etc.)
- *Programming languages* (C, C++, Visual Basic, Java, Python)
- *Network administration* (Novell NetWare, Windows NT, TCP/IP, Apache Server, etc.)
- *Web design* (HTML, DreamWeaver, JavaScript, ASP, Perl, PHP, CSS, etc.)
- *Presentation graphics* (PowerPoint, Harvard Graphics)
- *Desktop publishing/graphic design* (PageMaker, Adobe Illustrator, Adobe InDesign, Quark, Corel Draw, Adobe PhotoShop, Gimp, etc.)
- *3D Animation* (Maya, 3D Max, Blender, etc.)
- *Engineering/architecture-related* (AutoCAD, Inventor, SolidWorks, Revit, Sketchup, ArchiCAD, Pro E, Micrographics)

Many students are unsure about whether their skills with a given application are good enough to put on their resumes. Obviously, you want to be honest, but you also want to give yourself credit for what you do know. One suggestion for dealing with this dilemma is to break down your knowledge of applications under the categories of "Proficient with," "Familiar with," and "Exposure to." If you have tons of experience with Excel—including experience with pivot tables and vlookup—say that you are proficient with it. If you know how to do formulas, alter columns and rows, and create charts and graphs but not much more, you might say that you are familiar with it. While if you have only used it a few times or your experience is in the distant past, play it safe and say that you just have exposure to Excel. This way you can be honest without selling yourself short.

You also should take care to ensure that you correctly spell the names of any computer applications that you list under the heading of COMPUTER SKILLS or SPECIAL SKILLS. Use the following list as a quick reference when proofreading your resume. Although this is particularly important if you are applying for an MIS job, everyone should try to make their resume as perfectly accurate as possible... never an easy task when it comes to the bizarre spellings of many software applications.

Correct spellings of typical MIS terms (and acceptable alternatives)

Microsoft Word (MS-Word, Word)	Microsoft Access (MS-Access, Access)
Microsoft Excel (MS-Excel, Excel)	MacOS
Microsoft PowerPoint (PowerPoint)	UNIX
Adobe PageMaker (PageMaker)	Linux
TCP/IP	HTML
Lotus Notes	Dreamweaver
Windows XP (XP)	Windows Vista (Vista)
Windows Seven	C++
AutoDesk AutoCAD (AutoCAD)	Novell NetWare (Netware)

Note that it's also acceptable to include what version of a program you have worked with (e.g., Novell NetWare 3.x, etc.). This is especially true with operating systems such as Windows, as there is a big difference between, say, Windows NT and Windows Vista.

Also note that Microsoft Office is a family of Microsoft applications (Word, Excel, Access, PowerPoint, and Outlook) that some employers may buy as one complete package. If you have experience with Microsoft Office, though, we still suggest writing out all of the applications, as some employers may not be familiar with the term. Also, there are different versions of Office, so it may not be clear from that term if you know Access, for example, as that is not included in all versions of Office.

Now that you know how to capture your computer skills, let's consider other skills that you want to make sure to mention. In addition, you should include skills you have in the following areas:

- Language Skills: Fluent in..., Conversational ability in..., etc.)
- Laboratory Skills
- Licenses and Training (Real Estate, CPR, First Aid)

Here are several examples of what your SKILLS section might look like:

DRAFTING SKILLS

- Proficient with AutoCAD R14-2009 and Revit: model space, paper space, Xrefs, 3-D and file management.
- Solid foundation in both mechanical and architectural (residential & commercial) drafting including strength of materials and geometric tolerancing.
- Able to read blue prints and knowledge of building codes.

MULTIMEDIA SKILLS

- Adept with Cut Pro, Soundtrack and DVD Studio Pro
- Practiced in Maya and Photoshop
- Skillful with HTML and Pro Tools

SKILLS

- Proficient with Microsoft Word, Excel, and PowerPoint
- Familiar with Windows XP/Vista and Access
- Exposure to HTML and Dreamweaver
- Conversational in Spanish

If you have a very strong background in computers—meaning that your knowledge goes well beyond applications such as Microsoft Office—the recent industry standard is to break out your computer skills by category. This is fairly standard for students in MIS, Computer Science, Computer Engineering, and similar majors. Here's an example:

COMPUTER SKILLS

Operating Systems:	DOS, Windows XP and Vista, MacOS
Languages:	Visual Basic, HTML

Networking:	Windows Server, Novell NetWare, TCP/IP
Applications:	Microsoft Word, Excel, Access, PowerPoint, Lotus 1-2-3, Adobe PhotoShop, Minitab
Exposure to:	C++, Perl, SQL, Peachtree Accounting

CAPTURING SKILLS ON YOUR RESUME – A CO-OP PROFESSIONAL'S PERSPECTIVE

By Garry Oldham

Last spring a student came to see me and showed me her resume. It had almost nothing on it. She had missed the point; she failed to see that what she'd done at one job was applicable to the job for which she was now applying. In her last job, she had shown persistence, her ability to get along with others, and her ability to learn. It's my experience that students undercut themselves. They rarely see all the aspects of their prior jobs that have prepared them to be a better employee at their next job.

Unfortunately, women in our culture often don't see their skills. Women who have been homemakers and caretakers often write those experiences off; they don't give themselves credit for it. A recent student of mine was a grandmother who took care of a very fragile, granddaughter with special needs for many years. In this role she learned how to be an advocate, be organized, and how to plan, as well as how to respond to medical crises. She also became skilled at working with government entities and paperwork. Furthermore, she did this while running her own housecleaning business, but she discounted all of the work she did for her grandchild because it wasn't paid work.

Another problem women encounter when understanding their skills and creating their resumes has to do with how women are socialized in our culture. For women there are a lot of double binds; women are "damned if they do and damned if they don't." If a woman promotes herself, she may be seen as pushy, arrogant or aggressive. However, if she doesn't promote herself, her skills, she may not get hired or, if working, she may not get a raise. Women learn not to promote themselves; they learn to promote other people.

When women, well, all students, take the time to figure out their skills, it is confidence building. Not only does it change their resume but it prepares them better for their interview.

***Garry Oldham** is a faculty Cooperative Education Coordinator in Human Services at Lane Community College*

INTERESTS

Not everyone agrees that listing your interests on your resume is a good idea. Some experts argue that a job search is a very serious business and only information directly related to job experience, education, skills and abilities belongs on your resume. On the other hand, many experts argue that how you spend your free time reveals another dimension of your personality, as well as important skills such as communication skills, leadership, motivation and initiative, time management, resourcefulness, organization, and energy. Listing your interests on your resume is a chance to include activities, hobbies, and community involvement—to show you're well rounded. Interests humanize you—and anything that makes you seem more like a real person than just a name on a page will make an employer more inclined to give you an interview.

As before, try to be specific. Listing "dancing, reading, sports, and movies" is much less interesting than, say, "ballet, contemporary short fiction, ice hockey, and foreign films." A specific and unique list is much more likely to catch the eye of a potential employer. It also shows that you are serious about your interests and have some depth of character. This makes you come off as a three-dimensional person, and it also can make an employer want to get to know you a little better in the interview. As an ice-breaker question, interviewers may ask you about one of your interests...which is a MUCH easier first question than, say, "Why should we hire you for this job?" Better still, a potential employer may share one of your interests and believe (rightly or wrongly) that the two of you share a connection as a result. That can't hurt!

Make sure you list things in your INTEREST section that are related to the type of work you are seeking. For example, if you're going for a job that requires mechanical skills and you just happen to be passionate about restoring vintage cars, there is a clear connection between your interest and your preparation for the mechanical job. Another good idea is to list skills you may have gained by working with your family that contribute to your skills and abilities. Tamara has had many students who learned construction or machining skills working for a father or grandfather as they grew up. These skills are just as valid as those you gain in the classroom and have a place on your resume if they help paint a picture of you as a person with valuable knowledge and marketable skills.

If you include political or religious organizations or affiliations, be aware that this could work for you or against you. Choosing not to hire you for these reasons would be illegal, of course, but you still run a risk in including certain kinds of information. Imagine writing about your volunteer work for the Republican Party on your resume, then going into your interviewer's office and seeing an autographed photo of former President Clinton! In other words, try to be sensitive to the fact that others may not share your enthusiasms and may even be turned off by them.

Avoid anything that might be controversial or that may raise a potential concern. For example, it is best not to mention nightclubs, partying, hanging out with friends, or shopping. Depending upon the part of the country where you live and are seeking work, you might not want to list deer or duck hunting! You also want to show interests that require some intellectual curiosity or at least energy.

Although some consider the INTERESTS section to be optional or irrelevant, we strongly encourage you to include it. It can't hurt you, and it might help you. If you don't think you have the space, take a close look at the rest of the resume and ask yourself why you can't make room for this section. When we have students who are skeptical about including this section, we always ask them: "What

RESUMES – AN EMPLOYER'S PERSPECTIVE

by Mike Naclerio

An "Interests" section is a good icebreaker for interviews. It gives the resume a personal/unique touch and is an area I always seek out to open conversations with students in an interview.

Mike Naclerio *is the Director of Relationship Management at the workplace HELPLINE* would you prefer as the first question of your interview: "Tell me about yourself." or "I noticed that you're interested in contemporary fiction. Who are your favorite authors?"

Here are two sample INTERESTS sections:

INTERESTS

Cross country skiing, chess, current events, triathlons, and camping

INTERESTS

Expert gardener, skilled carpenter, hand quilter, performing cantor, and guitarist

OBJECTIVE: AN OPTIONAL SECTION

As for objectives, here is another area where professionals tend to disagree—including the co-authors of this book! Scott thinks objectives occasionally can be useful but usually are problematic or unhelpful. Tamara's experience is that a well-written, highly focused objective is like a great 30-second commercial which encourages an employer to read further. We agree that poorly written objectives either tend to say too much or to not say anything at all.

Think about this typical objective: "To find a computer network position with a growing firm where I can improve my skills and where there is opportunity for advancement." First of all, remember that employers hire to solve their problems. An objective like this focuses on how the employer can meet your desires for improving yourself and having opportunity. Another problem with this objective and ones like it, is that it really doesn't say anything that we don't already know: "To find a cooperative education position that will help me grow as an aspiring health care professional." Well, we hope so!

A good objective must describe how you fit the employer's needs. It should clearly state the specific functions and strongest abilities you can perform for an employer that can also be supported by your education and experience to date. Strong objectives are written in terms of your ability to help an employer gain their business goals such as expanding operations, increasing production, efficiency, quality, income, morale, sales, safety, etc.—anything that your education and/or experience has already shown you can do. In other words, you want to help employers envision you as a person who can help them advance their business interests. An effective objective avoids generalized virtues such as "honesty" or "dedication." And it never includes what an employer can do for you.

If you do choose to write an objective, it helps to begin by making a detailed list of the skills an employer is seeking for that type of job. For example, employers hiring drafters typically want someone with many qualities:

- good with CAD software
- very detail oriented
- has knowledge of the type of drafting (mechanical, architectural, electrical, etc.)
- prior experience in a related field such as construction or manufacturing

- has word processing and spreadsheet skills
- has well developed communication skills to be able to work with clients
- able to work both independently and as part of a team
- a good learner because drafters must constantly learn new software

In addition the employer wants what every employer wants: someone who is reliable, responsible, mature, and is a good problem solver.

Next think about what you uniquely bring to the employer that matches the list and use it in your objective to describe how you have the skills they seek based on your education and prior experience.

Here's an example of a good objective drawn from this list:

> "Mechanical drafting position where experience creating precision products, excellent drafting skills, and willingness to do what it takes to complete projects well before deadlines will contribute to company success."

This objective works for this student because he does have manufacturing experience where he has already proven he can complete projects before deadlines. Obviously, assertions in your objective must be true just like everything else on your resume.

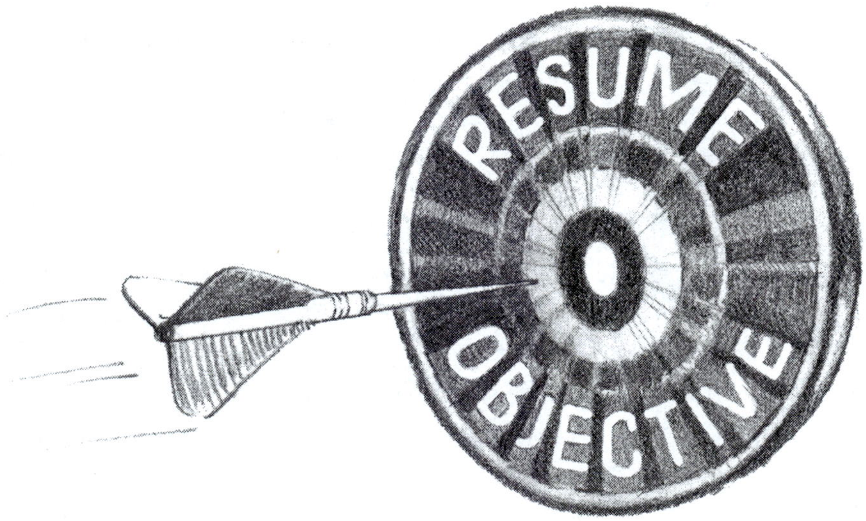

Here are two more good objectives:

> "Warehouse Position especially where knowledge of inventory and ordering methods as well as the ability to improve processes and services for staff and customers will be assets."

> "Administrative Assistant—where there is a need for strong communications skills, a pleasant manner in dealing with people, as well as excellent and accurate word processing/spreadsheet skills will be of value."

Notice that all three of these objectives avoid clichés and overused phrases like "team player" or "detail oriented."

Once you create your own list for your field, you can easily choose three or four skills and/or abilities you possess that are also of value to employers. If you choose to include an OBJECTIVE section, it is typically located as the first section immediately under your name and contact information. Best practice is to create a separate resume with a different objective for each type of job you are seeking. Computers make the creation of resumes easy so there is no excuse to do otherwise.

The sample objectives above are great as long as the person's resume is only under consideration for the type of job that the candidate is specifically targeting! While acting as a recruiting consultant, Scott received many resumes that had an OBJECTIVE section on the top of them. Almost without exception, the stated objective was to find a job that had nothing whatsoever to do with the job for which the candidate had applied! One job was a customer service representative, and there were candidates applying for it who listed an objective as finding a good mechanical engineering job.

Objectives can be a great way to zero in on a specific field... but even a well-written one can pigeon-hole you if your search is relatively broad. Always make sure that your objective aligns with all jobs that you are pursuing. If your search is broad, you may be better off without a stated objective.

REFERENCES

And, lastly, don't forget your references and reference page. As with other parts of a resume, there isn't agreement about including the phrase "References Available Upon Request" on the bottom. Tamara finds that employers know they can ask for references and thinks adding the line is a not the best use of space that could otherwise be used for pertinent information (like the INTEREST section.) Scott, on the other hand, supports having it on the bottom of the page. Regardless, we both agree that you must create a reference page, using the same heading as on your resume as well as the same type and color of paper. Be sure to contact your references first to ask their permission to be used as a reference. This will help your reference person to be more prepared and thus able to give you a better reference when called upon by an employer.

You should have at least three references and ideally around five. Try to include two or three professional/work references, one or two academic references, and one or two character references. A character reference is a coach, a religious leader, or a family friend who has known you since you were more or less in diapers, while a work reference is usually a direct supervisor. Include name, title, company, company address, telephone number, and, whenever possible, an e-mail address.

Ideally, the individuals you list as references are currently employed, even if they have changed jobs. If one or more of your best references are unemployed because of a plant closure or laid off due to the economy, the way to list the job titles of these individuals is to add the word "Former" in front of it as in "Former Hynix Production Manager." As long as you include the important items, the format isn't critical: some people center their references on the page, while others have them flush left. *Just make sure that whatever format you use is consistent with your resume and that the heading on the top of the page is identical to your resume—remember, they are a package.*

A number of Tamara's students have had trouble providing references because they left their last employer under less than positive terms or their supervisors from prior places have retired, moved away, died, or relocated to whereabouts unknown. If this is your circumstance, consider approaching former co-workers or people who left your former employer and now work for someone else. They don't have to be your manager to legitimately comment about your work, work ethic, and reputation. You may have worked with vendors, consultants, or contract workers who could also serve as good references. In addition, you may have some associates from volunteer work who have seen you in action. If you still come up short, you will simply have to explain that most of your former employers and co-workers are unreachable.

You should always bring a few copies of your reference page to an interview, so you can give them to the interviewer immediately, if asked. If you're asked to supply references, you don't want to reply "Um, uh.... Can I get it to you in a few days?" A sample of a basic but good reference page is included at the end of this chapter following the sample resumes.

SAMPLE RESUMES

At the end of this chapter, we have included a few sample resumes that you can review to see how other students have captured themselves on resumes. These resumes reflect varying degrees of education and job experience as well as many different majors, but they all are unique and effective.

Check out David Willhelm's resume on page 70. This is an example of the bulleted list form of resume, as opposed to the paragraph format. One nice thing about this resume is that he has used the font Arial. As mentioned earlier, employers see many resumes in Times New Roman, which looks fine. However, it won't stand out among all the other resumes that use Times New Roman. This is the resume of a young man with no real professional experience, yet it's packed with plenty of attractive attributes. With a clearly articulated set of skills, David comes across as a well-prepared individual despite his inexperience. Consistent with what we've covered in this chapter, note the use of powerful active verbs, strong qualitative details, and the use of transferable skills as opposed to simply listing responsibilities.

Look at Teresa Jones' resume on page 71. This is an example of a resume that effectively communicates her experience without the use of a skills list or objective using the paragraph format. Her job descriptions are concise, feature her range of skills, and highlight her awards and accomplishments. This resume also uses the Calibri font, another alternative to Times New Roman. Calibri is a good font for dense resumes because the letters are actually thinner than other fonts; thus, more letters fit on one line.

The third sample resume is a great example for international students. Look how much background information LaGuardia Community College student Eva Mendez has been able to pack on one page, all without overcrowding. By conserving space with her heading, she has managed to explain a great deal about her educational history, including relevant courses. She breaks out two different jobs with the same employer effectively. This resume will save her considerable time when it comes to the interview. While some students with international backgrounds are compelled to explain their personal history in the interview, Eva should be able to move right into why the employer should hire her. After all, they already know a good deal about who she is before she walks in the door.

Next we have another promising student from LaGuardia Community College. Here is a student whose job experience is longer and stronger than that of many college students. As a result, Pui Sze Ng opts against using the transferable skills within the job description: Her experience doesn't need as much selling as someone who has never had a professional job. Appropriately, she chooses to push her computer skills higher up on the resume, just after the education section. This is her top selling point, and she wants it to be noticed right away. The skills section breaks out her computer skills in a way that will be useful to her prospective employers: It's easy to follow both aesthetically and conceptually. Lastly, the resume is in a font called Verdana—always a good idea for an aspiring computer professional to show that she can get beyond the default font in Word!

As for the sixth and last sample, the first thing that catches your eye with Meghan Brooke's resume is that it is neat and eye-pleasing, with nice use of boldface and italics. She has opted for a different font called Arial Narrow, which is a nice change from the usual Times New Roman rut. This resume also shows how to display both a local and permanent address if you feel inclined to use both. As her job experience lacks work related to her concentration, she has chosen to use transferable skills throughout all of her job descriptions in order to highlight skills that an MIS employer might want to see. Meghan chose the paragraph format, probably because it saves a little space, but she could have used bullets just as easily. This resume attracted multiple interviews and a great entry-level co-op job for her.

As you can see, each of these five resumes differs significantly in terms of how to use font, boldface type, italics, centering, headings, and underlining. Some of the resume writers' choices may appeal to you more than others. There really is a great deal of flexibility in how you make your resume look, as long as you capture each of the required sections on page one of your resume, and as long as your resume is completely free of spelling mistakes or typographical errors.

Is it easy to write an effective resume? Not necessarily. As you hopefully know by now, you may have to be creative to show how some of your past job experience relates to the jobs you plan to pursue. But with considerable effort and a little assistance from your co-op coordinator and/or Career Services, you can write a resume that will help get you in the door for an interview.

MULTIPLE RESUMES

What if you are applying for jobs in more than one concentration? Perhaps you plan to apply for both mechanical and architectural drafting jobs, for example. The best option is to create TWO resumes: one emphasizing your skills for a mechanical drafting job, and another focusing on your aptitude in architectural drafting.

Is it "okay" to do this? Of course it is! In fact, trying to capture both of these interests in one resume is extremely difficult; you run the risk of coming across as someone who lacks focus or who is "jack of all trades, master of none." This should give you some incentive to consider writing more than one resume. One cautionary note, however: It is crucial that YOU keep track of which resume has been faxed or e-mailed to each employer. If the same employer receives one of your resumes from your coordinator and another when you arrive for an interview, this will definitely work against you! This is especially true given that many coordinators now use a computerized system for e-mailing resumes—make sure to discuss using multiple resumes with your coordinator before trying to do this.

When creating multiple resumes for related employment, much of the information on each of your resumes will be identical: Obviously, this won't affect your EDUCATION section much, and you still list your places of employment. But how you describe your job experience could vary quite a bit. On a mechanical drafting resume, you would emphasize the mechanical skills and knowledge in each of your work experiences: operating, troubleshooting and repairing equipment, exposure to engines, hydraulics, utilizing blueprints to manufacture products, etc. On an architectural drafting resume, though, you might describe the same job in terms of the architectural products manufactured like prefabricated walls, roof trusses, structural steel or precast concrete for bridges and parking structures. Or, if some of your previous job related to computers but some of it didn't, then move your computer-related duties to the top of the job description for the both resumes.

Even your interests might be reflected differently on each resume: You might take "restoring vintage cars" off of your architectural resume and add interests pertaining to building such as helping with Habitat for Humanity projects which may be perceived more favorably by an architectural employer. Keep in mind that we're not suggesting that you lie about your interests and your job experiences. Just remember to emphasize those things which will be relevant to an employer in that field.

AVOID TEMPLATES

We can't say this more emphatically, don't use a word-processing template! They may appeal to those who are lazy and/or fear that they don't know enough about word processing to make the format look good. Believe us, templates are not the answer. Templates make it extremely difficult for you to revise and update a resume, and they may force you into including or emphasizing items that are not appropriate for an aspiring co-op, intern, or graduate seeking a full-time job. A few times a year, we are shown resumes that were thrown together in a few minutes using the resume template in Microsoft Word. The typical Word resume template is not that attractive—the student's address is small and hard to read, and the experience section's format is rather odd in its emphasis. We have plenty of options here that will work better for you.

After you have written your resume use the following checklist to make sure your resume meets the successful resume standard.

RESUMES – AN EMPLOYER'S PERSPECTIVE

by Steve Sim

What impresses me on a resume? First of all, honesty impresses me. If you haven't done a whole lot of HTML development work, and you put that down as a skill set, be sure you can answer specific questions about HTML. Second, clarity impresses me. If you are clear enough on a resume where someone who doesn't know anything about you (or potentially even positions you're interested in) can read your resume and say you're qualified, then it's going to get to my desk. Third, effective use of space impresses me. Fonts and margins can change to fit your info. One should feel comfortable using them freely.

***Steve Sim** is a Technical Recruiter at the Microsoft Corporation*

RESUME CHECKLIST

- ☐ You have given careful thought as to whether your resume should be one page or two pages. If it's barely over one page, look for opportunities to condense it to fit on one page.
- ☐ The resume has been carefully checked for spelling and punctuation errors.
- ☐ Job descriptions are grammatically correct.
- ☐ There are no personal pronouns (I/me).
- ☐ Job descriptions do not begin with: "Responsibilities included" or "Duties consisted of" or anything similar to those constructions.
- ☐ Abbreviations of states are correct (e.g., OR not Or. or Ore.)
- ☐ The format is neat and attractive to the eye.
- ☐ The format is easily readable.
- ☐ All major components of a resume are included.
- ☐ Job titles are listed for each job description.
- ☐ Dates and locations of employment are included for each work experience, and they are written in the same format each time.
- ☐ Telephone number(s) and email are correct. (A common error because people tend to change cell phone numbers and e-mail accounts frequently.)
- ☐ Resume will be copied on 8½ X 11 inch paper in white or some other neutral color. (Ask your coordinator what format they wish to receive your resume. These days many coordinators prefer an electronic copy, not a hard copy. If they are faxing your resume, they may prefer plain white paper.)
- ☐ If you are required to submit your resume electronically, convert the file from Word to PDF and then check the PDF version to ensure that the conversion didn't create problems with alignment and formatting.

Appendix G is an extensive resume writing guide (rubric) that Tamara uses with her students. Use it to evaluate your resume drafts and it will help you change your resume from ordinary to exemplary!

YOUR RESUME IS A REFLECTION AND PERSONAL STATEMENT OF YOU!

Please note that these are formatting suggestions, not requirements. Your resume is a reflection of you, and as such, you should feel comfortable and proud of its contents. While writing your resume, you will be presenting your experience and achievements in the best way possible. However, there is no room for deceit or lies on a resume. Lying on a resume is akin to plagiarism and is not acceptable at any educational institution or in any professional workplace. Grade point averages, dates, computer skills, and achievements must be accurate and honest. You are building a professional reputation and should strive for a reputation known for its integrity.

While writing your resume, feel free to consult with friends, advisors, teachers, employers, and others whose opinions you respect. However, bear in mind that this guidebook and your co-op/internship or career services coordinator should be your number one resources. Again, be wary of your cousin's boyfriend who claims to be good at writing resumes—a person outside of your co-op program generally has no experience working with co-op students and employers and therefore may be not be a credible source of assistance. That said, do have several people proofread for format, grammatical and spelling errors. (Remind your proofreaders that resume grammar is not the same as an essay—no pronouns and sentences start with action verbs!) Many employers will discard your resume as soon as a typo is discovered, the theory being that if you cannot take the time to submit an error-free resume (which should reflect your best effort), then the quality of your work may reflect the same low standards. To put it more simply, an employer might think "If this is the best, I'd hate to see the rest!"

So invest your time wisely and do a superb job! There is no exact formula for a perfect resume, but these suggestions are based on experience, employer recommendations, and research. Learn to do your resume well now, and you will find that this skill will be helpful to you throughout your career. GOOD LUCK!

ACTION VERB LIST

COMMUNICATIONS

acted as liaison	demonstrated	lectured
advised	displayed	marketed
advocated	edited	mediated
authored	guided	moderated
commented	informed	negotiated
consulted	instructed	notified
corresponded	interpreted	presented

ADMINISTRATION

administered	distributed	managed

appointed	eliminated	motivated
arranged	executed	obtained
completed	governed	opened
controlled	implemented	organized
coordinated	instituted	overhauled
delegated	issued	presided
directed	launched	provided

PLANNING & DEVELOPMENT

broadened	devised	improved
created	discovered	invented
designed	drafted	modified
developed	estimated	planned

ANALYSIS

amplified	detected	forecasted
analyzed	diagnosed	formulated
calculated	disapproved	identified
compiled	evaluated	investigated
computed	examined	programmed

FINANCIAL/RECORDS MANAGEMENT

allocated	collected	logged
audited	documented	maximized
balanced	expedited	minimized
catalogued	invested	monitored
classified	inventoried	processed

TECHICAL/MECHANICAL/MANUFACTURING/ MAINTENANCE/CONSTRUCTION

adjusted	drilled	operated
aligned	drove	performed
analyzed	examined	polished
applied	fastened	positioned
arranged	filled	prepared
assembled	fitted	pressed

attached	fueled	pulled
bolted	gathered	recorded
built	identified	repaired
bundled	inserted	replaced
calibrated	inspected	rewired
changed	installed	riveted
clamped	joined	routed
cleaned	loaded	screwed
coiled	lubricated	sealed
connected	maintained	serviced
constructed	measured	set up
cut	modified	sketched
delivered	observed	smoothed
disassembled	oiled	soldered

MEDICAL

administered	charted	fed
admitted	collected specimens	followed HIPAA guidelines and safety protocols
applied medication	draped	labeled medication
assisted	dressed wounds	observed
bathed	examined	recorded

CULINARY/HOSPITALITY

adjusted	cleaned	prepared
arranged	cleared	presented
brewed	coordinated	rectified
calculated	delivered	relayed
carved	planned	replenished

GENERAL TERMS

accomplished	delivered	originated
achieved	expanded	performed
adjusted	handled	provided
assisted	increased	served
completed		

TRANSFERABLE SKILLS LIST

Ability to learn quickly	Positive attitude/Strong work ethic
Interpersonal skills	Quantitative skills (math, computation)
Computer skills (be specific)	Responsibility
Communication skills	Mechanical aptitude
Discretion and integrity	Dependability/reliability
Customer-service skills	Organizational skills
Willingness to do whatever asked	Ability to learn quickly
Patience	Ability to work in teams
Good judgment	Initiative/Self-starter
Attention to detail	Creativity
Ability to juggle multiple duties	Ability to work independently
Verbal communication skills	Willingness to take risks
Writing skills	Ability to identify opportunities
Ability to do research	Openness to new ideas
Persistence/Drive	Ambitiousness
Results-oriented personality	Eagerness to learn
Customer-service skills	Flexibility
Selling skills/Persuasiveness	Enthusiasm
Outgoing personality	Commitment
Ability to juggle responsibilities	Willingness to work long hours
Attention to detail	Ability to work in teams

TRANSFERABLE SKILL PHRASE CHEAT SHEET

If you would like to try building transferable skill phrases into your resume, try using this formula: Pick an accurate word from each column below in order to figure out how to graft a transferable skill phrase onto a bullet point or sentence in your EXPERIENCE *section.*

Verb	Adjective	Transferable Skill	Linking Word
Demonstrated	effective	ability to learn quickly	when
Displayed	excellent	communication skills	while
Showed	outstanding	interpersonal skills	

Exhibited	strong	attention to detail
Proved to have	solid	dependability
Utilized	very good	attitude
Exercised	consistent	organizational skills
Used	exceptional	patience
Possessed	positive	customer-service orientation
		willingness to do whatever asked
		ability to work in a team
		ability to work independently
		initiative

Step 1:

Capture what you did in simple, straightforward way:

- Cleaned out stalls at a horse farm.

Step 2:

Add quantifiable and quantitative details to make the job come alive:

- Working in a busy, family-oriented horse farm, cleaned out 23 horse stalls daily.

Step 3:

If you were GOOD at the job, identify the transferable skills you used in the job and use them to create a phrase using the above formula:

- Working in a busy, family-oriented horse farm, demonstrated positive attitude and willingness to do whatever asked while cleaning out 23 horse stalls daily.

You don't need a transferable skill phrase with every single sentence or bullet, but students without any directly relevant job experience probably should make sure to use at least two per job.... assuming you were GOOD at that job! One way or another, find ways to make your resume do more than list WHAT you did. Capture HOW you did it and WHY you did it well.

David Willhelm

123 N 45th Street
Springfield, Oregon 97477
(541) 766-0000 dwillhelm@yahoo.com

Drafting Skill Highlights:

- Highly skilled with AutoCAD 2007-2009
- Knowledge of ASME Y14.5 dimensioning standards
- Excellent visualization skills
- File management/ document skills: able to create section views and use Xrefs
- Leadership experience; eager and fast learner
- Broad software knowledge: Fluent in Windows XP operating system and familiar with Windows Vista

Education:

Lane Community College — Eugene, Oregon
Expected graduation — June 2010
Seeking two year **Drafting** AAS degree
G.P.A. 3.26

Related courses:

- CAD 1, 2, and 3D
- Mechanical Drafting & Design
- Geometric Tolerancing
- Strength of Materials
- Electrical Drafting
- Graphic Concepts & Engineering Information
- Architectural Drafting and Details
- Residential & Commercial Buildings
- Building Codes
- Hydraulics and Mechanical Systems
- Math 89 (Includes Trigonometry) & Math 111 (College Algebra)

Springfield High School — Springfield, Oregon
High School Diploma — June 2004

- Two years drafting including board drafting and AutoCAD

Experience:

Papa's Pizza — Eugene, Oregon
Waiter and Cashier — 2003 – Present

- Advise customers on menu selections; process cash and credit transactions
- Use safe/sanitary work practices and help lead by example
- Effectively perform in fast-paced environment where accuracy is necessary for customer satisfaction
- Demonstrate good communication with customers to ensure continued positive relations

Interests:

- Sketching, snowboarding, wildlife photography, and music

TERESA JONES

1825 Gilles Road, Eugene, OR 97401 | 541.643-9399 | jonest@yahoo.com

EDUCATION

Lane Community College — Eugene, OR
Associate of Arts Oregon Transfer Degree, Elementary Education Major — 2009
Awards: President's Honor Roll, John Dewey Education Award, and Graduation Keynote Speaker

CLASSROOM EXPERIENCE

Lane Community College — Eugene, OR
Teaching Assistant (college level) — 2008 & 2009

- Assisted and lectured in Foundations of Education 200 and 201 courses.
- Developed support material and lessons for whole class and small groups.

McCornack Elementary — Eugene, OR
Practicum Teacher (elementary level) — Spring 2009

- In second grade classroom worked with reading groups, led whole class discussions and created puppet show with student cooperation.

Meadowlark Elementary — Eugene, OR
Practicum Teacher (elementary level) — Fall 2009

- For second/third grade combination classroom, created two three-part lessons and executed them with whole class, facilitating discussions.
- Handled art projects and clerical duties.

Mapleton Elementary — Mapleton, OR
Instructional Aide/Library-Media Specialist (elementary level) — 2003-2007

- Handled numerous tasks on K-3 level, including teaching math and computer research in small groups
- Working in library, updated from manual to electronic checkout system, ordered all library books within school budget, and facilitated library checkout process for whole classes and small groups
- Created and facilitated Battle of the Books and Beverly Cleary Awards with grades 3-6 as well as organizing book fairs
- Conducted parent/teacher conferences, and handled recess duty.

Childbirth Educator (adult education)
Peace Harbor Hospital, Florence, OR — 1998-2000

TERESA JONES **PAGE 2**

RELATED EXPERIENCE

Star Mountain Waldorf School — Bend, OR
Afterschool Daycare Provider — 1994-1996

- Pre-K through sixth grade daycare and parent volunteer

Whitaker School — Eugene, OR
Parent Volunteer — 1996-2000

PROFESSIONAL DEVELOPMENT

Library conferences, literary conferences, math workshop, computer workshops, Teaching for Social Justice Conference

MEMBERSHIPS

Siuslaw Public Library Community Council — 2006-2007
Emerald Empire Reading Council-Oregon Reading Council
Rethinking Schools

ADDITIONAL EXPERIENCE

Direct-entry Midwife (currently non-practicing) — 1998-present

COMPUTER SKILLS

Proficient with MS-Word and PowerPoint. Familiar with Quicken, MS-Excel, and Adobe PhotoShop. Exposure to Adobe InDesign.

INTERESTS

Knowledge transfer, literacy, children's fiction, playing guitar, and hiking

Eva Mendez

11 23rd Place, Apt. 3D Sunnyside, NY 11012
646-555-3333 e-mail: evamendez84@gmail.com

Education

LaGuardia Community College/CUNY Long Island City, NY
Associate's Degree May 2011
Major: Education: The Bilingual Child
GPA 3.91 – Phi Theta Kappa Honor Society
Completed 48 credits toward an Associate of Arts degree
Relevant Coursework

Introduction to Bilingualism
General Psychology
Advanced Spanish Composition
Early Concepts of Math for Children
Sociology of Education
Children's Literature

LaGuardia Community College/CUNY Long Island City, NY
English as a Second Language – Level 6
September 2007 – May 2009

Universidad Central del Colombia Cali, Colombia
Bachelor of Arts, Communications; Sept. 2001 – Sept. 2003
specialization in Public Relations

Experience

LaGuardia Community College Long Island City, NY
English Language Center Lab Assistant August 2006 – June 2007

- Familiarized ESL faculty and students in the use of the language lab's computerized listening/recording equipment.
- Conducted student orientations to the language lab and participated in special teaching and learning projects.
- Supervised open lab hours for students' independent study.

Office Assistant September 2005 – June 2006

- Assisted the Center in helping students from Latin America adjust to living and studying in the United States.
- Guided students with information related to TELC programs and international student regulations.

Banco Popular del Colombia Bogota, Colombia
Consumer Banker/Financial Consultant June 2003 – May 2005

- Performed administrative and financial tasks for the Human Resources Director.
- Managed various financial operations including opening new accounts and providing information on loans and investments.
- Prepared banking instruments and completed monetary transactions for corporate and personal clients.

Skills and Interests

Proficient in MS-Word, Adobe Photoshop, QuarkExpress, and Netscape.
Familiar with MS-PowerPoint and Excel.
Strong marketing and organizational skills.
Fluent in Spanish; Proficient in Portuguese.
Interests: Latina writers, performing arts, black and white photography, basketball.

References Furnished Upon Request

Pui Sze Ng

57 Durutti Avenue, Staten Island, NY 10201
Phone 718-222-0000, Fax 718-222-9990, e-mail: puisze@yahoo.com

Education

LaGuardia Community College/CUNY, Long Island City, NY
Associate of Applied Science Degree – January 2012
Programming and Systems Major, Business Minor
Honors: Dean's List

Skills

Software	Programming Languages	Operating Systems
Word 97/00	Visual Basic 6.0	Windows 9.x/NT/00
Excel 97/00	Visual FoxPro 6.0	Windows Vista
FrontPage 97/00	C++	Novell NetWare 4.x/5.x
Adobe Photoshop	HTML	Macintosh OS 8.5

- Customizing computers, constructing PC systems, troubleshooting and implementing software applications
- Strong analytical skills
- Detail-oriented and dedicated to problem-solving
- Excellent interpersonal and organization skills

Work Experience

Manhattan University — New York, NY
Network Technician and End-User Support Specialist — August 2009 – Present

- Work with relative independence to meet CIS project deadlines, including the setup of computers and printers for the registration department, faculty, and student labs.
- Install and configure Windows Workstations, TCP/IP, and applications.
- Run RJ-45 CAT 5 wires and terminate into Keystone jack preparing workstations for LAN services and internetworking.
- Use a variety of equipment, such as wire scope and port scanner, and applications, such as IP browser, FTP, and IRC software to complete projects.

Robins USA — Long Island City, NY
Accounting Office Assistant — June 2008 – July 2009

- Used Excel to create accounting spreadsheets.
- Posted financial entries to journal and ledger utilizing customized software.
- Organized, sorted, and maintained financial records and profiles.

Interests

Technological trends via hands-on experience, online technology resources, computer technology magazines, gourmet cooking, jazz, outdoor activities.

References

Business and personal references available upon request.

MEGHAN C. BROOKE
e-mail: brooke.m@bigskycc.edu

Local Address	Home Address
145 Gallatin Street	6856 Camera Circle
Bozeman, MT 02115	Ocala, FL 22454
(907) 465-8822	(255) 788-8642

EDUCATION

BIG SKY COMMUNITY COLLEGE — Bozeman, MT
Associate's Degree in Medical Laboratory Science — May 2012
Cumulative GPA: 3.6 (4.0 scale)
Honors: University Honors Program, Dean's List
Activities: Health Sciences Club (Treasurer), Big Sky Student Ambassadors, Ultimate Frisbee Club
Planning to finance 60% of tuition and living expenses through cooperative education earnings

MANATEE HIGH SCHOOL — Ocala, FL
College Preparatory Curriculum — June 2009
Honors: Who's Who Among American High School Students, National Honor Roll, National Honor Society
Activities: Varsity Tennis, Ocala Packers Hiking Club, Students Against Driving Drunk

EXPERIENCE

KOHL'S DEPARTMENT STORE — Ocala, FL
Point of Sale Representative — June 2006-August 2008
Increased customer participation in Kohl's credit program by persuading customers to enroll. Exhibited close attention to detail while performing cash and credit transactions and calculating customer receipts. Demonstrated ability to learn quickly while using the credit computer and cash register. Greeted customers.

GOLDEN YEARS SENIOR CENTER — Ocala, FL
Volunteer — June 2004-Sept. 2005
Demonstrated warmth and caring when working with over 75 geriatric residents. Consistently exhibited patience while dealing with demanding population on a daily basis. Effectively juggled multiple duties by answering phones, delivering food and mail, and engaging in personal conversations with residents. Taught interested residents how to use Internet. Stocked supplies.

COMPUTER SKILLS

Knowledgeable in Microsoft Word, Microsoft Excel, Windows XP/Vista.
Familiar with Microsoft Access, Microsoft PowerPoint, and HTML.

INTERESTS

Skiing, ice hockey, camping, Scandanavian literature, drawing, and theater.

References will be furnished upon request

MEGHAN C. BROOKE
e-mail: brooke.m@bigskycc.edu

Local Address
145 Gallatin Street
Bozeman, MT 02115
(907) 465-8822

Home Address
6856 Camera Circle
Ocala, FL 22454
(255) 788-8642

REFERENCES

Mr. John Hannah, Store Manager
Kohl's Department Store
777 South Garfield Drive
Ocala, FL 22454
(255) 555-3388
e-mail: j.shumbata@kohls.com

Mr. Anthony Zamboni, Facility Manager
Golden Years Senior Center
5544 Manatee Highway
Ocala, FL 22455
(255) 555-3000
e-mail: azamboni@goldenyears.com

Ms. Susan Bacher, Family Friend
43 Locklear Cove
Kissimmee, FL 22103
(313) 555-1111
e-mail: krisdelmhorst@hotmail.com

Dr. Joseph Pepitone, Professor
Timothy Paul School of Nursing
Big Sky University
24 Lone Mountain Avenue
Bozeman, MT 90601
(906) 373-0001
e-mail: j.pepitone@bigsky.edu

Dr. Singha Piqaboue, Associate Professor
Timothy Paul School of Nursing
Big Sky University
24 Lone Mountain Avenue
Bozeman, MT 90601
(906) 373-0003
e-mail: s.piqaboue@bigsky.edu

CHAPTER 2 REVIEW QUESTIONS

1. Name at least four transferable skills that you have to offer a potential employer, and identify where you developed each skill.

2. Does it always make sense to list job experience in reverse chronological order, starting with the most recent job? Why, or why not?

3. What are the pros and cons of specifically listing your transferable skills on a resume?

4. What is the best way to indicate your varying degrees of knowledge of a computer skill or a language?

5. Name four or five specific interests that you have, choosing only ones that would add value to your resume. Also, list three interests that should NOT be included on any resume.

CHAPTER THREE

Strategic Interviewing

When we help students prepare for an interview, we are regularly asked the following question: "Should I try to make it sound like I would be a great candidate for this job, or should I be honest?"

Our answer is, simply, "Yes." Many future co-ops, interns, and full-time job seekers don't realize that this is not an either/or question: There is no reason why you can't be honest while effectively selling yourself as an outstanding job candidate. Learning to do so is a two-step process: You need to identify which of your skills, experiences, or personal characteristics might be attractive to a particular employer. Then you need to learn how to articulate these qualities to the interviewer in the process of answering questions... and asking questions!

By the end of this chapter, you should have a better idea of how to strategize for interviews: How to show the employer that there is a strong connection between your unique characteristics as a job candidate and the job itself, as it is described in the job description.

Mastering this art will boost your chances of obtaining the best jobs. Depending on your major, the job market, the interviewer's approach, and your school's way of doing business with employers, your interview could be anything from a brief "sanity check" to a grueling interrogation. Talk to the professional at your school about what to expect, but—when in doubt—always assume that the interview will be a challenging test of your ability to research, prepare, and execute strategically.

BASICS OF INTERVIEWING

Before your resume has been passed along to a potential employer, there are several basics that you should know about interviewing. While many may seem like common sense, sometimes we find that sense is less common than we would like to believe. Accordingly, see how you rate in terms of the following:

Voice Mail Messages

Making sure you have an appropriate voice mail message is an important start. Then you need to check it regularly during your job search. The best employers know that they need to act quickly if they hope to hire the best co-op candidates. If they have trouble contacting you, they may move ahead and hire someone else. At the very least, they may experience frustration in attempting to contact you. Obviously, this is not the kind of first impression you want to make. So check your voice mail and e-mail at least twice each day once you start the referral process.

There is a definite dilemma with cellphones for many students in this day and age. Even if you have a land line, it's sometimes reasonable to fear putting your home number on a resume due to unreliable roommates, family members, or young children answering the phone. Yet if you put your cellphone number on the resume, then you run the risk of having an employer call you while you're on a noisy subway or some other awkward situation. With a cellphone, you also have to worry about annoying delays, echoes, and garbled speech depending on the quality of your service.

There is no easy solution to this dilemma. Most students these days do use a cellphone. If you do, though, be careful about when and where you pick up the phone when you are in the thick of a job search. If in doubt about whether you should pick up the phone, just let it go to your voice mail—and then call back promptly from a quiet place with good reception.

Another point on this topic: Your voice mail message will give the potential employer their first opportunity to hear how you present yourself. As such, you want to leave a highly professional message, one that is clear and concise. For example: *"Hi, you've reached Tom Olafsson at 718-555-1234. I cannot answer your call right now, but please leave a message, and I will call you back as soon as possible."* There have been many horror stories about students leaving messages with loud music and obnoxious roommates saying ridiculous things: "Yo, we're down at the pub with a bunch of pitchers—Later!" We had one student whose girlfriend left a provocative message on his machine—not the best introduction to a potential employer! Sometimes it's not even clear whether the caller has dialed the right number. On a more subtle note, many students simply mumble, sound half-asleep, or fail to express themselves in an upbeat, professional manner.

Basically, a voice mail message won't determine whether or not you get a job. At best, it may be completely neutral. At worst, it can create the beginnings of doubt about whether you have the basic professionalism to communicate in a professional environment. And if life without a humorous voice mail message seems unbearable, you can always change your message back after you have started your co-op job.

Phone Etiquette

During your job search, answer all phone calls as if the person calling were an employer. Even if you have caller ID on your phone, treat unknown callers as if they are potential employers. This initial conversation will determine if you will be invited for the next step in the hiring process, usually an in-person interview. Recently one of Tamara's employers contacted her because he was particularly displeased with a phone conversation with a student she had referred to him. The employer said the student answered the phone with a 'Hey dude, what's up?" Needless to say the employer quickly ended the conversation and did not select this student for an interview.

While there is nothing wrong with simply saying "hello" when picking up the phone, you might take note of the caller and respond by stating your full name ("Rich Sugerman")—just as you likely would if you were picking up your phone in a professional office.

When speaking to a potential employer on the phone, make sure to be professional in your speech. Try to avoid "yeahs" and "uh-huhs." Speak with energy and enthusiasm—even if you're not sure if you want this particular job. You want your first conversation with a potential employer to be very positive and effective. If you're called to arrange an interview, make sure that you have your calendar on hand. Try to be flexible about what days and times you can meet. If you have another commitment, say so politely and suggest what days would be best for you. Tell the caller that you're looking forward to the interview and eager to find out whether this job would be a good match for your skills. Make sure to ask for directions to the interview, ask for the individual's phone number in case you must reschedule the interview due to an emergency, and confirm the date and time before you hang up.

Attire

Make sure that your professional wardrobe is in good shape before beginning the interview process. Many students have wound up buying a new suit or outfit right before going on an interview: In fact, one student forgot to take the price and size tags off of his new suit and was nicknamed "Tags" for his whole six-month co-op job! You don't want to be shopping before an interview when you could be researching the organization, so plan ahead.

Job seekers should wear nicer clothes for the interview then typically worn for work. The idea, of course, is to make that great first impression. Dressing up shows respect to the interviewer while also demonstrating that you are serious about your job search. What you wear depends upon what part of the country you live in and the industry to which you are applying. In general, the west coast is more casual than the east coast and bigger cities are more formal than small towns. If possible, go visit the business where you will be interviewing and observe how the staff are dressed to get a feel for what is appropriate. It is possible to dress up too much. For example, on the west coast, a student who shows up for a welding job interview in a suit would be considered way overdressed. If in doubt, check with your co-op coordinator.

Men and women applying to positions in conservative fields such as banking, finance, law, engineering, and other related professions should wear a suit, shirt, tie, dark socks the color of the suit, and dress shoes. Your shoes should be polished. Your shirt should be a light color, usually white, light blue, pink, light green, etc. Your suit preferably should be some shade of gray, blue, or black... NOT some unusual color like green, flamingo pink, or strong pattern like a dramatic plaid. Your shoes should be polished, and your socks should be close to the color of your suit. Go light on perfume or cologne or wear none at all; more and more offices are becoming 'fragrance free' due to staff sensitivities. As for ties, it is generally best to be conservative: Wear something that doesn't stand out too much.

To our knowledge, no one has ever failed to get a job because they wore a boring tie. This rule is especially true of jobs in conservative fields, such as finance and criminal justice.

For women, it is especially important that your clothing is not tight or revealing; the interviewer shouldn't be able to see your cleavage or your midriff. Makeup should not be excessive. Keep your nails short and avoid bright or specialty polishes. Although some women balk at wearing nylons—and there are co-op jobs where they are not necessary—you should always wear them for interviews if you are wearing a dress or skirt... even on hot summer days.

Jewelry, both men's and women's, should be kept to a minimum, especially if you have body piercings. It is best to remove visible jewelry from your tongue, nose or eyebrow. For folks with tattoos, cover them as completely as possible with your clothing. If hired, you'll want to find out what the company policy is about showing your tattoos before revealing them. Avoid wearing hats, head scarves, or other accessories—remember, the idea is for the interviewer to focus on your skills and abilities, not what you're wearing!

For interviewing in other fields, both men and women can wear nice slacks (solid color or tiny patterned are best, not jeans), a solid colored button down shirt, a belt, socks that match the color of the pants (no white athletic socks!), and polished dress shoes (not sport shoes or cowboy boots). Men can add a sport coat or tie (usually one or the other), and women should probably wear a jacket to help interviewers focus on them, not their body. For some fields such as fashion, multimedia or graphic design, showing a sense of style through your clothing is expected. Thus, you have a bit more flexibility and can dress a bit more creatively. However, it is never advisable to overdo it. In other fields such as construction, automotive, and manufacturing, coming dressed to "go to work" is considered ideal because it helps the interviewer imagine you doing the work. That does not mean showing up in a black t-shirt and black jeans. For all interviews, make sure your clothes are clean, neat (ironed is best), fit you well and are ones you feel good wearing. Feeling good in your clothes will help you project confidence; interviewing is uncomfortable enough without having clothing that is too tight! And, make sure you leave your hardware at home or in the car—take the sunglasses off your head and remove headphones from around your neck.

Some students object to these guidelines, feeling that their individuality is being compromised. Well, that's true. Basically, if having ear plugs, a mohawk haircut, or wearing funky clothes is more important to you than getting a job, go right ahead but be prepared to accept the consequences. Fairly or unfairly, potential employers will judge you based on how you present yourself at an interview. Are you really interested in "fitting in" and "being one of the team," or is it more important to make a statement about your individuality with your appearance? The choice is yours.

Hygiene

You shouldn't have to receive a gift-wrapped bar of soap from a friend, roommate, or co-op coordinator to know that hygiene is an important consideration. In an interview, hygiene is either neutral or a negative; it goes unnoticed or it distracts the interviewer from the task at hand.

You should shower or bathe before any interview. Make sure your hair is neat and clean. Use deodorant, and make a habit of having a breath freshener on the way to an interview. Smokers should avoid smelling of smoke by keeping their clean interview clothes away from smoke (immediately after laundering, hang in the closet in a garment bag or plastic bag from the cleaners) and by avoiding smoking in the car on the way to the interview, even if the windows are down. It can be a real distraction, and no one wants to work next to someone who has a hygiene problem or who reeks of smoke! And, as with perfume, more and more places of employment are going smoke-free so now is a good time to consider quitting.

Punctuality

Short of death—your own or that of an immediate family member—or severe illness, there is never really an acceptable reason to be late for an interview or to fail to show up altogether. Even arriving with a few minutes to spare can only increase any anxiety you feel about being interviewed. With this in mind, there are a few things you can do to avoid being late to interviews:

- Set your watch ten minutes ahead.
- Go to the office the day before to make sure that you can find it, and so you know how long it takes to get there. Frequently, the interviewer

will meet you in the lobby and ask you if you had trouble finding the office. Imagine what he or she will think of you if you respond by saying, "Oh, no... I drove out here yesterday to make sure that I could find the building, so I had no trouble being on time today." This is far preferable to beginning the interview with some excuse about why you're ten minutes late.

- Assume that the trip will take you 30 minutes longer than you expect it will. If you allow a great deal of extra time, the worst-case scenario is that you will arrive 30 to 60 minutes early. If you do arrive early, use the extra time to review the job description, review your research, and go over questions you would like to ask the interviewer. If you're completely prepared, take a brisk walk around the block to put any excess nervous energy to use. Don't go into the reception area an hour early—that can be awkward for the interviewer, who may feel obliged to see you sooner than the scheduled time. At most, arriving 15 or 20 minutes early is reasonable.

What to Bring; What not to Bring

Go alone to your interview; never bring your significant other, a friend, or your children. If someone gives you a ride, he or she should wait for you in the car or at another location. Carry a portfolio—any office supply store carries them, and they are a great way to keep your resumes, references, and interview notes organized—or briefcase to bring extra copies of your resume, reference sheet, notepad and any materials you might want or need during your interview. Avoid backpacks and fanny packs.

PREPARING FOR A SPECIFIC INTERVIEW

Working with a co-op/internship coordinator or career services professional, you will look at job descriptions and choose several jobs that you wish to target. So what do you do after an employer calls you and arranges an interview? For any employer, be sure to bring extra copies of your resume and the names, addresses, and phone numbers of your references on resume paper. But how do you prepare for an interview for one specific employer? Let's consider several steps in the preparation process:

Knowing the Job Description

First, make sure that you have a copy of the job description. Take it home with you, and memorize the specific skills that the employer is looking for in a job candidate. Start thinking about how the employer would think of you as a job candidate in terms of the skills needed for the job. What would the employer perceive to be your strengths? Your weaknesses? Try to understand what it was about your resume that attracted your employer as well as what concerns you may need to overcome to get the job.

One of the most underrated aspects of interview preparation is to research the job description. Many job candidates think of "interview research" as purely looking up facts and figures about the company. As mentioned below, this is important... but it also can be misguided. Think about this example: Let's say a job description mentions that you will be using a Crystal Reports database to do research on market segmentation for an athletic shoe company. Would it really be the best use of your time to memorize the company's total revenues, stock price, international offices, and so forth? Not really: If you aren't familiar with Crystal Reports or and/or with the concept of marketing segmentation, get on the Internet and use word searches until you come up with something. Anybody can say that they are a quick learner when they are being interviewed, but few people *demonstrate* their ability to learn quickly by doing appropriate research for an interview. Obviously, you can't learn a software application overnight, but with a little effort you can learn enough to have an intelligent conversation with the interviewer. That will help your cause much more than annual report data.

Researching the Organization

Doing strong research on potential employers is one thing that separates excellent job seekers from average ones. Start by asking your co-op or career services professionals. They may have student job descriptions that they can share with you; they may have visited the site. Best of all, they might be able to give you contact information for someone who has worked in that exact position! Imagine what you could ask that person to prepare yourself. This takes a little initiative, but this step can give you eye-popping information to use in the interview:

> "I spoke to Ben Birkbeck about his experience as a co-op, and I was excited to hear that there are opportunities to work closely with convalescing patients at your site."

You may want to ask about the supervisor's style, the nature of the work, the organization's culture, the possibility for employment after graduation or in future co-op periods, etc. You can even ask what the interview will be like!

For general company information, the Internet or your school library can be a valuable resource. Talk to a reference librarian if necessary about how to find company news. For publicly-traded companies, you can find recent news at websites such as Google or www.nasdaq.com or at any number of financial services websites. Once you have assembled several sources, look them up and take notes on what you read. Companies will be impressed if you do this homework before the interview.

Here are some other tips for searching via the Web.

- *Learn how to use more than one search engine:* The Internet contains a vast amount of information, and it's easy to get lost in the Web. Obviously, www.google.com is a great place to start for looking up a company website. You also could go to the News menu on Google in order to find any recent developments with that organization. That can be a great way to come up with some topical questions to ask at the end of your interview (although it's not wise to broach controversial topics, such as a lawsuit that the company is currently addressing).

When you do a search, watch out for companies that have similar names or various branches in different locations: Make sure you're researching the right one.

With some of the most powerful search engines—like Google—a few little tricks will greatly enhance the effectiveness of your search. For example, don't just type in John Hancock, because it will pull up every website that has the name "John" or "Hancock" in it... which is NOT very helpful. Instead, put quotes around the word: "John Hancock". This tells the search engine that you ONLY want URLs with that word combination.

- *Leave no stone unturned in your research:* In our experience, students give up far too easily when doing research for an interview. Here's an example: A small company interviewed six of Scott's students one time. Five looked in the files, looked in the library, looked on the Internet, and found NOTHING. They gave up. The sixth student did all of the same things and also found nothing. But he kept trying. He looked at the job description again, and saw this phrase: "We provide software solutions for the vending industry." He decided to go back to the library and back onto the Internet, learning as much as he could about the vending industry and how software was utilized in it. He learned a TON about the industry, the competition, and key issues that probably were facing his potential employer. Then he walked around campus with a notebook, looking at the vending machines: Who made them? Who serviced them? How sophisticated were they in terms of software? Armed with this information, he was able to have a sophisticated conversation with the interviewer about vending. And, of course, he got the job. So remember, you can use the Internet to research the industry and the competition as well as the company itself.

STRATEGIC INTERVIEWING – A CO-OP STUDENT'S PERSPECTIVE

by Ted Schneider

RESEARCH, RESEARCH, RESEARCH! It is extremely embarrassing to show an interviewer that you have not prepared by researching the company or its clients. During my Microsoft interview, the interviewer asked me to "describe an issue facing Microsoft currently – besides the unfair business practices/ monopolization issue." As you may have guessed, I had nothing to say.

***Ted Schneider** was an Accounting/ MIS student at Northeastern University, Class of 2002*

In similar ways, you need to think creatively about your research: If the product/service is consumer-oriented, go see it in action or how it is displayed and sold. Talk to people who might use the product or service, and ask them their opinions of it. Get a real understanding of the company.

Any information that you can dig up may prove useful in the interview. Later in this chapter, we will show specific ways that you can impress an interviewer with the fruits of your research.

MATCHING YOUR SKILLS TO THE EMPLOYER'S NEEDS

The most crucial aspect of a great interview is demonstrating that your skills and personal qualities are a great match for what the employer needs in a co-op worker. You may have excellent grades, terrific skills, and a great attitude, but if you can't explain why YOU are a great MATCH for THIS job, you may be out of luck. You need to have concrete reasons that reflect specific information on the job description. If a co-op candidate fails to strategize in this way, the employer may tell the co-op coordinator something like this: "Susan seemed like a great person with good skills, and I really liked her attitude. But I'm not convinced that she meets our needs."

How can you avoid being "close but not quite" when going after a job? Consider the following example. The Littlefield Rehabilitation Center has a nursing co-op job available for a student with "great empathy and patience, some experience working with the elderly or disabled, a basic understanding of nursing, and a willingness to work long shifts."

Student 1 and Student 2 have identical skills: Both are solid "B+" students who have only limited experience with the elderly. Both have taken only prerequisite coursework in nursing, but they do have volunteer experience working in hospitals during school vacations.

In the interview, both students are asked the following question: "Why should we hire you for this position?"

Student 1 says:

> "I'm a hard worker, and I've always wanted to work for a rehabilitation center. I think this job would give me a lot of good experience, especially the exposure to the geriatric population. So I look at this as a great opportunity."

Student 2 says:

> "I know you're looking for someone who is extremely patient and empathic. Here are my references—please call my supervisor at the hospital and ask her specifically about those qualities. As for working with the elderly, my experience is limited—but in preparing for the interview today, I talked to some students who worked at your Center; it sounds like you are doing some amazing things with treatment! Looking on the Internet, I was surprised to find that a third of your beds are utilized by younger patients recovering from head injuries, so I've already started reading up on subarachnoid hemorrhages and their clinical manifestations—I want to be ready to hit the ground running in this job! As you can see on my resume, my real strength is working with people, whether

> I've worked as a hospital volunteer or as a waitress. So I think I bring a strong background to this position."

Who would you be more inclined to hire? Neither student has excellent skills, but Student 2 did a much better job of showing the employer the connections between her skills and the job description. Student 1 answered the question more in terms of why she or he would like to have the job instead of focusing on why the employer would want to hire her. As such, the employer might see this student as a far better match for the job... even though the two students have identical skills!

By tying your answers to the job description, you show the potential employer that:

- you are industrious enough to prepare effectively for an interview
- you are persuasive, self-confident, and sensitive to the employer's needs
- you have an awareness of what your skills are and how ready you will be to do the job well—right from the start

One good tip is to go into any job interview with a solid strategy featuring three or four compelling reasons why the interviewer should hire you to do that specific job. Being focused like this will make a big difference. If you want to get more practice in strategizing, consider trying the bridging exercise, Appendix E, at the back of this book.

We will consider more examples when we look more closely at interview questions.

VERBAL AND NONVERBAL INTERVIEWING SKILLS

Obviously, interviewers are very interested in what you have to say. However—especially in some fields—employers are interested in how you say it. Many interviewers may not consciously notice what you're doing right or wrong in this sense, but these behaviors still may have a critical impact on whether or not you get a job offer.

Verbal Skills

Keep in mind the following when interviewing.

- *Speak at a reasonably loud volume.* Sometimes students who get nervous end up speaking all too softly. Make sure the interviewer can hear and understand you. If you're not sure, ask.
- *Don't speak too fast.* If you speak quickly, the interviewer may miss the strong points that you are making, or simply fail to remember. Slow down: especially when making an important selling point about yourself. When asked a question, don't be afraid to pause before answering or between giving each of two or three points about yourself. Don't be afraid of pauses: Brief silences can be effective in allowing points to sink in or to emphasize something strongly.

It's easy to overlook just how *hard* it is to be an interviewer: All at once, the interviewer has to listen to your answer while trying to assess your answer and think about the next question to ask. If you never come up for air or give time for your points to be digested, the interviewer won't remember much of what you've said. One interviewer told Scott that he "uses silence effectively" as an interviewee. Scott thought that was a strange compliment at first—aren't interviews all about what you say? Really, though, she was just saying that he was giving her enough time to juggle all her various thoughts as an interviewer.

Another point to consider is that many, many interviewers have no formal training in conducting a good interview and are often as uncomfortable with interviewing as you are. The more at ease you are during the interview, the better for both of you.

- *Watch out for "verbal tics."* We all have verbal tics, y'know? Um.... you should, like, try to not use them during an interview, y'know? Yeah, they like make you seem totally immature and unprofessional, right?

  Seriously: Almost everyone has a tendency to fill the empty seconds between phrases and sentences with little bits of meaningless slang. Doing this occasionally will go unnoticed, but doing it repeatedly can become a major distraction. In practice interviews, we have heard students use the word "like" as many as 12 times in one lengthy sentence! Many people don't even believe they use these phrases constantly until they see themselves on videotape. Slowing down your speech will help reduce these annoying, meaningless phrases. If you fail to reduce these phrases, you may come off as very young, inarticulate, immature, or unprepared. It takes practice to get out of these habits, but it's worth it, y'know?

It's also especially easy to lapse or relapse into these habits when being interviewed by someone who is younger. Even if you feel like you connect with an interviewer who is of comparable age, don't slip into unprofessional, informal speech habits.

- *Speak with a professional tone.* Save your slang expressions for conversations with friends and significant others. When describing your job experience, for example, avoid terms like "stuff" and "things." Be precise; use a broader range of vocabulary.
- *Vary your tone.* Avoid speaking in a monotone. Make your voice sound excited when talking about things that interest you. This will keep the listener interested.
- *If English is not your primary language:* Make sure that you know how to answer typical interview questions in English. Speak loudly and slowly, and cheerfully offer to repeat something or rephrase something if the interviewer doesn't seem to understand you. If asked about your understanding and use of English, discuss what you have done and will do in order to improve your communication skills in English. If appropriate, you also might mention previous job experiences in which employers were concerned about your English skills but eventually found that this was not a problem for you or your co-workers.

Nonverbal Skills

People can often say a great deal in an interview without even opening their mouths. Therefore, pay attention to the following guidelines:

- *Handshakes:* Shake hands firmly when meeting the interviewer or anyone he or she introduces you to. Keep your thumb up as you extend your hand to shake. If you are a man, give women the same firm shake you'd give another man—no limp wrists or just clutching fingertips. If you tend to get sweaty palms when you're nervous, try to wipe off your hand frequently (and subtly) while waiting for the interviewer to arrive in the lobby.
- *Eye Contact:* As much as possible, make eye contact with the interviewer. Don't stare, but don't let your eyes wander around the room at any time; you may be perceived as having a short attention span or as being uninterested in the job. Look long enough to notice the color of his or her eyes. If you have difficulty with eye contact, some experts suggest looking at the space right between someone's eyes instead. Tamara's students report this works well for them.
- *Body Language:* Sit up straight, and lean forward a little when being interviewed. Don't slouch, lean way back, or fold your arms: This

comes off as being uninterested, defensive, laid-back, or unfriendly. When you're not using your hands or arms to help express a point, keep them on your lap. Don't put them in your pockets, as you may distract the interviewer by jangling change. Avoid drumming your fingers, clicking your pen, or fiddling with your hair, jewelry, or clothes, and never chew gum. Try to smile!

"So... do I get the job?"

- *Using notes/Taking notes:* There is no simple answer to this question. In some fields, job interviews are comparable to making a formal sales presentation. In this case, failing to use notes may indicate that you have done little preparation for your interview/presentation. You will give the impression that you are "winging it," which—even if you're good at it—may not send the message you want to send. Conversely, other business employers might feel that relying on notes indicates that you are not adequately prepared.

  When moderating a co-op employer discussion panel a few years ago, Scott was intrigued to hear that some employers are very impressed when an interviewee takes notes during the interview. These employers felt that the note takers were showing sincere interest and good attention to detail. They cautioned, however, that you need to be judicious in exactly what you write down. Otherwise, note-taking can be very distracting and also may keep you from making adequate eye contact.

  In most cases, using notes or taking notes will not be necessary in business interviews. But if you are afraid of "blanking out" or failing to cover several points, you might try using them... as long as you are not reading directly from them or looking at them constantly. Scott tells students to think of notes the way a tightrope walker thinks of a safety net: Knowing that the notes are there makes you less nervous—and less likely to need them! If you are unsure about what is most appropriate for your field, ask your coordinator. We will talk specifically about how to use notes later in this chapter.

INTERVIEWING – A STUDENT'S PERSPECTIVE

by Mark Moccia

I fit the "sweaty palms" prototype perfectly on my first interview. I previously worked in an office environment, although I did not have a formal interview because my mother hired me! I thought I would not be as nervous because of the ease with which I handled my practice interviews. Despite my glowing confidence from the day before, I was nervous from the moment I woke up that morning. When I arrived at the office, I was sweating as if it were 100 degrees outside; the only problem with this is that it was only 75 degrees and cloudy! I experienced all the nightmares that come with nervous first interviews; I stumbled over words, dropped things on the floor, and apologized 50 times, along with many other little, embarrassing moments.

The most important lesson I learned from this interview is to relax and be yourself. I was trying too hard to impress the interviewer (who was the president of the company, which did not help matters) when I should have been selling myself more. It is important to impress the interviewer but you have to earn this right through hard work. You simply cannot impress the interviewer with your "uncanny multi-tasking ability" if you have never experienced multi-tasking.

It is important to figure out your strengths and sell those to the interviewer. It is also important to figure out your weaknesses and what you are doing to improve on them because interviewers will ask that question frequently. Finally, as mentioned earlier, the more research you perform on the company before the interview, the more questions you will have for them at the end of the interview when you hear the dreaded, "Do you have any questions for me?" This was pretty ugly for my first interview; I believe my response was, "Uh, uh, no. I do not believe I can learn anything else from this interview." BIG MISTAKE!

***Mark Moccia** was an Accounting/MIS student at Northeastern University, Class of 2002*

TURNING NERVOUS ENERGY INTO AN ALLY

Some people enjoy interviews, but most people experience at least some nervousness about them. Feeling nervous is a completely normal and rational reaction to going on an interview. After all, you want to make a good impression, and you want to make sure you get the best possible job for each co-op period. You care! That's a good thing.

One big mistake that many individuals make is believing that their goal should be to eliminate any nervousness that they feel. The more they try to force themselves to be relaxed, the harder it becomes to do so.

Here is a more helpful strategy: Remember that nervousness is nothing more than energy. The last thing you want to do is go into an interview without any energy! The trick is to use your nervous energy in positive ways. One proactive idea is to try to make time for some vigorous exercise earlier in the day to use up excess energy and to get in the right mindset.

If you begin to feel nervous during an interview, put that excess energy to use by:

- speaking louder and with more enthusiasm
- using your hands to be more expressive instead of keeping your arms folded
- focusing harder on the interviewer, listening closely to what he or she is saying
- pushing yourself to come up with excellent questions and answers

Perhaps most importantly, remember another important fact about nervousness: *People can never tell exactly how nervous you are if you don't tell them.* In mock interviews, many of my students will openly admit that they're nervous. This is a mistake. The interviewer can rarely tell if a student is nervous. Even if nervousness is evident, the interviewer typically underestimates how nervous the interviewee is. Admitting nervousness sometimes makes the interviewer focus on trying to determine how nervous the person is instead of really listening to his or her answers. In some cases, talking about nervousness may make the interviewer feel awkward or nervous too. Regardless, discussing nervousness only moves you both further away from focusing on whether you are a good match for the job.

Here are a few other ideas about how to keep nervous energy from becoming a negative force for you in interviews:

- Formulate a specific strategy for each interview: Come up with at least three specific reasons why YOU should be hired for THAT specific job description.
- Prepare yourself thoroughly by considering how you would answer typical questions and by doing extensive research about the company. We will go over these typical questions shortly.
- Allow yourself plenty of time to travel to the interview location.
- Practice your interviewing skills by working with your co-op/internship coordinator or with the Career Services Department.
- Practice answering questions with a friend, roommate, or family

member. Remember that these individuals generally aren't experts. Practice with them to get used to saying your answers out loud rather than to seek useful criticism.

It's hard to overemphasize the importance of thorough preparation. In the classroom, when are you most nervous before taking an exam? It's when you really haven't studied and aren't prepared. The same is true for interviews: When you know your stuff, you'll be much more at ease.

People who learn to use their nervous energy effectively come off as energetic, enthusiastic, motivated, and focused in interviews... even though they have butterflies and knots in their stomach the whole time!

ORDINARY QUESTIONS, EXTRAORDINARY ANSWERS

Although it is impossible to anticipate every question that an employer will ask you in an interview, you should be prepared to answer the typical questions that arise in many interviews. Preparation makes an enormous difference in being able to deliver extraordinary answers to ordinary questions.

Individuals with little interviewing experience seldom give "bad" answers to questions. However, many people fail to understand the difference between a pretty good answer and an extraordinary one. In this section, we will dissect the most common interview questions and show you specific examples of mediocre, ordinary, and outstanding answers to these questions.

1. "Tell me about yourself."

In one form or another, this is a fairly common opening question. You may be asked about your background, or about what kind of person you are. Many people—particularly those who have failed to prepare—dislike these questions and struggle to answer them. The question seems incredibly broad and general: There are a thousand things you could talk about. However, those who are well prepared look forward to this kind of question. Basically, the interviewer is giving you a very open-ended question: You could choose to talk about almost anything in your response.

Why do interviewers ask this question? For one thing, it's an ice-breaker, a way of easing into the interview before asking tough questions about your skills. Another reason employers ask this is because it's a quick way to test your judgment. What you choose to say about yourself says a great deal about your personality and character.

There are many possible ways to answer this question effectively. Here are some guidelines to bear in mind:

1. *Don't waste time telling interviewers what they already know.* Many students answer this question too literally, telling the interviewer where they go to school, what their major is, what their hobbies are, and so forth. By now the interviewer very likely has reviewed your resume, and rehashing these basic facts gets you nowhere.

2. *If you're not given a specific question, focus on why YOU are a good candidate for THIS specific job.* An open-ended question is always a good opportunity to sell yourself. Talk about what the job description requires and why you represent a good match for these requirements.

3. *If you are an unconventional candidate for a job, discuss why you are interested in this job and why you are a strong candidate.* This is especially important if you have returned to school to change careers. For example, if you've been a nurse and you are now working toward an Associate of Arts degree in accounting, you should explain why you are changing careers, why you are excited about an opportunity in your new field and how this job relates to your career goals. In other words, anticipate an employer's concern and deal with it enthusiastically.

Let's look at some possible answers to *"Tell me about yourself."*

Mediocre answer: "I live in Brookfield; I'm an accounting major; I like sports, reading, and rollerblading, and I'm in the middle of my second year at Lane Community College."

Ordinary answer: "I'm a hard worker, and I've got solid grades. I think this job would be really interesting, and I'm eager to learn from this experience. I'm persistent, and I expect a lot of myself."

Extraordinary answer: "My goal is to use my accounting skills to help your organization meet its goals while also helping the community. As you can see on my resume, I have excellent grades in my accounting coursework and prior experience volunteering for community organizations. I am dedicated to proving myself as a bookkeeper for an organization like this that brings value to our city."

Can you see how different these responses are? The first tells the interviewer almost nothing that couldn't be inferred from reading the resume. The second conveys a positive attitude but tells the interviewer nothing about why the person would be good for THIS job as opposed to any other position. The third response shows that the job candidate read the job description carefully and has thought a great deal about why the position is a good match for his or her skills and traits. It also shows initiative by referring to research that the candidate did to prepare for the interview (provided the candidate really DID do that research). With this kind of response, you can go a long way toward showing an employer how your skills connect with a given job opportunity.

But what if the employer really was asking the question to find out more about your interests outside of work? Well, he or she can always ask a more specific follow-up question, which you can answer accordingly.

2. "I see on your resume that you're interested in __________. Tell me more about that."

This is another common ice-breaker question. Some employers may ask about your interest in books or skiing or whatever in order to help you relax and have a less artificial conversation with them.

This type of question also illustrates why we strongly recommend that you list some of your hobbies and interests on your resume. Basically, an employer is hiring an individual: not just a list of skills and qualifications. Talking about your hobbies and interests gives you an opportunity to make yourself a real person in the employer's eyes: hopefully, a person they would enjoy working with for a lengthy period of time. If you're lucky, you may have an opportunity to build rapport with a prospective employer if the two of you happen to share an interest. Also, believe it or not, this type of question can also help you sell yourself for the job, sometimes in subtle ways.

For example, one of the first questions that Scott gets asked in most interviews is about his interest in writing fiction. When asked about it, he's delighted: For one thing, it gives him a chance to speak about something with great enthusiasm. More importantly, though, this type of question allows him to convey personal qualities that may be very useful in the job at hand. If a job requires creativity, communication skills, persistence, patience, listening skills, etc., he can mention these qualities as aspects of fiction writing that have proven valuable to him.

Let's look at some examples relating to a fictional student named Pete Moss, a graphic design student who lists his interests as follows: Photography, camping, skiing, and volunteer work. Check out some possible options for Pete if he's asked about his interests during a marketing interview:

"I see on your resume that you're interested in camping. Why does that interest you?"

Mediocre answer:	"Yeah, I just like being in the woods. It's relaxing, quiet and I can hang out with my fiends."
Ordinary answer:	"Yes, I try to go as often as I can in the summer. I find that it's a good way to clear my mind on the weekend, so I can return to work on Monday with a good focus."
Extraordinary answer:	"Besides being a relaxing way to recharge my batteries, camping is enjoyable to me because it requires a combination of characteristics: resourcefulness, good judgment, planning, stamina, and thinking on your feet. Some trips can be quite challenging, and I like to challenge myself."

An employer who hears the first answer might wonder whether Pete can handle being indoors long enough to handle the job! At best, this type of answer won't hurt you. The "Ordinary answer" is better: It shows that Pete values a balance between work and other interests, and that he sees his weekend time as a way to be more energized in the workplace. However, the "Extraordinary Answer" reflects a job candidate who really "thinks marketing" and is able to make some subtle but creative connections between his career interests and his personal interests. With this answer, he never says anything directly about being a good candidate for the job, but the employer may start thinking that Pete's individual traits fit nicely with a graphic design position.

But what if Pete had been asked about one of his other interests? Let's consider some options:

Photography: "Photography appeals to my creative side, which is a very strong aspect of my personality. I also enjoy photography because I like the challenge of trying to capture something in a picture. It's like marketing, where you're trying to capture the nature of a product or service with one simple slogan or image. I like that."

Skiing: "I haven't skied for very long—only three or four years—but I really enjoy everything about it. I like researching different ski mountains, finding out which appeals to me, and trying to sell my friends on which one I think is the best. On the mountain, I like taking on challenging terrain without sacrificing technique. I've improved very quickly."

Here we see two different approaches. In the photography example, Pete ties his interest in photography directly to its relevance in the field of graphic design. In the skiing example, though, Pete is more subtle. He describes many aspects of skiing that are appealing to him, but the interviewer also can see that he's demonstrating many traits that are useful in a graphic design job: researching, salesmanship, reasonable risk-taking, an outgoing personality, and a focus on results. The interviewer may be more likely to think of this student as a job candidate without even realizing why he or she feels that way!

Whatever your interests are, think about how you would talk about them if they come up in an interview. Are there connections you can make between your interests and a co-op position? If you can learn to do this well, an interviewer may be pleasantly surprised at your ability to turn a simple ice-breaker question into another showcase of your abilities.

3. "Why should we hire you for this job?"

If the interviewer has a more aggressive personality, you may hear this exact question in an interview. If not, you may find it in a more polite form (i.e., "What is it that makes you a good candidate for this job?"). In either case, the question an employer is really asking can be broken into many possible questions:

- How much self-confidence do you have?
- Are you a good match for this job?

- Do you know if you are a good match for this job?
- Can you articulate your strengths clearly, confidently, and realistically?

Answer this question directly, focusing on your experiences, attitude, and aptitude in relationship to the job requirements as explained in the job description. In other words, don't just tell the employer why you're a good person, or a good candidate for any co-op job. Likewise, don't make the mistake of concentrating exclusively on why the job would be good for you. Focus closely on why you are a good match for this co-op job. And if you don't have everything they're looking for in terms of skills, present a strategy for overcoming this obstacle.

Mediocre answer: "Working at this job would really give me the experience that I currently lack. It would build my skills considerably."

Ordinary answer: "I'm hard working; I have good grades; I'm eager to learn more, and I learn quickly. I also have good job experience that relates well to this position."

Extraordinary answer: "According to the job description, you want someone who knows AutoCAD, and who has strong communication skills. In my class, I was the AutoCAD expert, and I help most of my friends with that and other software at school. As for communication skills, I encourage you to contact any of my previous employers. They'll tell you that I not only have excellent communication skills: I also was well respected by my coworkers. I also noticed that you prefer someone who has used Revit. Since reading the job description, I've familiarized myself the basics of this application and am confident I could hit the ground running by the time I start work."

The first answer gives the employer absolutely no incentive to hire the job candidate. Even worse, the candidate focused only on what the job can do for him instead of vice-versa. The "Ordinary answer" is more positive, but it's rather generic: If an interviewer talks to ten students, this kind of answer will turn up three or more times. To stand out, you have to push your skills. In the "Extraordinary answer," the job candidate talks with confidence about past job experiences and shows a keen awareness of what the prospective job demands. If the employer didn't see these connections when looking at the resume, he or she will be clear on them now.

4. "Why did you choose to become a Physical Therapy Assistant (or dental hygienist, etc.)?"

An employer who asks this kind of question hopes to learn more about how focused, enthusiastic, serious, and mature you are. There are many good ways to answer this question, but there are also several bad ways. Thus, some helpful hints:

- *Show that you have a career plan.* You don't want it to sound as if you're only majoring in a field because some advisor or relative suggested it or that you're only in it for the money. Don't be vague when presenting your reasons. Relate the career plan to the job. For example, if you are interviewing for an entry-level veterinary technician position, describe your love of animals as well as your desire to learn as much as you can so that you'll be able to earn additional certifications, meaning that you will become both more skilled and more valuable to the practice.

  On the other hand, be very cautious about mentioning future plans to return to school to further your career. Let's say you are a drafting major and have notions of going back to school to earn an advanced degree—architecture school, for example. When interviewing, for example, for a drafting positions with a construction company, keep in mind that they are hiring you to solve their need for drafting work. If you tell them about your plans to become an architect, they will most likely be concerned that you'll be leaving soon to go off to school again. They will envision the time that they will invest in training you without getting a return on that investment. As such, they may not hire you, opting instead for someone who appears to be a better long-term fit. Not all employers think like this; some are eager to help emerging professionals. However, in general, keep your advanced degree plans to yourself when interviewing for entry level positions. Don't give up your dream; it just isn't the right time to share that part of your career goal with a potential employer.

- *Show some excitement.* One option is to tell the interviewer a short anecdote about what first excited you about your field of study. You might mention a high-school job experience, a previous internship, a classroom experience, or some extracurricular activity that inspired you to major in your given concentration.

- *Make sure to connect your response to the interviewer's job description.* If you're seeking a job within your concentration, this should not be difficult. However, if you're pursuing a job in a different concentration or major, you are very likely to be asked about this discrepancy. Basically, if you're a psychology major, why are you interviewing for a job as a webmaster, for example? There may be plenty of good reasons, but you will need to make the connection. Otherwise, the employer may perceive a mismatch between you and the job.

Here are some sample answers for a student who is asked why he or she chose physical therapy as a major.

Mediocre answer: "I dunno; I think it's kind of interesting. My dad says that the economy stinks for just about everything except the health sciences these days, so I figured it would be the best way to make a lot of money."

Ordinary answer: "I've always seemed to do well in my science courses, and I've enjoyed working with people in various jobs over the years. I think it's just a nice fit for my abilities."

Extraordinary answer: "I think I've always been a natural for the physical therapy field: Heck, I had to undergo physical therapy at the age of five, when I broke my arm falling off my bike. I'm great with people; I'm caring, and I really want to be in a healing profession that can help others in the way that I was helped as a child. I can't imagine another major that would fit so nicely with these qualities."

What if someone is interviewing for a marketing job but actually majors in, say, general studies (in other words, a two-year transfer degree)? The interviewer may ask: *"Given that you don't have any specific coursework in marketing, why are you interested in a this position?"*

Mediocre answer: "Well, I just figured I could do the job... ."

Ordinary answer: "I think it would be interesting, and it would give me broader experience in business in general."

Extraordinary answer: "The skills associated with earning a transfer degree include those I need to become a successful businessperson. My psychology courses prepared me to understand the mentality of customers. My speech course helped me learn how to pitch to a specific market niche, and you can see that I have a good mind for numbers by the good grades I earned in my math classes. I have spent many years working in a family business. I'm confident I have the foundation to be successful in marketing."

5. "I see on your resume that you worked for Organization X last summer. What was that like?"

Employers have much to gain by bringing up one or more of your previous job experiences. They want to:

- determine whether your experience at that job makes you a better candidate for this job
- see how well you can articulate what another organization does and what your role was for that organization

- give you an attitude check of sorts by seeing if you focus on negatives when asked an open-ended question about a previous job experience

Keep these things in mind when working on an effective response to this question. Most interviewers will ask you about prior job experience, and you want to be ready for it. Follow these guidelines:

- *Describe what the organization does.* Unless the organization is very large or well known in its field, you may have to use a sentence or two to explain the nature of the work done by the organization. Show the interviewer you can capture the big picture of what a company does.
- *Describe what you did at the organization.* You probably did numerous things in your job at Organization X. Focus primarily on what you did well, what you enjoyed, and—most importantly—how it relates to the job for which you are currently interviewing.
- *Go beyond what is stated on your resume.* The interviewer can read, so you have to say more than what is written on your resume. This is why it is so important to tie your work experience to the description of the job for which you're applying.
- *ALWAYS focus exclusively on what was positive about the work experience.* Even if you hated your boss and found the job boring or unsatisfying, focus on the positives about the experience. Nobody likes a complainer or whiner, and the interviewer may start wondering if you might have significantly contributed to the problem and therefore would be a "risky hire."

STRATEGIC INTERVIEWING – AN EMPLOYER'S PERSPECTIVE

by Steve Sim

If I can add any perspective on interviews, I'd have to say one thing: each and every experience you listed on your resume or talked about in an interview should have taught you something. Whether that lesson is how to do something right every time or how to do something right the next time, it's a lesson learned. Be prepared to talk about it.

***Steve Sim** is a Technical Recruiter at the Microsoft Corporation*

Here are some responses interviewers might hear in response to *"Tell me about your job at Organization X."*

Mediocre answer: "Well, I did some pretty tedious office work: You know, answering phones, sending faxes, things like that. It wasn't much fun, and my boss was a pain, so I definitely want something different this time."

Ordinary answer: "I worked for Organization X in Anytown. I worked in an office and did a lot of administrative support work: xeroxing, answering phones, basically doing anything to help out the team."

Extraordinary answer: "Organization X makes galvinators, which are electronic parts used in the automotive industry. I was an Administrative Assistant, responsible for handling many clerical jobs in the Finance Department at Organization X. The job was a good entry-level experience; the best thing about it was just having a chance to work alongside finance people and getting to pick their brains about the company's financial operations. That's why I'm interested in the position at your company: I'll get more exposure to the world of finance and get a chance to use some of the skills I've picked up in my business classes over the last six months."

Obviously, all three responses reflected a job that was not too demanding or exciting. The extraordinary answer, though, shows that you can be honest about this kind of job while still focusing on the positives of the experience.

6. "What would you say are your strengths?"

This question makes some interviewees uncomfortable: People often don't like feeling that they are bragging about themselves, fearing that they will come across as egotistical. Our culture is full of messages about being modest, such as "don't toot your own horn" or "don't be a show-off." These can be difficult to overcome. But remember: if you don't sell yourself in an interview, who will? Interviewers ask this question to assess your self-confidence, maturity, and self-awareness in addition to how well your strengths match up with the requirements of a job.

Here are a few guidelines to bear in mind when answering this question:

- *Be honest.* On the one hand, don't exaggerate about your abilities. If you say you have a given technical skill, many employers will follow up with a question to assess how well your knowledge matches up with your claim. Or—if you do get hired by saying you have a skill when you actually don't—the truth will come out shortly after you start the job. Lying about your credentials is grounds for immediate dismissal with most employers.

  On the other hand, be honest about what you can do. Many co-op candidates sell themselves short when asked about their strengths. If asked about their experience with computers, for example, many candidates will say they don't have any... overlooking the fact that they have taught themselves many software applications and, sometimes, even programming languages. Yes, self-taught skills count when you are asked about your strengths, skills, or experience in a given area.

- *Describe your strengths in terms of the employer's needs.* One common mistake in answering this question is failing to tailor your reply to the employer's needs. Sure, your strengths may include fluency in speaking Swahili and Swedish, great speed in using Adobe Photoshop, and the ability to program in Visual Basic, but how are these skills going to help yourself as a candidate for a medical office assistant position?

  Before the interview, decide which of your strengths should be emphasized. If a welding/fabrication position primarily requires mechanical aptitude, welding skills, and the ability to do mathematical calculations, you should strategize accordingly. In addition to citing examples of experience that show your mechanical aptitude you also might cite a strong grade in a machining class. In contrast, you might not focus on your PC skills or your warehouse experience. However, you might cite these skills heavily if interviewing for a position requiring these talents.

Let's consider some possible responses to the strengths question. Let's say that the job in question is a bookkeeping job requiring a high level of accuracy, an ability to work as part of a team, and the ability to quickly perform complex calculations.

Mediocre answer:	"I guess I'm a good worker, and I've done pretty well in most of my classes. I'm really good with computers too, especially spreadsheets and stuff."
Ordinary answer:	"I'm a real self-starter; I'm motivated and eager to learn. I got an A – in my accounting class last term, and I have strong writing and presentation skills."
Extraordinary answer:	"I consider myself a real team player: In my last job in construction I was part of a four-person framing team that consistently finished each job on time and on budget. I've always been a natural with numbers, and am confident I can do any calculation necessary for this position. My ability to calculate accurately helped me earn outstanding grades in all of my accounting courses."

Although the second answer discusses many bona fide strengths which may help the candidate land a job somewhere, it goes into little detail regarding strengths that will prove beneficial to this employer. The extraordinary answer covers all of the areas mentioned in our mini-job description. Of course, this answer is only effective if the candidate is prepared to "walk the talk." A shrewd interviewer may follow up this question by giving the candidate a simple problem that requires calculation. Be prepared to back up any claims that you make in an interview.

7. "What are your weaknesses?"

Less experienced interviewees dislike this question, probably because they're afraid of exposing a legitimate weakness that the interviewer will use against them in making a hiring decision. Or the interviewee may worry about giving an answer that really isn't an honest weakness, which may come off as an insincere response.

The good news is that this is not a difficult question to answer as long as you are prepared to answer it. You'll need to think it through beforehand because coming up with a good answer on the spot is quite challenging. Here are some basic guidelines in answering this question:

- *Start off your answer by acknowledging your strengths.* You don't want to dwell on negatives more than necessary when answering this question, and you want to reinforce your strengths to make sure the interviewer understands them. One way to make sure you acknowledge your strengths is by starting your answer with "although" or "despite":

> "Although I have solid skills and experience in areas X, Y, and Z...."

- *Avoid cliché responses.* Frequently, interviewees will cite "working too hard" or "being a perfectionist" or "being too focused on the job to the detriment of having a social life." This kind of answer comes off as a cliché, at best, and insincere and defensive, at worst. In a way, you're telling the interviewer that you feel a need to dodge the question, as if you have something to hide.
- *Choose a legitimate weakness, but not one that would keep you from getting a job that you want.* There are many ways to do this. The best answers are based on truth; your weakness needs to be an honest weakness that is also a non-fatal flaw. Always keep the job description in mind when thinking up good weaknesses. Consider these options:

1. Admit something that is obvious, such as "I talk fast, especially when I get excited" and then make sure you say that you monitor yourself and consciously work on speaking more slowly.
2. Say something that is both positive and negative such as "I have high expectations of myself." Be careful with this type of answer because it can come across as canned.
3. Describe something you have worked on and changed like "stopped smoking" or "lost weight."
4. Reveal something about your work preference, such as "I burn out if I have to work 60 hours a week on a regular basis." You can go on to explain that you get your work done efficiently, that your strength is in prioritizing, and that you have no objection to working long hours when necessary as long as it isn't every week. This kind of answer may keep you from getting a job... but it might be a job that you wouldn't have wanted anyway.
5. Say something that is not critical or relevant to the job. For example, if you're applying for a nursing job that requires good interpersonal skills, strong communication skills, and great attention to detail, your weakness could be the fact that your computer skills are limited to word processing and doing research on the Internet. Sure, you don't know databases, but you may not need to for this particular job. Or, if you're a computer science student looking for a software development position, you probably wouldn't have a weakness such as shyness held against you. If a job description mentions the need for someone who is able to work independently with little supervision, you could discuss your inexperience

in working with groups. If a job description mentions a hectic, unstructured work environment with unpredictable demands, you could state your weakness as follows:

> "I find that I tend to get bored easily if I'm forced to do the same job day in, day out. I don't deal with a steady routine and a rigid structure, which I find stifling and monotonous. So I think that would be a real weakness for me in some work settings."

- *Computer skills are almost always a great choice when looking for a weakness that is sincere without being fatal.* No matter how much you know about technology, there is always going to be a long list of computer skills that you lack. Even better, many will be completely irrelevant to the prospective employer. If you're an arts and sciences major, you could tout your MS-Office skills but acknowledge that you have never done any Web design or programming. If you're a computer science major applying for a programming job, you could talk up your C++ background while admitting that you know little or nothing about network administration. As long as you aren't dwelling on a skill that might be valuable to the employer, this is a safe option.

- *Remember that you aren't expected to know everything.* Perhaps the easiest way to deal with a question about your weaknesses is to acknowledge what the employer already knows about you: that is, admit that while you have a strong foundation of knowledge in your field of study, you still have a great deal to learn before you could be considered an expert in finance or computers or accounting or whatever field you are pursuing. As long as you are enthusiastic and can convince the interviewer that you have aptitude for learning new skills, this kind of answer will work for you with most jobs. After all, you're applying for a job as a student or soon-to-be graduate who is in the process of learning a given field. As such, employers would expect that your learning is incomplete.

- *As mentioned, emphasize what you have done or what you will do to improve your area of weakness.* Who would you rather hire? A person who doesn't admit to having any weaknesses, or a person who tells you about a weakness and how he or she has worked to overcome it. This is a good strategy for anyone, but especially for students who struggle with the English language. Just saying that you're weak in English won't help you. However, if you explain that you have only been in this country for three years, and that you have been taking courses and practicing regularly to improve, and that you enjoy working on your English skills, you will impress some interviewers: most of whom know only one language!

- *Try to anticipate any concerns or perceptions employers have about your weaknesses as a job candidate.* This ties in with the previous example

> about problems with speaking English. Most likely, an interviewer can tell if English is challenging for you, and he or she may wonder whether this will hurt your ability to do the job. You don't want the employer to be distracted with thoughts like this. So what you can do is bring up the concern yourself—maybe even in responding to a first question such as "Tell me about yourself." If you can anticipate the interviewer's concerns and eliminate them early in the interview, the interviewer is more likely to focus on your strengths.

One business student who worked with Scott did this very effectively in interviews. Due to a physical disability, this student needed metal crutches to walk, and his gait was awkward. The student knows that interviewers are probably curious about his disability and know they shouldn't ask him direct questions about his condition because it is could lead to charges of discrimination if he isn't hired. Not only are they probably wondering what's wrong with him, they are also wondering about lots of other things such as can he get around the workplace, for example.

The student figures that if the interviewer is thinking about his crutches, he or she is *not* giving him the attention he deserves as an individual. Maybe the interviewer isn't really listening to his carefully-prepared questions and answers. So right when the interview starts, the student says, "You're probably wondering why I'm on these crutches." He explains what happened (a motorbike accident), and he assures the employer that the disability doesn't keep him from being able to take a computer apart and put it back together again. Now the interviewer can focus on the student as a job candidate, not as a medical curiosity.

Let's consider some possible answers to *"What are your weaknesses?"*

Mediocre answer:	"I don't really know much about [sociology, journalism, etc.] since I've only taken some classes, and I don't really have any kind of real job experience."
Ordinary answer:	I guess it would be that I'm a perfectionist. I have a hard time letting go of a project unless I think it's just right.
Extraordinary answer:	"Although I have done extremely well in my human services coursework, I would say my weakness is that I haven't yet had an opportunity to work directly in the field. But I hope to build on the interviewing and case management skills I've learned in the classroom by getting some practical job experience in a position such as the one at your organization. There's always more to learn, and I'm confident I can do so quickly."

8. "How are your grades?"

If your grades are good, you probably won't be asked this question because your grade point average will be right on your resume. Obviously, the best solution to this question is to have good grades to begin with! If your grades are not good enough to put your GPA on your resume, though, you'd better be ready to answer this question.

Do employers care about your grades? Generally, yes. Many don't care if your grades are mediocre as long as you can do the work. Others, however, may require a GPA of 3.0 or better, and others believe that grades are a good predictor of job performance. Therefore, you have to be ready to address this question.

Once again, preparation will help you handle this type of question more effectively. Here are a few strategies that may prove helpful:

- *If your grades are good in the field for which you are applying, discuss those grades explicitly.* In other words, if you have a 2.4 GPA, but your grades in your culinary classes are all Bs or better, then focus on those grades if you're applying for a culinary job.
- If your grades have improved significantly over the last few academic terms, acknowledge that you got off to a slow start but have improved significantly.

Even though the statistical evidence shows that there is almost no relationship between grades and job success, employers don't necessarily know or believe that.

Anyway, here is the range of responses to "How are your grades?"

Mediocre answer:	"Not too good. I have a 2.4."
Ordinary answer:	"Well, they're okay; they could be better. I've done pretty well in classes in my major."
Extraordinary answer:	"I am doing very well in my multimedia courses, earning all A's and B's. My average in these classes is 3.2. If you talked with my instructors in these classes, they would tell you that I produce very high quality work and turn in all my assignments on time.

9. "Tell me what you liked LEAST about your job at Organization X."

This request is basically a check of your attitude and your tact. Don't be tempted to bash your former boss, your co-workers, your lousy job, etc. Doing so will make you come off as a complainer or as someone who dislikes work.

For example, Scott interviewed a young woman for a medical writing job several years ago. When he asked her about her previous job, she was only too happy to go on for a full 15 minutes about her horrible employer. Since this horrendous job was also in medical publishing, Scott finally put on a very concerned face and asked her "Do you think your previous experience has made you too bitter to continue to work in this industry?" She immediately realized her mistake, but it was too late. She had already been interviewed by the company president, who afterwards dismissed her with a simple sentence: "She's a whiner." Scott never did hear her discuss her qualifications, which, actually, were quite good.

Instead of harping on the negatives, your best bet is to acknowledge that the job had many good aspects, but that you felt you wanted to broaden your experience and move on to something that would provide you with a bigger challenge and that more closely fit your long-term career goals.

Here are some sample responses for this request:

Mediocre answer: "They made me do all kinds of busywork that any idiot could do. Also, the pay was bad, my boss was totally clueless about how to manage me, and my co-workers were pretty useless, too."

Ordinary answer: "It was an okay place to work, but it got kind of dull after awhile. And since I was just a co-op student, I had to do a lot of jobs that other people didn't want to do. Basically, it was just a way to make money for school."

Extraordinary answer: "The job was definitely a good entry-level experience for me; I learned a great deal about __________, which I think will prove useful in my next job. I just believe that I could only learn so much in that job, so I decided it would be in my best interest to pursue something more challenging and interesting. Plus, I chose to go back to school to become a ______ and I'm really ready to work in this field.

10. "What are your long-term career goals?"

A variation on this one would be, "What do you see yourself doing in _____ years?" When employers ask this type of question, what they really want to know is many different things:

- *How focused or goal-oriented is the job candidate? Is she or he someone who plans ahead? Is she or he ambitious?* After all, you wouldn't want to hire someone who's just looking to make some quick cash, or someone who isn't achievement oriented.
- *How well do the career goals of the job candidate fit the organization's needs?* In other words, will you stay employed long enough to make it worth the time and effort to train you? If you're applying for an automotive repair position with the long-term career goal of opening your own repair shop, you probably don't want to share this because the employer may not want to train his future competition. As with all interview questions, you shouldn't lie. At the same time, you are not obligated to tell an employer absolutely everything you might possibly do in the future. After all, your career goals may change after you've been in the working world for a while.
- *Does the job at hand really make sense as a match, given the job candidate's long-term goals?* If you're applying for a psychology position in an

after-school program, but your long-term career goal is to become an entrepreneur, you had better be ready to explain why you're interested in the psychology job now. "I just really, really need a job" is not the best reason! It is entirely possible to explain the apparent disconnect, of course, but you have to give some thought as to how a job would fit into your career plan before you go out for that interview.

- *How mature and realistic is the candidate?* Your answer can reveal a great deal about your maturity and perception of yourself. If you don't have much of an answer, you may come off as someone who lacks focus and maturity. If you say that your goal is to someday be an administrative assistant, you may come off as lacking confidence or ambition. If you say that your goal is to be CEO of Microsoft, you may be seen as a dreamer, or as hopelessly naive... particularly if you have shown no initiative in acquiring computer skills.

That said, let's look at the range of replies an interviewer might hear to a question about long-term career goals. We'll assume that the student is interviewing for an entry-level bookkeeping job for a small company that manufactures furniture.

Mediocre answer:	"I haven't given it much thought. I just need a job, basically."
Ordinary answer:	"I hope to gain some valuable experience in accounting during my co-op jobs, then I'll pursue a BA in business and maybe go on to get my CPA."
Extraordinary answer:	"I really enjoy accounting and hope to do the best job I can for you and stay with your organization as long as it is a good fit for both of us. Over time, I'd like to continue taking additional courses to improve my skills and hopefully become more valuable to you. I have considered earning a BA and maybe a CPA but that is well into the future. Right now I'm focused on doing accounting work for an organization such as yours."

But what if you don't *know* what your long-term goals are? Don't lie about that. But do give some general sense of your priorities and why the job for which you're interviewing is a good step with that in mind:

> "Right now I know that I want to have a career working with kids, but I think a number of possibilities are plausible in the long run. Regardless of where I land, though, I know that it's really important to have a variety of experiences with children in different settings and with a range of ages and abilities. So I'm excited about this job working as a classroom aide, as it would be a great first step toward any number of careers with children."

11. "What kind of hourly rate are you looking for in this position?"

The issue of pay can be an awkward matter in an interview. It's natural for you to be wondering about the pay rate or hoping for a specific figure, but your best bet is to not bring it up unless the employer does. Even then, you have to be careful about what you say. You don't want to get ruled out of a job for being greedy, but you don't want to accept $11.50 an hour when they would have been delighted to give you $14.

So how should you handle this question? First of all, always check the job description, do some online research to find out what the pay is for similar positions, and ask a co-op coordinator what the pay rate is before you go in for an interview. If the job pays $11.00 an hour, and you can't afford to take a job that pays less than $13.00, it's better to find out ahead of time and decline an interview rather than wasting everyone's time. In general, co-op students tend to be paid at the lower end of the scale for similar work.

In many cases, the issue of pay in a co-op job or internship is fairly rigid and non-negotiable. Some positions pay a certain figure, period. Others offer varied pay... but the pay only varies depending on your year in school; again, the pay rate is non-negotiable. Some internships don't pay at all, depending on the field and the organization.

In an equal number of instances, however, the pay rate is a range that can vary depending on your skills, your prior experience, the employer's alternatives to hiring you, and your desirability as a candidate. The co-op coordinator will usually—but not always—have an accurate sense of what the realm of possibility is with pay. Find out before the interview.

If you *do* know what the pay rate or pay range is, you can acknowledge this in response to the question: "My understanding is that the job pays something from $13 to $15 an hour. I'd be comfortable with something within that range."

This kind of response doesn't pigeonhole you as someone seeking a high or low pay rate and indicates that money isn't the most important consideration for you. For a co-op job, you never want to mention money as the reason you want a particular job, or as the main way you will decide between Job A and Job B.

If you *don't* know what the pay range or pay rate is, your best bet is to reply with a question: "Is there a pay range that you have in mind for the position?" Usually, there is, and many employers will provide you with a range. When you are told the range, it is best to not show any surprise, positively or negatively.

If you're pressed for a specific dollar figure, another option is to evade the question until an offer is presented: "Money isn't the main factor in my decision. But I plan to interview with other companies, and if I get more than one excellent opportunity, then money could be a factor. But once you make me a specific offer, I will give you an answer within three business days." Experts in salary negotiations will tell you the first person to give a number is at a disadvantage. You want to discuss salary only when they are absolutely convinced they can't live without you. It is at this point that you have negotiating leverage and not until then.

This kind of response indicates that money is not the top objective. More importantly, it helps you to project yourself as a person who has options and who considers himself or herself to be an attractive candidate. You want to show that you're strongly interested in the job, yes, but not desperate to get it!

Unfortunately, gender also plays a role in determining compensation. Men tend to expect and set a higher salary goal and ask for it when offered a job while women are generally more likely to accept the initial offer. A valuable resource to help women overcome wage inequity is a book written in 2003 by Linda Babcock and Sara Laschever entitled *Women Don't Ask* (Princeton University Press). Babcock and Laschever provide evidence that one of the major reasons women often do not achieve the same level of income as men in the same job is due to their inability or unwillingness to even ask for a higher wage when a job offer is extended.

Obviously, there are many other possible questions you might be asked in an interview. You'll find 21 more examples of interview questions in Appendix D which were created by Linnea Basu, a co-op coordinator at Northeastern. One accounting employer consistently asks job candidates to "define integrity." Some interviewers may ask candidates to name someone that they think of as a hero. We have heard of one employer who asked a job candidate to tell him a joke! In short, you cannot prepare for every specific question that you possibly could be asked.

But when you are asked an unusual question, don't panic: just think, how can I use this question to show that I am THE candidate who is the best MATCH for THIS job description. Whether you're defining integrity or describing your ideal job, this is something that you can focus on.

DEALING WITH DIFFERENT INTERVIEWER STYLES

Another challenge in preparing for an interview is that you may come across many vastly different interviewing styles. Sometimes, students return to the co-op office feeling frustrated because the interviewer never shut up and didn't really give them a chance to sell themselves. Others may have a different frustration: The interviewer barely talked at all, and they felt extremely awkward. So it may be useful to consider how to deal with different types of interviewers.

First of all, keep in mind that many interviewers are NOT experts in interviewing. They may not know the best questions to ask to determine how good a candidate you are. You may find this disappointing, but that's the way it is. You may have to overcome an interviewer's weaknesses or personality if it keeps you from selling yourself. Here are some tips for dealing with several types of interviewers.

Type 1: "The Interrogator"

This interviewer puts job candidates on the spot. The Interrogator asks blunt questions, such as: "Why should we hire YOU for this job?" Or "What makes you think you know computers well enough to work here?" Alternatively, he or she may like to pose a challenge for you: "Here's a set of numbers. Figure out the present value of this sum of money if it's invested for 10 years at 8% interest." One interviewer likes to toss a beeper on the table and ask the potential computer engineering co-op: "How would you go about developing a new operating system for this beeper?" Sales interviewers may pull out a 79-cent pen and say, "You have one minute to sell me this pen."

You should always be prepared for an intense interview. Assume that you're going to be challenged with difficult questions, and that you may be asked to back up your answers with real-life examples.

Most interviewers will not be this tough: particularly with co-op candidates. Still, you have to be prepared for the possibility. And although many job candidates tremble at the thought of facing a high-pressure interviewer, the Interrogator is not the toughest to face. The Interrogator puts you under the microscope and evaluates how you handle tough questions or problems, but this gives you an opportunity to show how you can step up to a challenge and handle it.

Some information technology employers will sit a student down at a broken computer and have them attempt to fix it. The interviewer sits and notes how the candidate attempts to tackle the problem as much as the result. More and more employers are administering skills test to verify that students have the skills they claim to have. Be prepared to demonstrate your software skills, welding skills, etc.

Type 2: "The Buddy"

This interviewer is very different from the Interrogator. The Buddy will have more of a conversation with you about the job, asking questions in a non-threatening way, showing interest in who you are as a person, etc. Most students prefer this kind of interviewer, naturally, but you have to be careful. Some wily interviewers will intentionally take on this friendly tone because they know you are likely to let your guard down. With the Buddy, you might be likely to confide more of your weaknesses, shortcomings, and problems, because their friendliness seems so trustworthy. The Buddy will get you to admit that you got a C – in your accounting class—and will even sound sympathetic—then the Buddy will turn around and nail you when it comes time to pick the best candidate.

If the interviewer is casual and friendly, you should relax too: but be a little cautious. Don't ever forget that you're trying to sell your strengths and show why you're a good match for the job: even if you're doing this with a smile on your face and a more relaxed tone of voice. Friendly conversation can set a nice tone for an interview: Just make sure that your conversation gets beyond small talk.

Type 3: "The Nonstop Talker"

Although the Interrogator may sound like your worst nightmare, The Nonstop Talker is actually the most difficult and frustrating type for most interviewees. You may sit through an interview that feels more like a lecture, barely getting a chance to say anything to this interviewer. At least the Interrogator gives you a chance to say something in your defense!

The Nonstop Talker may not be immediately recognizable. Many good interviewers will begin by telling you a great deal about the job and the organization before asking you questions. The Nonstop Talker may talk about these things, too, in addition to himself or herself, the previous co-op student that worked at the company, and a whole bunch of other topics. Applicants for one job came back and reported with some amazement that the manager talked about his ex-wife! The next thing you know, the interviewer has used up all of the scheduled time, and you've done little but nod a lot. Of course, this is a low-pressure interview, but you run the risk of coming across as part of the office furniture: In other words, this type of interview may mean that they like you and have basically decided to hire you, but it also may mean that you are completely forgotten by the interviewer.

When interviewed by the Nonstop Talker, you have to walk a fine line: Don't interrupt, but DO take advantage of any break in the monologue by asking a question that brings the Talker around to considering you as a candidate. During a pause, you might be able to politely say: "Can I ask you a question? I'm very interested in this job. What would be useful for you to know in order to find out whether I'm the best candidate for the job?" Another strategy is to acknowledge and flatter the Talker's talking while changing the focus of the talk: "I've certainly learned a great deal about you, this job, and the organization. In fact, from what you've said, I think this opportunity would be a great match for my skills because...." At this point, you can tailor your response to what you've learned from the nonstop talking... as long as you were listening carefully! This strategy works especially well toward the end of the interview and can be used effectively at the time the interviewer asks if you have any questions.

In short, try to get the Nonstop Talker to focus on you. He or she may still talk a great deal, but at least it might be about you and your ability to do the job.

Type 4: "Silent But Deadly"

This interviewer is the opposite of the talker, but this style can be equally frustrating. The Silent But Deadly interviewer will ask very few questions, and the questions may be very vague or general. So why is this interviewer potentially "deadly?" Basically, he or she gives nervous job candidates every opportunity to hang themselves! Consider the following dialogue:

Interviewer: "So... tell me about your weaknesses."

Job Candidate: "Although I have a good understanding of computer networking from class work, I need to learn more in order to master networking: specifically, I'm looking forward to learning more about setting up and maintaining networks in a real life environment which is why the job with your company appeals to me."

Interviewer: "Hmmmm......"

Job Candidate: "Um, and I guess you want another weakness?"

Interviewer [nods]: "Uh-huh..."

Job Candidate: "Hmmm.... okay, let me think... Um, I guess I'm not that strong when it comes to network security.... I'm not as good at setting up firewalls as I should be."

Interviewer [nods, says nothing]:

Job Candidate: "And.... I suppose that getting a C+ in my Linux operating systems class wasn't that strong."

Do you see what can happen in this situation? The job candidate started off with a strong answer but then interpreted the interviewer's silence as a negative: The candidate assumed that he or she failed to answer the question adequately. As a result, the candidate supplied more information. In this case, it was information that can only hurt the individual's chances of getting a job.

Most Silent But Deadly interviewers act this way because it reflects their personalities. But some shrewd interviewers may use this as a deliberate strategy to see if you will hang yourself if given enough rope. This is especially common when asking about weaknesses or reasons for leaving a previous job or situation.

Either way, your strategy is simple. If the length of the silence starts to feel awkward, ask a clarifying question such as: "Does that answer your question?"; "Is there anything else you'd like to ask me?"; "What else would you like to know about me?" Unless you're asked a specific question requesting more information, have faith in your answer; don't assume that silence or apparent indifference means that you have to say something more.

During Scott's last job search, he was interviewed by a very quiet, introverted gentleman. After each of Scott's answers, the manager would let a solid ten seconds go by; once, he waited for a good 20 seconds, as if he were curious to see how Scott would handle that. But Scott believed he had given a strong, definitive answer, so he simply waited. Finally, the interviewer said, "Is there anything you'd like to add?" Scott replied, pleasantly, "I think I covered everything. Was there something else you would like to know?" Ultimately, Scott was offered the job. So it just goes to show you: There is seldom one "right" way to handle an interviewing challenge. It's always difficult to feel that you need to carry both sides of any conversation. But if you can take charge of the situation by offering to explain why you're a good match for the job, what you have to offer the organization, and by asking questions that reflect your research, you may succeed in bringing this interviewer out of his or her shell.

Type 5: "The Big Picture Person"

This interviewer is prone to asking very open-ended, general questions, such as:

- Tell me about yourself.
- What do you want to do with your life?
- What are your career goals?
- What kind of person are you?

Students often hate these questions because there seems to be no clear-cut way to answer them. Again, though, remember the rule: When asked about something general, answer in a way that shows why you are a match for this specific job. What kind of person are you? "I have a great deal to offer to a small medical office like this one. I have excellent grades in my anatomy and physiology classes, and I have solid experience working hands-on with people as a volunteer at the small hospital in my hometown. If you hire me, you will be employing a person who has a solid base of experience as well as someone who picks up new things quickly and does work without complaining." If that's the kind of job description in question, that's the right kind of specific answer to a "big picture" question.

Type 6: "The Human Resources Interviewer"

If you are interviewed by someone from the Human Resources (HR) department, you may or may not be asked questions relating to your technical skills. An experienced HR person may have enough expertise to ask you about specific tasks, but it is not uncommon to come across an HR interviewer who knows little about engineering, nursing, or social work. Alternatively, the HR interviewer may have that knowledge but decide that such questions are better left to the person who would be your supervisor if you're hired. Either way, the HR interviewer is more likely to ask the classic interview questions as described in the previous section. The questions may be more "warm and fuzzy," as the purpose of this interview may be to "screen" candidates to determine who will go on to the next phase of the interview process. Be prepared for a structured interview, and don't get too technical in your responses unless the interviewer seems to be looking for that. Save your more technical answers for the interviewer who is a network administrator or mechanical engineer—someone who is an expert in your field, whatever it is.

Type 7: "The Behavioral-Based Interviewer"

Some organizations swear by the Behavioral-Based Interviewing (BBI) approach, and for good reason: Studies have shown that this style is generally more effective in determining whether someone is a good match for the job. In particular, Big Four accounting firms such as Deloitte and Touche and PricewaterhouseCoopers often use this approach. Microsoft and other corporations also use these questions to determine if you have specific "core competencies" that are considered to be vital to success at the organization in question: drive/results orientation; passion for learning; ability to work in a team; ability to handle conflict effectively; good ethical judgment; etc.

The behavioral-based interview features questions that require specific stories in response. This makes it much more difficult for the interviewee to come up with a slick-sounding, canned answer: Instead, he or she must recount something that they really experienced in the classroom or at work. In answering, the interviewee is urged to walk the interviewer through the specific situation and to detail what they were thinking, feeling, and doing in dealing with it.

Here are some typical BBI questions:

- Tell me specifically what your greatest accomplishment in life thus far has been.
- Tell me about a time when you had to overcome a challenge or obstacle when working as part of a team.
- Tell me about a time when you felt really successful in something at work.

- Describe a situation in which you faced an ethical dilemma and how you dealt with it.

If you're not too forthcoming or struggle initially, the interview may add, "Just walk me through what was going on step-by-step..." or something like that.

The key to these interviews is to have several good, specific stories that you are ready to share. Think long and hard ahead of time about which stories will best showcase multiple positive qualities—some stories are better than others! Describe the situation specifically first, then logically walk the interviewer through how you handled the situation step-by-step, wrapping up with a description of what ended up happening due to your actions. Naturally, you'll want to choose ones that have a positive outcome.

Practice the telling of your behavioral-based stories ahead of time. Last summer, Scott's nephew interviewed for an engineering position—his first job out of college. Ahead of time, they gave him a list of core competencies that they seek in applicants and told him that they would be looking for him to share some personal experiences related to those competencies. Scott told him that this was like going for a test where you have been given the questions a week in advance! However, the first time he told Scott his stories, they weren't good enough. He had to try out some stories to figure out which ones would be the BEST stories to showcase his strengths. After extensive practice and preparation—and despite limited internship experience—he went in and nailed the interview, and it turned out to be the only offer he got in a tough economy. Without strategizing and practicing for a behavioral-based interview, it may not have happened.

Whether or not you ever have a behavioral-based interview, having extremely vivid and specific examples to share is always a smart idea for use with all types of interviewers: It brings alive your ideas and tells employers what you really mean when you say that you can learn quickly or work independently or be a strong team player. For a great deal of information on behavioral-based interviewing—including several terrific student examples—check out Appendix F in the back of this textbook.

Type 8: "The Olympic Judge"

The Olympic Judge likes to let you know how you're doing throughout the interview. As you might imagine, this can be encouraging, disconcerting, or both. This interviewer may come out and say, "Good answer!" However, this individual may also shake his head or frown or say, "Well, I don't know about that."

Dealing with immediate negative feedback can be very challenging to your confidence. How can you handle it? Most importantly, don't ignore it. If an interviewer reacts negatively to one of your answers, ask a clarifying question: "Is there a concern you have about that answer?" Once you understand why the interviewer reacted negatively, try to acknowledge the concern and address it as best as you can. For example, if you're asked to cite your experience in records management, and the interviewer reacts negatively to your response, you might handle it like this:

Job candidate: "I noticed that you had a negative reaction to my answer. What is it about my records management experience that concerns you?"

Interviewer: "Well, I'm concerned that your knowledge is primarily theoretical since you don't have any real work experience doing file management."

Job candidate: "I think it's fair to say that my knowledge of file management does come from my coursework. But one of the great things about the classes I've taken is that they required that we work through "in-basket" activities that simulate real work situations. During my education I've had many opportunities to practice and get good at file management."

The candidate could then go on to tout some specifics about proper file management practices. Would this be enough to turn around the Olympic Judge's perception? Maybe not, but it would at least give you a chance. It shows assertiveness, desire to get the job, and sensitivity to the concerns of others.

A variation on the Olympic Judge interviewer is the person who asks you to judge yourself: "On a scale of 1 to 10, with 1 being terrible and 10 being fantastic, how would you rate yourself in terms of...." The interviewer then asks you to rate your communication skills, your analytical ability, your interpersonal skills, etc.

This kind of question tests your honesty, realism, and savvy: Rating yourself uniformly high comes off as insincere or unaware, but who will hire you if you give yourself low ratings? When answering this question, make sure you do yourself justice, but make sure to rate yourself lower in certain areas: particularly those that seem less related to the job that you want. Don't rate yourself as a 1 or 2 in something unless you really know nothing about it (i.e., you're asked about C++ programming, and you've never done anything like it). For most generic characteristics, stick between 6 and 10. Bear in mind that your coordinator would not send your resume out for a position if he or she believed that your skills were not a reasonable match for the given job. Have confidence in your skill level, and show it with ratings that are realistic and positive.

PANEL, GROUP AND TELEPHONE INTERVIEWS

In addition to encountering individuals who vary widely in terms of their interviewing style, you also may come across some interesting variations when it comes to interview format. When we say the word "interview," most people visualize a one-on-one, face-to-face meeting. However, there are three notable exceptions to that rule, and you are very likely to experience some or all of them eventually.

Panel Interviews

Panel interviews, where you are interviewed by two or more interviewers, can occur in any industry. In most ways, panel interviews are like one-on-one interviews in that you need to highlight your knowledge, skills, and abilities. To succeed in a panel interview, you'll also want to follow these additional techniques:

1. *Start answering questions while making eye contact with the person who asked the question.* Then briefly make eye contact with the other interviewers before finishing your answer by looking back at the person who asked the question.

2. *When you ask questions at the end of the interview, direct questions to the person who appears to be the leader of the group.* Typically this is the individual who makes the initial introductions or asks the most questions.

3. *If the interviewers follow the good/bad cop scenario, remain cool and calm.* Don't let them fluster you: They may simply be attempting to determine how you'll react in stressful situations.

4. *Collect business cards from all interviewers so that you will be able to send thank you notes to each interviewer.*

Focus each letter differently depending upon the job title of the interviewer. For example, emphasize teamwork and productively to the supervisor of your department, but note your ability to work collaboratively when writing to someone from another division. You also could allude to specific questions that the various individuals asked to customize each note.

Group Interviews

Some employers figure they can hire the best workers for a team environment by using group interviews. In a group interview, there may be anywhere from three to 25 people all interviewing at the same time in a room! Inevitably, many interviewees find this format strange and confusing. The key is to make yourself stand out from the pack even though you won't know what to expect. Prepare as you would for all other interviews with these additional tips:

1. *Arrive early to give yourself time to meet and introduce yourself to the interviewers before the interview begins if possible.*
2. *Group interviews are often interactive so listen carefully to instructions and follow them accurately.*
3. *Demonstrate your leadership skills by acting as a "facilitator."* Instead of being loudest or attempting to show that you're better by being critical or negative when other job candidates speak, find ways to coordinate others and/or delegate tasks. For example, say "I like your idea. Who else agrees with that?" Or "That idea is definitely a good start. To build on that, I also would suggest an additional element, which would be..." These responses show that you are confident, respectful, and willing to listen to others. Include quieter people by asking their opinion. Behaving in this way demonstrates you are a team player with effective communication skills.
4. *Be courteous to your fellow interviewees, even if it appears they are trying to take over the interview.* Group interviews are designed to see how you interact with other people and in stressful situations. Project positive energy, even if others don't. Remember, no one can intimidate you without your permission!
5. *Make eye contact with everyone at some point.* Avoid focusing your attention on one person.

Frequently, the group interview is merely a first-round interview. If it goes well for you, typically there will be at least one additional interview.

Telephone Interviews

In this digital age of recruiting, phone interviews are frequently used to screen candidates in order to decide who will be invited for in-person interviews. Prepare for a phone interview just as you would for a regular interview. While you're engaged in any job search, be ready to telephone interview on a moment's notice. You never know when an employer might call and ask if you have a few minutes to talk. If you do get a phone call from an employer and are not prepared to talk, let the call go to your voice mail so you have at least some brief amount of time to reflect on your interview strategy and to focus.

Sometimes employers may have only one or two clarifying questions that would take just a few minutes. Or they may want to do the full 10-60 minute phone interview with you, and they *want* to have you do it extemporaneously. Consequently, they aren't interested in rescheduling. That said, most employers want the candidate to have a quiet place to talk and think and are willing to make a later appointment. If you are good on the phone you may want to go ahead with the interview. If you are driving or otherwise preoccupied, it is best to suggest an alternate time. A good way to ask for a rescheduled interview is "I'm very glad you called. I have about 10 minutes before I have to leave for another appointment. Is that enough time, or may I call you back either later this afternoon or tomorrow morning?" This way, you are showing your interest in the position, being clear about your current availability, and suggesting a time to connect later.

These tips will help you ace a phone interview:

1. *Use a landline if possible.* You don't want to risk having problems with cell phone service. Even at their best, cell phones often have awkward delays or echoes. If you don't have a landline at home, consider asking your coordinator if you can make a call from the school. If that is not feasible, just make sure you are in an area with the best cell phone service as possible. Before you begin the interview, check to make sure your phone battery is not about to run out.

2. *Avoid distractions.* Find a quiet place to interview and stay there! This can be tricky if you have young children or other family members at home who need your attention. Don't be embarrassed if the quietest spot is the bathroom—no one can see you! Set up your interview for a precise time so that you can minimize possible distractions. For example, if your phone interview is scheduled between 4pm and 4:30pm, be sure that no one has company over during that time, the kids are fed and occupied or a sitter will watch them.)

3. *Have your resume and interview notes in front of you.* One of the real advantages of a phone interview is that you can lay out several pages of notes on a desk or table along with your resume and job description. This can be very handy if you blank out on anything. Just be sure to spread them out so you don't have to pick up any of the papers, as the rustling will be audible over the phone. Also, have a pen and paper handy to take notes. If you are being interviewed by a committee and they are all on the other end of a conference call, you will want to write down each person's name/role down so that you can refer to it later. Use your interview notes to ask questions at the end of the interview.

4. *Remember that your voice is your only means of communication.* This is both a positive and a negative. In a conventional interview, you can use body language, eye contact, posture, and even attire to convey attentiveness, enthusiasm, and interest. On the phone, you don't have to worry about any of those elements. Scott often tells students that they can wear pajamas and fuzzy bunny slippers for a phone interview if they're more comfortable that way. Likewise, you can close your eyes if it helps you concentrate better. On the other hand, though, your voice has to do all of the heavy lifting for you in a phone interview. It needs to convey your energy, interest, professionalism, and listening skills.

   Accordingly, speak clearly and a bit more slowly. In a face-to-face interview it is easier to understand what is being said because you and the interviewer can both see each other's mouths move. Additionally, smiling and nodding can indicate that a point is understood. Because you aren't able to do this over the phone, you'll want to speak very clearly. Take your time and don't rush your answers. It is absolutely okay to say "I'd like a moment to get my thoughts together" or "That's interesting... Let me think about that for a moment.' Beware of jokes or remarks, as they are much easier to misinterpret over the phone.

5. *Consider how your facial expression or posture may affect your tone.* First off, smile. According to experts, smiling has a positive effect on the tone of your voice. Secondly, give some thought to your posture. Some people find that standing while talking helps calm them or puts them into the mindset of putting on a presentation.

6. *No eating, drinking, smoking or chewing gum!* It's okay to take small sips of a drink you have nearby in case your mouth is dry but nothing else. Remember that phones amplify sounds.

7. *Stay on the phone with the interviewer.* If you have call waiting, turn it off in advance if possible by pressing *70 before your dial. If it's not possible to disable your call waiting, don't answer any other incoming calls and definitely don't allow yourself to give in to any other distractions when on a cell phone or cordless phone with the interviewer.

8. *Give verbal signals that you are engaged in the conversation.* As you would in a face-to-face interview, use typical conversational short interjections that don't interrupt such as "I see," "that's interesting," "okay," "great," and "yes."

9. *Don't discuss compensation.* If the interviewer asks about your current salary or desired income, indicate that you will be happy to deal with those questions in an in-person meeting. Then inquire what salary range has been budgeted for the position. If the job requires relocation, it is important to know the compensation range so you don't waste time pursuing a job that doesn't fit your needs.

10. *Remember, your goal is to set up a face-to-face interview.* If you have not been invited to an interview by the end of the conversation, take the initiative. Consider saying something such as "This sounds like an interesting opportunity and I believe I could make a contribution. Can we get together to continue this discussion?" Write a thank-you note the same day. Follow up with a phone call within two to three days to reinforce your desire to secure an in-person meeting. Given that it is difficult to evaluate an opportunity properly over the phone, go to the interview. It will give you more practice, and you will have a better understanding of the job and the work environment through an in-person interview.

For Individuals With Hearing Loss/Deafness

Although phone interviews are possible via relay service or TTY, all too often companies are not prepared to communicate in these ways or comfortable doing

INTERVIEWING – AN EMPLOYER'S PERSPECTIVE

by Mike Naclerio

The goal of interviewing is to determine a "mutual" fit between the company and potential employee. Too often, candidates view interviews as situations where they have to prove to a company that they are worthy of a job offer without turning the tables. It's important to "interview the company" to see if the company is good enough for them (i.e., does the company have an appropriate level of ethics, will the position be satisfying, what type of people work there, etc.). So, candidates should not lose sight of this opportunity: Ask questions!

***Mike Naclerio** is the Director of Relationship Management at the workplace HELPLINE*

so. As unfair as it may be, the candidate may have to suggest alternatives to the speaking-and-hearing phone interview. If TTY is used, a hard-of-hearing candidate may want to send a note in advance to the interviewer indicating some basic TTY vocabulary. It is up to you whether or not you want to educate the employer about communicating via TTY or relay.

In the computer age, another suggestion would be to have a real-time conversation via chat technology. Companies may have specific areas on their website where employees can meet from different locations in real time. Such a site would be an ideal venue in which candidates and employers can interview.

TURNING THE TABLES: ASKING THE RIGHT QUESTIONS DURING AN INTERVIEW

Many job candidates think of interviewing as an audition for a part. This perception has some truth to it, but it's not the whole story. In an interview, you are trying to show that you're the best person for the job. Additionally, though, you're trying to determine whether the job is a good match for you. In that sense, interviewing should be a two-way street.

The nice thing about asking questions in an interview is that it helps to achieve both of these goals. Asking smart questions is a great way to show the interviewer that you are:

- prepared for the interview in terms of researching the job and the company
- excited about and interested in the job
- determined to find out whether you think this job is the best match for your considerable talents

All of these things reflect favorably on you as a job candidate. Likewise, asking questions is a great way for the interviewer to show you whether:

- the job is what it appears to be in the job description
- the job is something that you will be excited about doing for several months and possibly as a regular position after your internship or co-op is complete
- the job is indeed a good match for someone with your level of skills

Don't underestimate the importance of determining whether the job is what you really want. More often than not, individuals who end up disliking their jobs failed to ask the right questions during the interview. Basically, they didn't have a realistic sense of what the job requirements would be. As a result, they end up being bored or overwhelmed. But isn't it the employer's fault for failing to communicate this to the job candidate, you might say? True, a great interviewer will do this effectively. However, if an interviewer fails to do so, it's your responsibility to ask if you want to ensure that misunderstandings are avoided.

What questions should I ask?

Many internship and co-op candidates—even many experienced professionals—struggle to come up with good questions. When they are given the opportunity to ask questions during an interview, they will try to think up some on the spot, then decline the opportunity.

Like so many things in interviewing, this element requires preparation. You should have as many as eight to ten questions ready to ask before you even arrive for the interview. Why so many? Because several questions that you had beforehand may be answered during the course of the interview. Most interviewers won't simply ask questions; they'll talk a little about the company and explain a little more about the job. Thus, you need to have numerous questions ready.

What are the "best" questions to ask? In our opinion, the best questions are the ones that:

- force the interviewer to imagine you in the job
- show that you did some meaningful research and have given serious thought about the position
- reflect your attitude and values positively
- require more than a yes or no answer

Let's consider what this means. If you want the job, it is certainly in your best interest to make the interviewer imagine you in the job. You can do this by using the words "I," "me," and "my" in your question. For example:

- What would my typical day be like in this position?
- Who would train me when I begin this job?
- When could I expect to receive performance feedback?

These are good questions, but the very best ones are those which also reflect a positive attitude and strong values. Consider these:

- What could I do between now and the first day of the co-op to be ready to hit the ground running in this job?
- I definitely want a job that challenges me and keeps me busy. Given that, can you give me a sense about whether this position would be right for me?
- If I excel in this job, would I be able to have more responsibilities added to my job description?

Here are some other good questions:

- What would you say is the most challenging part of this job?
- In preparing for the interview, I talked to one of your former interns.

INTERVIEWING – A STUDENT'S PERSPECTIVE

by Gabriel Glasscock

As expected, your first few interviews will be a little nerve-wracking. But that's to be expected. It's impossible to know exactly the type of interviewer you will have. So try not to prepare too much for a certain type of interviewer. Rather, invest your time into knowing as much about the job as possible. Find good potential conversation starters. I found it good to start a conversation on relevant job-related topics (where appropriate). This shows the employer that you are not just interested in the job but the field as a whole, and it also eases some of the tension. Look them in the eye, and use good body language.

Expect the unexpected. One time, I was at Snell Library at 8:30 p.m. in the middle of an intense group session. I got a call from a recruiter for an excellent position in Florida with a Big Five firm. We had been playing phone tag for a few weeks and she was to make a decision the next day on whom to hire: I had to interview over the phone outside the library in the freezing cold of December. I knew this would be my one and only 15-minute chance at this job, and I had to sell myself RIGHT THEN, without any preparation at all. Unlike most interviews, this was not prearranged: The interviewer wanted to see how well I could think on my feet.

The main thing is self-confidence. They were looking for a trainer in Java. When she asked the infamous "Why should we hire you?" question, I had to be creative. Although I had no prior experience with Java, I convinced her that my experience with Visual Basic would help greatly with learning Java, as both are object-oriented programming languages. Understanding transferable skills—and knowing how to use and express them—is an essential quality for an interviewee and also one of my favorite parts of this guidebook.

Any time an interviewer gives you the floor to ask questions, ASK QUESTIONS. Always have several prepared. I used the "Why do you like working here?" question with the Big Five recruiter, and she loved talking about that. Ask questions that show you have an interest in working there in your specific job and in being a part of their company.

***Gabriel Glasscock** was an MIS student at Northeastern University, Class of 2002*

He told me that he loved the job because many new projects arose while he was working for you. Would you say the role will be the same this time?

- In researching your company, I read your organizational credo. It's very impressive. I'm curious as to how the credo affects business decisions on a day-to-day basis. Can you tell me more about that?
- I saw online that your company merged with another organization four months ago. How has that affected the company thus far?

- What would you describe as the most rewarding aspect of the job?
- In the research that I did to prepare for today, I noticed that your company is trying to (i.e., implement a new marketing strategy, adopt a new process of providing quality care to patients). How has this development changed things in this department?
- This job involves several different responsibilities: Which do you think would require most of my time?
- Why do YOU like working for this company?

Asking these kinds of questions will show the interviewer that you are serious about the job, and that you value yourself highly enough to know that other options may be more attractive to you than this one. Because this is true, you need to see if the company meets your needs as well as you meet theirs.

It is also especially important to ask how you'll be evaluated. It is amazing how many people don't ask. You don't want to agree to play a game and not know how the game is scored. A good question to ask is:

> "It's important to me to get an outstanding evaluation in my co-op job: What could I do to really stand out as an exceptional employee in this job?"

One last note: Be sure to follow up on your questions. Listen to the employer's answer, and respond to it positively. Here's an example:

Interviewee:	"What could I do to earn an outstanding evaluation working here?"
Interviewer:	"Well, more than anything we want someone who is willing to do whatever it takes to get the job done—even if that means staying really late or coming in on Saturdays from time to time."
Interviewee:	"That's great to hear. I have no problem putting in extra hours: I just want to be a productive part of the team, whatever it takes. Actually, if you want to call my previous supervisor, she can tell you about my willingness to work overtime or come in on short notice. I think I would stand out in a similar way here."

ENDING ON A HIGH NOTE

If you have ever taken a psychology class, you may have heard of a phenomenon called the primacy/recency effect. Research has shown that when individuals are presented with a significant amount of information, they tend to best remember what they are exposed to first and last; the middle tends to get hazy.

We already discussed how to get off to a good start. Now let's discuss how you can cap your interview with a strong ending. Here are a few basic guidelines:

Take charge of the transition from asking questions to closing the interview.

Don't wait for the employer to figure out that you have no more questions to ask. The best approach is to bridge from asking questions into closing the interview. After you've had your job-related questions answered, simply say: "I have just one more question. When do you plan to make a hiring decision?"

Ask the interviewer what the next steps will be.

After you learn when the decision will be made, ask the interviewer what his or her preference is regarding next steps: "Would you like me to call you next week about the decision, or should I just wait to hear from you?" If the interviewer says that you can call, make sure to get a business card, or, at least, a phone number you can call.

An alternative way to close the interview is to offer a concise summary of your fit for the job.

Sometimes, as the interview comes to an end, you realize you didn't have the opportunity to highlight one of your skills or mention something you think will influence the hiring decision. The best approach in this situation is to give a brief summary that explains why you are a good fit for the job, making sure to add any items not already covered during the interview, and express your interest and enthusiasm for the position. Just because this is your time to ask questions it doesn't mean you can't also make some brief additional comments. Then you should proceed to ask about next steps.

Thank the interviewer for taking the time to meet with you.

Even if you're not interested in the job, be graceful and polite. Acknowledge the fact that the interviewer has devoted part of his or her day to talk to you. Show some appreciation for the experience, and mention something specific about your conversation that was enlightening. One possibility would be: "Thank you for taking the time to meet with me today. I learned a great deal about the nursing practices in a geriatric care facility. I think that someone with my interpersonal skills and strong grades in the sciences would be a great addition to your team, and I look forward to hearing from you."

Shake the interviewer's hand before leaving, and make sure that you haven't left behind any personal belongings.

If you have any doubts about whether or not you handled questions well, write them down soon after you leave. Then you can discuss them with your coordinator.

AFTER THE INTERVIEW: FOLLOW-UP STEPS

To some degree, your follow-up steps may vary depending on the employer's needs or preferences. In all circumstances, respect any request that an employer makes of you, whether it's getting a writing sample to her or additional references to him, calling on a particular day, or not calling at all.

Most people would agree that writing a thank-you note or letter or e-mail would be appropriate at this point. But one dilemma is whether a handwritten card is better than a less formal e-mail. My rule is that if a decision is not going to be made within the next two or three days, then it's better to send a brief letter or card if you mail it by the following morning. But if a decision will be made within 24 hours, then opt for an e-mail.

More than anything, though, make sure that any such note or e-mail is absolutely perfect in terms of grammar and spelling... especially when writing the name of the manager or organization. Sending no thank-you letter at all is better than sending one with errors.

Keep your thank-you note simple and professional. A safe approach would include the following steps:

- Thank the interviewer for taking the time to meet with you on Thursday (or whatever day it was).
- Say something positive about the interviewing experience: something you learned about the company, its products/services, the job, etc. This demonstrates you were paying attention.
- If you want the job, briefly reinforce your interest in the position and why you would be a good match for it. If you don't want the job, skip this part of the thank you note.
- Encourage the interviewer to contact you if any additional information is needed. Be sure to include your phone number and e-mail in your thank-you note. Make it easy for the employer to contact you with a job offer!

Here is an example of how one might format a thank-you e-mail:

> Subject: Thank you for your time
>
> Ms. Bacher,
>
> Thank you so much for taking the time to meet with me this morning. I enjoyed

learning about the new directions Deloitte will be taking in the next five years. I was especially pleased to hear about the variety of activities that would be in store for me if I am hired for a co-op position this January. It sounds like an exciting time for the firm.

I am very interested in the position and I believe that my bookkeeping experience, attention to detail, and strong academic performance in accounting would make me a strong contributor to your organization.

I look forward to hearing from you soon. Please feel free to contact me if you have any additional questions.

Thanks again,

Leigh Kelley
523.353.4093
kelleyl@comcast.com

A pleasant and timely thank-you note can't turn a mediocre candidate into a great one. But it can make all the difference if the employer is struggling over the decision or believes that several candidates could do the job.

SPECIAL CONSIDERATIONS FOR MARKETING INTERVIEWS

Generally, most of the information that you have read so far can prove useful when interviewing for any job. As we also have alluded to, however, there are some critical differences between marketing interviews and those for jobs related to other majors.

Why are marketing interviews different? Frequently, marketing employers expect a more aggressive approach. Since sales and marketing are closely related, the marketing employer will closely examine your ability to sell yourself: If you can't persuasively sell yourself in an interview, they believe, how can you be expected to sell that company's products and services? You really have to prepare your "interview presentation" with this in mind. Here are some tips:

- *Generally, it is a good idea to bring notes to a marketing presentation.* As noted earlier, this would be a real no-no for many interviews, but many marketing employers believe that a lack of notes reveals a lack of preparation. Thinking on your feet is one thing, but "winging it" for an important presentation is another one entirely!

  A short section on how to prepare and use notes can be found on page 127.

- *Be aggressive.* There is no room for shyness in a marketing presentation. Your self-presentation should be energetic, persuasive, and geared toward pushing the employer for a commitment.

- *Ask for the job.* Again, this is something you would not do with most non-marketing employers. But in a marketing interview, conclude your sales pitch with an attempt to close the deal. Your ability to close this deal may reflect your aggressiveness in closing in a selling situation on the job. If you want the job, ask for it. If you can do the job, tell them.

- *Seek closure.* At the end of the interview, ask the interviewer when they expect to make a decision regarding the position. Keeping this information in mind, it is generally recommended that you follow up with the employer after your interview. Be aware that there is a fine line between being persistent and being a nuisance. Some marketing students have failed to get jobs because they failed to follow up with interviewers. Others have been turned down because they called too often and alienated the interviewer.

Accordingly, remember these guidelines:

- *After making clear that you want and can do the job, ask when a hiring decision will be made.* Then plan your follow-up efforts accordingly.
- *If the interviewer tells you when you should call back to follow up, honor their wishes.* If they tell you not to call until next week, then do so.
- *Don't be a pest.* Job candidates have lost jobs because they kept calling until the employer got fed up with it. Limit follow-up calls to one or two per week.
- *Remember that the policy of following up after an interview often doesn't apply if you're interviewing for non-marketing jobs.* Some marketing students pursuing opportunities in finance, accounting, etc. have come across as pushy and obnoxious by repeatedly calling interviewers. If you are interested in opportunities outside of marketing, remember that the recommended follow-up procedure is to simply send a thank-you letter to the interviewer(s), and perhaps one phone follow up.

In any job interview, of course, you need to sell yourself persuasively. In a marketing interview, though, you can do so much more directly. But again, remember this warning for marketing majors who apply for non-marketing jobs: Be sure to tone down your presentation, or you may be perceived as pushy, arrogant, or obnoxious. As always: If in doubt, ask the coordinator who works with the employer about what approach would be most effective.

USING NOTES IN INTERVIEWS

Although there are some potential pitfalls to consider when using a notes page in an interview, we have come around to believing that almost any student could benefit from using notes—if done properly. The single best thing about notes is that they are a safety net if you are concerned about "going blank" due to negative nervous energy. Your notes will not include word-for-word answers, but they will feature enough words to jog your memory if you blank out. And if you don't go blank at all, nothing says that you have to use them just because you prepared them.

Of course, there are some major blunders you could make by using notes. The biggest one would be to write out detailed answers to common questions and to bury your head in your notes page during the interview, reading answers to the interviewer. That definitely would come across as being less prepared for the interview, and it would cause you significant problems with eye contact, natural speech, and connecting interpersonally with the interviewer.

So let's walk through how to create and use a notes page. How should your notes look? One former colleague suggests having your notes on an 8 ½ x 11-inch piece of paper, which is divided into four quarters:

- One quarter features key strategic points you intend to make about why you are a good match for the job. For example: "Excellent team player." Beneath each point, write words to help you remember a specific example that shows that strength in action (Example: Banana Republic – "Black Friday").
- One quarter has key notes about the job or company that you learned by researching the position.
- One quarter has eight or ten questions that you might ask, so you can be sure that all of your questions won't be answered in the course of the interview.
- The last quarter is left blank, so you can use it to take notes on what the interviewer says during the interview.

Write your notes in large print or—if on computer—print them out in a large font, so that they are easy enough to read without having them leave your lap or a tabletop. Don't wave your notes around. Keeping them on one piece of paper will help you from fumbling around during the interview to find what you need. A portfolio can be handy when using notes: You can buy one which has a flap for your resume and references on one side, with a clipboard for your one page of notes on the other side. Hand over a fresh resume and references when sitting down, then fold over the portfolio so your notes page is right in front of you.

A sample of a good notes page can be found on page 131. For this example, let's assume that the candidate is pursuing a PC support job in a corporate environment.

Lastly, what if an employer questions you on why you are using notes? The biggest thing is to avoid being defensive about it. If you try to hide the fact that you have a notes page or come across as if you're doing something wrong, then it will be perceived negatively. Simply say that this interview is important to you and that it is important for you to feel prepared: You wanted to make sure that you got across everything that mattered in terms of why you are a good fit for the job.

SAMPLE NOTES PAGE

STRATEGY/STORIES

Point #1: Passion for technology
Supporting Story: The Week I built new computer for myself at age 15

Point #2: Ability to learn quickly
Supporting Story: Day I fixed dad's crashed computer despite no experience with Macs.

Point #3: Customer-service skills
Supporting Story: Night I handled 8 tables at Applebee's when many called in sick.

Point #4: Team player
Supporting Story: My role in MIS301 group project on servers.

QUESTIONS

1. What could I do between now and January 2 to hit the ground running in this job?
2. How specifically could I earn a great evaluation?
3. Chance of a position after graduation?
4. Any new technological initiatives planned for the coming year?
5. Opportunity to take on additional work?

RESEARCH POINTS

— New investment product, Alpha Edge, just released

— 650 people in Boston office

— Previous intern said ability to work Saturdays is a plus

— Intern also said transition to MS-Vista is planned

— Hiring five co-ops: hardware, software, customer service roles

NOTES

HANDLING JOB OFFERS

Right now, you might believe that the least of your problems is how to deal with job offers. Just getting a job offer may seem improbable for the time being. However, your job situation can change quickly, and you need to know how to handle job offers. Over the years, we have been amazed at how many times an employer has called to tell us that they offered a job to someone, only to have the response be a low-energy mumble, indicating only that the person would have to think about it. In extreme cases, we have seen an employer pull back an offer in this situation, figuring that they don't want to hire someone who only wants the job as a last resort.

So don't take this small step for granted! Here are some quick tips.

Be Proactive

As soon as you get home after an interview, you should write down the pros and cons of accepting a job offer with that company. Without thinking about any other options that you may or may not have, is this a job that you would accept? In other words, start making up your mind BEFORE you get the offer.

ALWAYS Start Out by Thanking the Person for Making You the Job Offer.

If someone is not sure if they want to accept a co-op job, they often quickly state that they'll have to think about it or that they aren't sure. This is impolite, at best. You should be flattered to receive ANY job offer: whether or not you choose to accept it. You also may mention some aspect of the interview that you found enjoyable. Consider this example:

> "First, I'd like to thank you for offering me this position. I enjoyed getting the chance to hear what you had to say about working for [ORGANIZATION]."

AFTER thanking them, gracefully tell them what your situation is.

If you definitely know whether or not you want the job, AND you're clear about the position and pay, this will be easy. The hard part is knowing what to say when you're really not sure what to do or if the job is good but not necessarily your top choice. We suggest handling this situation carefully: You don't want to treat any employer like a second or third choice, but you also don't want to give someone the impression that you probably will take a job when you don't feel that way. Also, you have to be sensitive to the employer's needs. It's not fair to keep an offer dangling for weeks while you make your mind; if you ultimately say "no," then the employer will miss out on other good students. Many coordinators believe that you should make up your mind within THREE BUSINESS DAYS OF RECEIVING AN OFFER. In other words, if a company makes you an offer on Thursday, you will need to say yes or no by the following Tuesday.

Here is an example of the simplest way to keep an offer on hold without making a potential employer feel like you're shopping around for something better:

> "I promised my co-op coordinator that I would discuss things with her (or him) before making a final decision, but I definitely will get back to you in no more than three business days, and sooner than that if possible."

Here is another way to keep an offer on hold without alienating a potential employer:

> "Let me tell you what my situation is: I'm considering a few other employers right now, and I want to be fair to those other employers and give them a chance to make me an offer. But I WILL give you my decision within three business days, and sooner than that if possible. Is that okay?"

An employer has every right to ask you to make a decision faster if possible. However, you also have the right to talk to your coordinator before saying yes or no. If you feel that an employer is trying to corner you into making an on-the-spot answer, let your coordinator know. This generally does not happen and should not happen.

Be clear on what you are being offered.

If the employer has not told you what your hourly pay rate would be, NOW is the time to ask or to confirm what you believe the pay rate to be. Do so before you accept the job to avoid any misunderstandings. Likewise, you should be clear on what hours and days they expect you to work, your start date and end date, and what your responsibilities will be, so everyone is clear about this.

Be careful about pay rate issues.

In many cases, the pay rate will not be open to negotiation: You should know whether or not it is before you bring up the matter. And even if there is some room for negotiation, there are some good reasons to avoid doing so: Pushing for more pay can send the message that you care more about the money than about the learning experience.

When there is some room for negotiation, you probably should not take matters into your own hands. Talk to your coordinator to find out if there is any latitude regarding pay. In some rare cases, a coordinator may be able to negotiate a higher pay rate. This takes skill and experience, however, as handling this the wrong way can backfire quickly.

The same is true in cases when you are offered less than the job description indicated or less than your coordinator told you to expect. If this occurs, thank the employer for the offer, tell him or her that you need to talk to your coordinator before reaching a final decision, and contact your coordinator immediately about the situation. Perhaps the situation has changed, or the company simply has made a mistake. Either way, get your coordinator's advice before proceeding on your own.

If you're not sure what to do, contact your co-op or internship coordinator immediately.

It's hard to predict every dilemma that you may face when getting a job offer. But if in doubt about what to do, seek the advice of your coordinator. In some cases, a coordinator may be able to get a faster response from a second employer if you need to make a decision about an offer from a first employer. If it's a matter of being indecisive, your coordinator probably will not tell you what to do: Instead, she or he may try to help you walk through the different pros and cons of the offer or offers. In the end, though, it's your decision.

Follow up with ALL employers once you have made a decision.

After you have made a timely decision, make sure that you communicate that decision to EACH employer that is waiting to hear as well as to each co-op coordinator that you have worked with to obtain the job.

ALWAYS be polite when turning down a job offer.

Usually, people feel awkward when they have to turn down a job. This is understandable: Employers may be very disappointed to hear about your decision. But usually they are understanding if you are professional and gracious about it (see the sidebar box). Consider this example:

> "I just wanted to let you know that I decided to accept a job with another company. It was a tough decision: I just felt that this other job was a slightly better match for me in my current situation. But I do appreciate your offer, and I hope that you can find a good candidate for your position."

DECLINING A JOB OFFER – A CO-OP PROFESSIONAL'S PERSPECTIVE

by Rose Dimarco

A student who was in her third year interviewed for a job and she got it, but she felt she was more compatible with a very different experience, so she turned it down. But she sent a thank-you note—even though she rejected the offer. She praised that employer—she did not want to burn that bridge.

It turned out that she eventually interviewed again with that employer. It was the same interviewer, and she remembered—very positively—that rejection. So she ended up with a second chance at the job.

***Rose Dimarco** is a cooperative education faculty coordinator in Physical Therapy at Northeastern University*

Once you have accepted a job offer, you CANNOT go on other interviews or consider other job offers.

There are NO exceptions to this rule. Think of it this way: Accepting a job and continuing to interview is like getting engaged and continuing to go on dates. It doesn't make sense, and it's just plain wrong. Or, if you'd like to think of it another way, how about this: How would you feel if a company makes you an offer on November 1st, you accept the offer and stop pursuing other jobs; maybe you even turn down another good job or two. A week or two later, the company calls you up and tells you "Sorry, but somebody else came along who turned out to be a better candidate." Colleges would not work with an employer who behaved in this way, and, likewise, career professionals will not work with you if you treat an employer in a similar way.

That said, you absolutely SHOULD call back any employer who is interested in interviewing you, even after you have accepted a job. It's professional and courteous to follow up on any interview request, and it is not hard to get across the situation:

> "I wanted to thank you for your interest in interviewing me. However, I have accepted a position with another employer, so I am no longer available. But I do wish you luck in finding a good candidate, and I will keep you in mind for the future."

Once you have accepted the offer, make sure to see your co-op coordinator one last time.

Let your coordinator know as soon as you have a job lined up: That's why 24-hour voice mail and e-mail exists. Your coordinator generally will ask you to come in to complete an agreement form and to go over success factors for your position.

DRUG TESTING

It's important to know that some employers make offers that are contingent upon the candidate's ability to pass a drug test successfully. Though many employers do not require this, drug testing is on the rise. Many organizations, especially those in health care, manufacturing, and in local or federal government—require drug testing for all new hires. Eventually you're likely to encounter this issue.

Why do companies drug test? Generally, it's not a moral issue. People with substance abuse problems can be costly to organizations in terms of absenteeism, tardiness, and turnover. Companies don't want to invest time, money, and energy developing a co-op or new employee who may not prove to be a productive worker.

If you do use illegal drugs—or if you use any prescription drugs *without* having a prescription—you may have time to change your behaviors. Many companies now use hair tests to test for drug use—these tests are harder to fool than urine tests. These tests generally will reveal if you have regularly used drugs over the last three or four months. If you don't want to limit your opportunities, make changes in your behavior well in advance of the term you expect to do your co-op.

In some fields, drug testing is not just a part of the hiring process—it's an ongoing part of being a professional employee. Think about if you need to make a lifestyle choice—unless using drugs illegally is more important to you than being eligible for as many great opportunities as possible.

Scott had the unfortunate experience where one of his students was offered one of his very best positions—a job that would have provided an incredible learning experience as well as about $19/hour plus one week of paid vacation. The student failed the drug test because he had smoked marijuana within the last several months. He asked me if the company would let him retake the test in a few weeks—he really wanted the job. Of course, the drug test was a one-shot deal, and he missed out on the opportunity of a lifetime with that employer.

Most if not all co-op coordinators do not want to know if a student is using illegal drugs of any kind. Our role is to be advocates for students with employers, and it puts us in a very difficult situation if we know about illegal drug use. Tamara advises her students to avoid or decline even applying for a position if they don't think they will pass a required drug test. She suggests the best way to tell her that they decline to apply is to tell her that they are interested in the position but have chosen not to interview for personal reasons. Anything more is too much information!

FINAL THOUGHTS ON INTERVIEWING

Remember, you can't control many aspects of interviewing. You can worry all you want about the quality of the interviewer or the caliber of the candidates who are competing for the job, but that won't change anything. Your goal should be to walk out of the interview feeling good because you did terrific research, employed a smart and thought-out strategy, answered questions honestly and enthusiastically, and asked provocative questions to wrap up the interview.

It's a terrific feeling to come out of an interview knowing you gave it your all. If, after that, another candidate gets the job because of superior experience, you really can't have any regrets—especially because your effort will pay off for you down the road, probably sooner rather than later.

One great fact is that it's really amazing how little the average person knows about interviewing. Both Tamara and Scott have helped hire co-op faculty for their institutions and are often surprised at how poor some of the interviewees have been. They ask questions that make it obvious that they didn't do one iota of research, and they clearly haven't begun to think strategically about why they would be good for the job and how they would approach the position. And this is for a job in which you must be able to teach students how to interview! Tamara has been on hiring committees for Lane Community College's President, Vice

President, Chief Information Officer and several division managers, and she expected applicants at these levels to have developed strong interviewing skills but sadly, many, many have not. In any event, if you can really learn and apply the concepts in this chapter, you'll be way ahead of most interviewees—including many who may have considerably more professional experience than you.

Lastly, give some serious consideration to doing one or more practice interviews, especially with peers who are also learning the principles of good interviewing. At the very least, stop and think about what interview questions you hate answering, then see if you can practice them with your coordinator. Reviewing your strategy for a specific interview is something that most coordinators can do if a practice interview is not possible. The worst thing you can do is to assume that you have nothing left to learn about interviewing.

CHAPTER 3 REVIEW QUESTIONS

1. If you were researching in preparation for an interview, what are two ways in which you can go beyond the job description to learn more about the job and the organization?

2. Which statement most appropriately captures how to approach an interview?

   A. Be able to summarize your strengths as an individual.

   B. More than anything, be sure to tell the interviewer what he or she hopes to hear.

   C. Try to just relax and be yourself—don't get too worked up about it.

   D. Try to make connections between your background and the job description.

   E. Be sure to give the interviewer plenty of personal background about yourself.

3. Imagine you are interviewing for your first co-op job: For that job, how would you answer a question about your weaknesses?

4. What does the chapter describe as the most difficult type of interviewer for most interviewees?

   A. The Nonstop Talker

   B. The Silent But Deadly Interviewer

   C. The Olympic Judge

   D. The Big-Picture Person

   E. The Interrogator

5. Write a brief but effective thank-you note that would be appropriate to send to an interviewer as a follow-up step.

6. Write two great questions to ask at the end of any job interview. For each question explain why you choose to ask it. In other words, explain how the question will reflect positively on you or how the information you will gain from asking the question will help you decide if the job is right for you.

CHAPTER FOUR

Keys To On-The-Job Success

By the time you have prepared your resume, gone on numerous interviews, and finally accepted a job offer from an employer, you may feel like it's time to kick back and relax and let the money come in from your job. However, nothing could be further from the truth: Accepting a job offer doesn't mean you've reached the end of all your hard work. All it means is that you've reached the end of the beginning.

When you have accepted a job, you need to start thinking about living up to your interview... and then some. In other words, anyone can walk into an interview and state that they are punctual, conscientious, hard-working, willing to learn, and happy to help out with some of the less glamorous tasks associated with a job. But it's very different to actually go out and live up to these statements all day, every day, for three months, six months, or longer.

Our goal in this chapter is to point out why your job performance matters and to help you get the best possible evaluation from your co-op employer or internship supervisor. Some of the points we make here may seem like common sense, but we have learned that sense can be rather uncommon when it comes to some behaviors in the workplace. If you follow the guidelines in this chapter, you can prevent most co-op problems before they happen... which is infinitely easier than trying to fix something after it breaks.

WHY YOUR PERFORMANCE MATTERS

The best interns and co-op students realize that there is a great deal at stake when you're working in a job. An "outstanding" or "very good" evaluation from an employer means that:

- *You are a person of integrity who remembers your interview and delivers what you said you could deliver.* You come off as a hypocrite if you say that you are punctual, for example, and you start showing up late to work. Right away, the employer might start wondering what else might not be exactly true in what you said in your interview.
- *You are intelligent enough to realize that today's supervisor is tomorrow's reference.* Think about interviewing for a future job: It's nice to say "I'm an excellent worker with a great attitude," but it's highly effective and powerful to be able to say "I'm an excellent worker with a great attitude, and I would encourage you to contact my

previous employer if you'd like to confirm this." Some employers may even call your previous employer without telling you: You don't want bad performance to come back and haunt you when seeking future employment.

- *If you are asked about a previous job in an interview, you want to be able to say in all honesty that you did a great job.* Interviewers can often tell how successful you were in a previous job by how you describe it. A common interview question is "If I were to ask your previous supervisor about what kind of employee you were, what would he or she say?" You have to be honest in these situations, and you want to be able to mention many positives.
- *You can feel good about yourself.* It's much more fun to do things well than to do things poorly. If you can complete your job with a sense of pride and accomplishment, you will have more confidence and will be better prepared for challenging jobs in the future.
- *You'll learn more and get better work to do.* The harder you work—the more you go "above and beyond" the basic requirements of the job, the more likely you are to learn more and gain valuable exposure to more sophisticated aspects of your field. You'll also show your employer that you're capable of handling bigger and better challenges.

The last point merits some more consideration. Scott always tells his students that there is often a domino effect while on a co-op job or internship. When you first start work, you may be given low-level work to do. This is rarely because supervisors believe that you're an idiot until you prove otherwise, so don't look at it that way. Rather, employers know that it's difficult to be a new employee. They want to make sure that you feel comfortable at the beginning by giving you work that will be relatively easy while also watching your attitude and attendance.

What happens next? That depends! If you get those simple tasks done efficiently, effectively, and with a positive attitude, eventually this tends to get noticed... and your manager may start giving you better work to do, tasks that weren't even on your job description.

Of course, this domino effect works the other way occasionally. A few years ago, Scott visited two co-op students at work. When he met with them, they were irritated: "This is a terrible job," they said. "There's nothing to do; they just give us data entry work that anyone could do. This should not be a co-op job."

Scott was surprised. Many students had worked for this employer before, and the verdict had been that it was a good job. Yes, there was some downtime, but you were allowed to use that time to teach yourself computer skills using resources that the supervisor made available to you. Of course, some good jobs do turn bad, so Scott approached the supervisor with an open mind. "How's it going with the co-ops?" he asked. He looked at Scott and shook his head. "I wish we could get these two to do something!"

At first glance, this seemed as if it would be the easiest problem to solve in the history of cooperative education and internships! Here we had two bored co-ops with nothing to do and a manager who was itching to get them to work. Naturally, it wasn't that easy. It turned out that these two co-ops were insulted by the low-level tasks that they initially were given. How did they respond? They did the work slowly and poorly, so the manager assumed that they weren't able or willing to handle anything more challenging. He continued to give them grunt work, and their performance never improved.

LEARNING AT YOUR CO-OP SITE – A CO-OP PROFESSIONAL'S PERSPECTIVE

by Merrill Watrous

One of my students chose to do her co-op with a kindergarten teacher who was a new employer in our program. I knew nothing about her. After working in the classroom for several days, the student reflected on what she had learned in my education classes and realized that her mentor teacher was not very skilled.

The student and I discussed her situation. I wanted to move her to another classroom, but the student chose to stick it out. She was surprised to observe that all the children were happy and nobody fought during one part of the day; this happened when the teacher taught drawing. My student wanted to stay in this classroom to find out more about how this teacher taught drawing and to discover why her students enjoyed it so much. As a consequence, my student learned about a uniquely successful approach to teaching art she might never have experienced otherwise. I was impressed by the way my student found something positive to embrace in a challenging classroom that others might have abandoned earlier in the term. I share this experience with co-op students today to help them understand that learning can be found in unusual spots if you look for it and remain open to it.

Merrill Watrous *is a faculty Cooperative Education Coordinator in Education at Lane Community College*

Admittedly, maintaining a strong work ethic and an excellent attitude can be challenging in some work environments. You may be a student who is doing a co-op to test out a field as a possible career. As such, you may learn that you don't want to be a legal secretary or a computer programmer. That's fine, but bear in mind the following: A mediocre co-op can do a great job in a job that she or he loves, but a great co-op continues to do a great job *even after realizing that he or she is working in the wrong field.*

Sometimes you probably will be asked to do work that is less fun, less interesting, and less educational than you had hoped. In fact, one unpleasant fact you have to accept is that almost any job you will ever have may require you to do some things that you don't enjoy. But if you can take on all work assignments with a pleasant and cooperative attitude, your employer will remember this and often will reward you with better assignments as well as an excellent evaluation.

Tamara regularly has first-term students who are hired for an entry-level drafting job and who end up making mechanical design recommendations to the engineers by the end of the term! You never know what doors might open to you if you do a terrific job on whatever you're asked to do.

Occasionally a co-op student will find himself or herself in a co-op where, overall, the learning environment does not offer as much learning as either the student or co-op coordinator initially expected. If you find yourself in a situation like this, remember there is always something that can be learned. Look for the learning opportunities and capitalize on them; don't expect learning opportunities to always be immediately evident.

MAKING THE TRANSITION FROM STUDENT TO WORKER

Don't underestimate the fact that you're undergoing a significant transition when you go from being a full-time student to working and being a student simultaneously. In that situation, you will be continually making the transition from your role as student to your role as a worker and it's useful to give some thought to these role changes.

As a student you may believe that you have every right to skip class: After all, your grade may be the only thing that suffers. Likewise, the student lifestyle can be quite different for some individuals. We're sure that some of our students stay up till 2 or 3 a.m. more often than not, waking up at the last minute to make a mad dash to their 8 a.m. class or maybe sleeping through it.

Your role becomes more complicated when you're a co-op. Yes, you're still a student, but that role is trumped by your most important role: You are viewed as an employee and a service provider to your employer. This should be obvious when you're drawing a paycheck, but it's also the attitude that you need to take into an unpaid internship or co-op.

A good way to think of the transition is an analogy to running: The classroom is more of a sprint, while a co-op job is more of a marathon. In the classroom, you may be able to be very successful with periodic bursts of effort at the right time. On co-op, the individuals who do best are those who are able to sustain a consistent effort for several hours, weeks, and months. It means that you need to figure out what you must do to be sure that you're not only showing up but that you're arriving rested, alert, and ready to put in a full day's work of good quality.

A few years ago, Scott had a student with a 4.0 GPA who was fired from her job, and he has seen many other top academic performers fail. Likewise, we have had many co-op superstars whose GPAs were in the 2.0 to 2.4 range. Once you get your co-op job or internship, grades no longer matter; you have a clean slate… but you also will have to prove yourself day in and day out. Remembering that the employer is your customer and acting accordingly should help you make this transition effectively.

THE FIRST DAY OF WORK

On your first day of work, you'll probably be excited, nervous, and eager to show that you can be a productive employee right from the start. This is perfectly normal. However, bear in mind that few workers—whether co-op or otherwise—can be immediate heroes. Be patient. If you're introduced to people, do your best to come across as positive and agreeable. You're going to want to have good relationships with many people besides your supervisor, and you can cultivate those relationships by making an effort to be friendly and learning their names. This may include going out to lunch with people even if you'd rather be working, and it definitely includes saying "Good Morning" and "Good Night" at the start and end of the day.

You also may have an orientation or training session to attend. Even though you might be dying to dive into the job itself, take advantage of these sessions. They can help you get acclimated and learn what it may take to be successful in that environment. In addition, you may learn important safety protocols that are vital to your well-being. You'll have plenty of opportunity to work before you know it.

CO-OP JOB SUCCESS – A STUDENT'S PERSPECTIVE

by Ted Schneider

- Meet as many people in your workplace as you can. And I do not mean this in only the superficial, "networking" type of way. If your co-workers are willing, do social things with them outside of work. I found that working closely with good friends on co-op was not at all distracting. I actually think that I performed much better when I worked for people who I liked and respected.

- An old one but still so true: Do not ever go to work late if you can help it. I knew people on co-op who were very good at what they did, but would fail to be promoted due to their tardiness. I also find that managers are much more flexible about giving time off if you are on time.

- Wear the right clothes. Wearing questionable or even semi-questionable attire makes you look like a fool. Enough said.

- Make sure to find a balance between asking for too much help and asking for too little. It's a difficult skill to master – I certainly haven't yet.

Ted Schneider *was an Accounting/MIS student at Northeastern University, Class of 2002*

UNCOMMON SENSE: WHAT IS AND ISN'T ACCEPTABLE IN THE WORKPLACE

As stated earlier, there are many aspects of work life that internship and co-op coordinators would like to believe are common sense: Things that everyone should know without being told. However, we have found that this is not always the case. As a result, here are some critical recommendations regarding how to avoid problems in the workplace. Some may appear obvious; others are less so. HOWEVER, no one should have to tell you these things once you have started your job. It is your responsibility to know these things ahead of time!

1. You must be on time to work.

After you have accepted your offer, be very clear about what time you are expected at work. Then make sure you are *always* there at least 15 minutes before that time.

When you become a co-op, intern, or full-time employee, you undergo a tremendous role reversal. Some students may be used to showing up late to classes. This is a bad habit, but you could argue that it is your choice: You have the right to not show up on time for classes. However, when an employer is paying *you* to arrive at a specific time and to work a specific number of hours, you do ***not*** have that right. Unless an employer specifically tells you that you can come in when you want to, you have to live by that employer's rules. For example, you can't just decide that you'll come in 30 minutes late and then eat your lunch at your desk instead of taking a 30-minute break at noontime. Most non-paid co-ops and internships are set up with the same expectations that students will work a set schedule. Being non-paid is no excuse for tardiness nor is it permission to leave early!

Another point to remember is that too many interns and co-op students fail to leave any extra time in the morning to allow for possible traffic, parking problems, car trouble, or whatever. If it takes you 25 minutes to get to work, assuming that you catch every train or traffic light just right, then you probably should allow for at least 45 minutes to get to work. If you have to use this kind of excuse more than once over a three to six-month job, you need to change your habits: These excuses get old very quickly.

Lastly, remember one critical point: *Just because your co-workers arrive late, don't automatically assume that it's okay for you to do the same.* Scott recalls one memorable student who had been given a warning by his employer because of repeated tardiness. The boss told Scott that the student sometimes came in by 9 but other times it was more like 10. When Scott talked to the co-op student about it, he thought that he was being unfairly singled out: "I see quite a few full-time people coming in at 10 or 10:30 every day!"

When Scott looked into this, it turned out that the student was missing a few key facts: For one, he didn't take into account that those individuals reported to a different manager, and he didn't know that these people were software developers. They had an understanding with management that they could come in late because they often stayed until 8:00 or 9:00 p.m. at night, well after Scott's student left by 5:30! For another thing, the student had misinterpreted something his manager had told him when he was hired. When she said that it was possible to have a "flexible schedule," she meant that you could work from 7:30 to 4:30 with an hour for lunch, from 9 to 6 with an hour for lunch, etc. She did NOT mean that you could change your schedule every day, or that you could start your day later than 9:30. Ultimately, Scott had to tell the student that sometimes policies are not always fair. Sure, the manager could have done a better job upfront about communicating the "unwritten rules" of that workplace, but she didn't. That simply means that the student needed to step up and be sure that his assumptions were correct.

2. If being late or absent is absolutely unavoidable, give your employer as much advance notice as possible.

There may be rare situations in which being late or absent is absolutely unavoidable. These primarily include car accidents, serious illnesses, or deaths in your family. These things can't be avoided at times. However, you need to call your employer before the official workday begins. That may mean leaving a voice mail or answering machine message early in the morning before you show up: not after your shift has begun, when everyone has already been wondering where you are for several hours. If you have a flat tire on the way to work, for example, use your cellphone or find the nearest possible phone so you can call in and give your estimated time of arrival. Always carry the phone numbers of your supervisor and the front desk just in case something like this happens.

Unless you are completely incapacitated through illness or injury, YOU should be the one to call in: not your roommate, your mother, your roommate's boyfriend's sister's cousin or anyone else. And if you don't say how long you will need to be out, and you remain sick or otherwise unavailable the next day, you need to call your supervisor again each day until you return.

3. Keep personal phone calls to an absolute minimum.

Working in an office with your own phone and phone number does not give you the right to have extended conversations with friends, family, and significant others throughout the workday. Beyond using your phone for business, you should generally use your phone only if you need to contact your co-op/internship coordinator, your physician, or to contact a family member in the event of an emergency.

One good way to avoid temptation is to not give your work number out to anyone besides your parents, your spouse or partner (if applicable), and your co-op or internship coordinator. If you do need to make a five-minute phone call once or twice a week to arrange for plans after work, that probably would be acceptable in most workplaces. But otherwise you should avoid it whenever possible.

Over the last several years, cellphones have become incredibly common. They also have become increasingly entertaining, as many professionals now own BlackBerrys, Droids, or iPhones that offer the constant temptation of text messaging and Internet access. As you have undoubtedly noticed, many people don't hesitate to use their cellphones in inappropriate places, including classrooms and—most incredibly in my opinion—restrooms. When you are working in a co-op job, your friends and family obviously will already know your cellphone number, and some people probably won't hesitate to call you during the workday. It's important to remember that making personal phone calls on your cellphone is really just as bad as making such calls through your company line. So unless you specifically need to use your cellphone for job-related purposes—which is not uncommon with PC support jobs, for example—you generally should turn off your cellphone before you walk in the door at work and keep it off until the end of the day. At most, you might check your messages during your lunch break.

Also, watch what you say over any type of phone while at work—even during your lunch break. Employers have accidentally overheard co-op students say the darndest things (e.g., "personal" comments from boyfriend to girlfriend or vice-versa) when the student/caller thinks no one is listening.

4. Use your computer for work-related activities only.

Like a modern-day telephone, a computer on your desk can be highly tempting to some interns, co-ops, and full-time employees. Most computers have at least some games (such as Minesweeper and Solitaire) on Windows, and more and more computers have Internet access, which can be an irresistible on-line temptation to some—especially those with e-mail accounts through gmail, Yahoo or Hotmail. More recently, Facebook has become increasingly popular, and its chat option has been known to lure many employees away from their tasks. In general, many professionals—especially younger employees who have grown up with high levels of computer usage daily—find it difficult to break the technology habit at work. However, it's very important to do so—if you want to juggle your homework with e-mail and instant messaging for hours on end, that's up to you. But when your role has changed from student to employee, you're generally being paid to be at work, you shouldn't be using personal e-mail or instant message on company time. You aren't being paid to chat with friends, after all. Even in an unpaid internship, this sends the wrong message to your co-workers and supervisor.

Unless your supervisor tells you that it's okay for you to use the Internet or World Wide Web as part of your job, you should avoid going online. If you don't have Internet access at home, most colleges have computer labs for student use where you can do e-mail and surf the web, or you can go to the public library. As a last resort you could ask your supervisor if it would be okay to come in early or stay late in order to navigate the Internet or send e-mails with a clear conscience.

Tamara and Scott have both had several students fired from co-op jobs primarily because they were frequently on the Internet and spent a great deal of time writing e-mail or instant messages to friends during the work day. In late 2006, Scott heard about the first—but probably not last—students fired for managing their fantasy football teams on their work computers. Bear in mind that it's relatively easy for a computer network administrator to be able to see what applications anyone on the system has open, and it is completely legal and easy for organizations to monitor the e-mails that their employers send and receive to determine whether they are appropriate. Entertaining yourself on the computer during work hours certainly doesn't say very much about your initiative, drive, and judgment. Don't take chances—surf the 'net and do your text messaging at home or on campus!

Even if you have a BlackBerry or some other Personal Digital Assistant (PDA), don't think of that as a way to "get around" the advisories above. Refrain from using any technological activity that is not work related. Even if no one sees you doing it, I guarantee that your decreased level of productivity will be noticed eventually if you're unable to curb your technology addiction at work.

We will discuss the specifics of professional e-mail and IM etiquette later in this chapter.

Although this behavior is not excusable, these problems are most likely to arise when there is not enough work to do in a given job. Therefore, we will address that next.

5. If you don't have enough work to keep you busy, talk to your supervisor as soon as possible.

If your supervisor needs to come around and see you playing a game, staring at the ceiling, or talking on the phone in order to find out that you don't have enough work, you already have made a significant mistake. If you anticipate running out of work, try to give your supervisor as much notice as possible. It's perfectly fine to ask your supervisor what you should do if you run out of work: especially if your supervisor isn't always readily available. Asking for more work when necessary shows that you are mature, that you take initiative, and that you have a good work ethic. All of these things reflect positively on you as an employee. Basically, *learn* from your work environment. Something ALWAYS needs to be done. Be proactive. Say something like, "I've finished 'X'; should I move onto 'Y'?" Your supervisor may be too busy to find a project for you and may be appreciative if you offer suggestions.

One challenge with such a conversation is to make sure that you don't come across as a whiner. Even if you're bored because of a lack of work, it probably won't be productive to go in to your supervisor and say, "I'm bored; I have nothing to do." Try to frame it positively by emphasizing your ability and willingness to take on more challenges on top of your current responsibilities.

It is always best to find out in advance who your supervisor would like you to go to for assignments in their absence. If you aren't sure and if your supervisor isn't available, ask co-workers if there are ways you can assist them rather than just sitting around. When you do so, you'll be seen by your co-workers as a collaborative individual who understands teamwork. You'd be surprised how often supervisors consult co-workers when it comes time to fill out your end-of-term evaluation!

As noted earlier, many entry-level professionals have begun a job with relatively low-level responsibilities but managed to end up with much more demanding jobs—simply by getting the easy stuff done quickly and correctly and then enthusiastically requesting more work to do. Show that you're hungry for a challenge.

6. If you consistently have MORE work than you can do and do well, you should discuss this with your supervisor.

Most good jobs will keep you very busy. But if you find that you are working so hard that it is affecting the quality of your work, your health, and your enthusiasm for the job, you need to discuss this with your supervisor before it becomes a major problem.

Obviously, the best way to deal with this problem is to avoid these situations in the first place by using your interview to ask the appropriate questions about workload and expectations. But you can't always anticipate this problem. Some employers hire a part-time person thinking that the work can be done in just 10-20 hours a week, only to find that this is unrealistic. In other situations, a manager

CO-OP JOB SUCCESS – A STUDENT'S PERSPECTIVE

by Mark Moccia

In order to get the most out of your job, you must bring a strong work ethic to the table. Once your employer sees you are willing to work hard, they will be impressed. Then, after you have shown the ability to work hard, you can polish your "working smart" skills: By this I mean getting things done quickly AND more efficiently for the company/department.

It is also important to learn the preferences/personality of your boss immediately. It is important to know whether your boss is the type that wants assignments done in five minutes or 30 minutes. A question I still ask to this day is, "When do you want this done by?" This avoids any confusion as to when you are supposed to finish an assignment and also avoids potential conflicts.

Speaking of conflicts, if you encounter one at work then it is important to alert your immediate supervisor. While fellow co-op students might lend an ear to your problems, they might not always have the best solution because they are just as inexperienced as you. If the conflict is with your supervisor, bring it to the attention of your co-op advisor quickly. I have heard stories of co-op students who feel invincible because they are only on assignment for three or six months and imagine that the company cannot fire them because it would look bad for the company. This could not be further from the truth; if you have direct conflicts with your supervisor or are not performing to your potential, you can be fired just as easily as a full-time employee. I encourage co-op students to use their best judgment in these situations and avoid "blow-ups" at all costs. If you can do this, work hard, and bring a positive contribution to your time on the job, a good reference and evaluation will follow.

***Mark Moccia** was an Accounting/MIS student at Northeastern University, Class of 2002.*

may give an intern a full workload on limited hours in an attempt to simply save money. If talking to your supervisor doesn't improve the situation—or if you're unsure about whether you really are being asked to do more than what could be considered reasonable, call your co-op coordinator and get his or her input. Together, you can determine the best course of action.

7. If you're confused or unsure about how to do one of your assigned tasks, say so. When you are assigned a task or given specific instructions, take careful notes so you won't have to request the same information again.

The worst thing you can do if you're unsure about how to do a task is to just forge ahead and hope for the best. Usually, people are reluctant to ask questions because they are afraid of appearing stupid or ignorant. But remember: appearing ignorant is MUCH better than demonstrating your ignorance by doing your job poorly. Making mistakes on the job can be very costly to a company. Good employers expect you to ask for help when you need it to avoid these costly mistakes. Don't be afraid to ask a supervisor or co-worker to repeat or clarify instructions if you didn't understand the first time. On the other hand, don't go running to your supervisor or co-worker with a question every ten minutes. Over the course of an hour or two, jot down your questions and then go to your supervisor with several questions at once. This is more efficient for both of you, and it will help you to be viewed as a person who understands that your supervisor's time is valuable.

A corresponding point relates to what you do with information or instructions when given to you. A smart intern shows up on the first day of work with a calendar for marking down due dates, deadlines, and meetings. A smart co-op student also brings a notebook and some writing materials so he or she can jot down specific instructions, guidelines, job requirements, computer procedures, and anything else you need to know. Nothing frustrates an employer more than a student who claims that he or she doesn't need to write things down, and then winds up making mistakes or sheepishly asking for the same information some time in the future.

8. Always keep your desk and/or work area reasonably neat and well organized.

This means keeping food and drink to a minimum in your work area. Keeping some mints or granola bars in your desk and a coffee cup on your desk is okay, but leaving food wrappers or food in plain sight at any time other than lunch is something to avoid.

Also try to keep items on your desk well organized. If asked to produce some paperwork, you shouldn't have to do a scavenger hunt in your desk or office to find it. If you're unsure about ways to organize your work materials efficiently, ask your co-workers for advice.

9. Always use good judgment regarding attire and hygiene in the workplace.

You need to convey a professional image every single day that you are on your

FROM STUDENT TO EMPLOYEE – A CO-OP PROFESSIONAL'S PERSPECTIVE

by Bob Tillman

I tell students that if you only learn two things when you go out on your first co-op, it's going to be a huge success: If you learn when to ask a question when you should, and when to keep your mouth shut when you should, you're really light years ahead. When you figure out, "This is a problem that I ought to be able to solve on my own" and know "What are the resources that are going to help me do it?" you're way ahead.

Another thing you learn out there is that there's a whole language out there that you haven't been exposed to, and you have to learn it. And the last thing is, "What are the other learning opportunities that are going on around you that aren't directly sitting on your desk?"

In engineering, if you can't do the routine work—checking calculations, adding numbers, checking drawings—you're never going to get more advanced work.

***Bob Tillman** is a cooperative education faculty coordinator in Civil Engineering at Northeastern University*

CO-OP JOB SUCCESS – AN EMPLOYER'S PERSPECTIVE

by Steve Sim

There are two things to keep in mind when coming for an internship/co-op at Microsoft:

1. *Know your limitations.* This is a fact at MS. There will always be someone who knows more about business, technology, marketing; etc. than you here (especially technology). Knowing your limitations also makes you aware of how these people can help in your development.

2. *Don't be afraid to fail.* You're here to learn about how we do things. MS is a place where we do things, if anything, for the right to learn how to do that thing better. You'll always be challenged to do something right the first time, and possibly, you do it right the first time. Or did you? Have you tried everything possible? Who's to know that better than you?

***Steve Sim** was a Technical Recruiter at the Microsoft Corporation*

co-op. The standards may differ from one workplace to another. Some places allow "business casual" attire, for example. But be careful in how you interpret dress codes. Casual attire generally still means that you should wear a collared shirt and nice pants, not blue jeans or shorts. Sometimes you can get away with dressy black sneakers, but not always white sneakers. Women should always avoid low-cut blouses, halter tops and tank tops. Open-toed shoes or sandals are a bad idea for men and may or may not be okay for women, depending on the particular work environment. For office environments you should always wear clothing that is clean, wrinkle-free, and without any holes in it and that fits you well–nothing too tight or too baggy. Work environments such as machine shops and construction sites have specific dress requirements, especially for safety reasons, which may include wearing coveralls, keeping hair pulled back, and limiting jewelry—heed them! For men in casual environments, you should still shave each day. Keep in mind, you want to both fit in at the work place while also presenting your best self; a job offer at the end of your co-op may depend upon it. It's not a bad idea to look at how your co-workers dress, but you want to err on the conservative side—don't assume it's okay to dress a certain way just because one or two co-workers choose to wear extremely informal attire at work!

Another point here: You may think nothing of wearing an eyebrow ring or a nose ring or a tongue stud, but an employer may find these items to be unprofessional. Save your unusual jewelry for after-hours and weekends.

10. Don't misunderstand the meaning of the words "casual work environment."

As stated above, you may be able to wear more comfortable and informal clothing in some work settings. But don't think that "a casual work environment" means that *everything* is casual. Just because the company president wears jeans and jokes around with you when he or she visits your desk or cubicle, it doesn't mean that it's okay for you to pop into his office and joke around with him or her. Likewise, a casual work setting is not a place where work is done in a casual, laid-back manner. In fact, there are many very intense organizations that allow casual attire. Remember, casual work environments are just like all other jobs in one important way: You still can get a poor evaluation or get fired by not living up to your interview and by not living up to the company's expectations and standards.

Another point about casual environments: It is *never* acceptable to wear headphones in any workplace unless your boss specifically *suggests* it. This is true regardless even if you are working on your own, doing boring, monotonous work. Wearing headphones on a job sends a clear message that you're not really paying attention to what you're doing and that you don't care if you look unprofessional. Even if co-workers wear headphones, don't make the same mistake.

11. When asked to do something that you don't enjoy, do so without complaining or sulking.

Scott visited one employer who was Director of MIS for a prestigious organization. He mentioned that a co-op student from another university (not Northeastern, thankfully) complained when he was told to do a fairly monotonous and time-consuming task with the computer system. The employer told Scott, "The thing that I asked him to do is something that I have to do pretty often, and I'm the Director of the whole department! And he tells me that *he* shouldn't have to do it?"

There's a valuable lesson here: Sometimes students are quick to assume that they are given boring tasks to do because they are "only students." This can be an erroneous assumption at times. Sometimes, you may be asked to do something simply because it has to get done, and it doesn't matter who does it. Employers appreciate any employee who does routine, unglamorous, necessary tasks without complaining, whining, or sulking.

If an employer asks you if you enjoy doing a certain task, be honest but be pleasant about it. If you don't like doing a given task, you might say, "Well I don't mind doing it, but it's not my favorite part of the job..." Be ready to point out some other tasks that you would be excited about doing.

12. Go above and beyond your basic duties.

One reason some students fail to get great job evaluations is because they basically show up on time, do their job in a competent, acceptable way, and go home when their required hours are over. If you want to get a very good evaluation, you

A TALE OF TWO INTERNS

By Dr. Sarah David

Taking the extra step to go above and beyond the call of duty can really pay off. We host a number of interns and part-time employees in our office. This particular semester, we had the opportunity to host two interns. They were both very bright and eager to learn. Intern #1 always took the initiative to identify what needed to be done in the office, always willing to volunteer and take on extra tasks and made an extra effort to get to know employees who worked in the office.

On the other hand, Intern #2 also did a good job, did what was asked but did not take the extra initiative to do any extra tasks. The work Intern #2 completed was continuously being questioned and this individual had to be corrected on numerous occasions regarding the same tasks. When we had a full-time opportunity open up guess who immediately was thought of to fill the position? You guessed it... Intern #1! In all situations you have a chance to demonstrate your personal brand and what you want to be known for in your profession and your work. Intern #1 exuded a brand of reliability, hard work and working well with a team. This is a tale to remind you to always do all things with excellence and to the best of your ability even if it is only for a short while. You never know when you might be offered a full-time opportunity due to your efforts."

Dr. Sarah David *is a Certified Personal Branding Strategist, National Certified Counselor and Certified Career Management Coach. She teaches a Career Exploration class in Human Development where she serves as a Counselor and Professor at Lone Star College – Tomball*

ABOVE AND BEYOND – A CO-OP STUDENT'S PERSPECTIVE

by Katie Van Meter

Be passionate! Enthusiasm really shows in your work, in addition to making things more fun for you and your co-workers. If you don't have enough to do, then ask for more tasks. If you don't get any suggestions, then think outside the box! If you figure out an area of the company that isn't getting filled, and then manage to fill it, you're on your way to becoming an invaluable employee. I did this at my co-op by getting my company, with permission of course, into the social media stream. I began with a Facebook page. When I got positive feedback from my supervisor and the fans of the games my company was creating and selling, I broadened out in to Twitter, Vimeo, and YouTube. It was nice to be given the freedom to try something new and rewarding to communicate with people who love our games.

***Katie Van Meter** was a Simulation and Game Development student at Lane Community College, class of 2009*

need to go beyond this. You need to be willing to put in extra hours if necessary. You need to show some pride and excitement in what you do: If you're asked to do something, give them even more than they expect in terms of effort, ideas, and attitude. Always think about ways in which you could do your job more efficiently, whether it involves helping your supervisor, your co-workers, or just the tasks you do on your own. This sidebar box is a great example of this phenomenon.

13. Understand what an employer's expectations are regarding time off from work.

Before you begin any job, you should make sure you have total clarity regarding your start date and end date as well as time off from work. In many cases, co-ops and interns—or full-time hires for their first six months on the job—have NO vacation time coming to them! So don't assume that it's going to be fine to take a Spring Break if it falls in the middle of your work term; don't imagine that there will be no problem if you want to take a week off in the middle of the summer.

What days do you get to take off? Any days that are official holidays for your employer (e.g., Memorial Day, Labor Day). Technically, that's all that an employer is required to allow you to take. But can there be exceptions to this? Sometimes, yes, but you shouldn't count on it. For example, a student who works in a position that is far away from his or her home may ask his or her employer if it would be okay to conclude a work assignment prior to Christmas rather than going home and coming back for three or four days before the assignment technically ends. The employer may or may not grant this request.

What can you do to improve your chances of having a request for unpaid time off granted? Do the following:

- *Keep such requests to an absolute minimum.* If you know you're going to ask for time off after Christmas, for example, don't press your luck by looking for additional time off earlier in the work period.
- *Only ask if you have an excellent reason for requesting time off.* Besides religious holidays, it may be reasonable to ask for a day off to attend an out-of-state wedding, for example. Or if you've been working many extra hours during tax season in an accounting job, it may be reasonable to ask for a day off when things slow down once again. Generally, though, you don't want to ask unless it's an absolute necessity. You never know when you might really need the time off.
- *Do such an outstanding job during the work period that your employer will be willing to give you time off.* An outstanding worker definitely has a much better chance of having requests for time off granted when necessary. In some cases, an employer even raises the subject to offer a reward to an extremely productive worker.

Look at it this way: If a worker has a bad attitude, is late or absent frequently, does mediocre work, and constantly needs to be supervised, an employer is bound to look at a request for time off as the final insult.

14. Keep your internship or co-op coordinator informed about any major problems, dilemmas, or unpleasant situations that arise.

The majority of students will not have any major problems arise during their work experiences. However, there is always the possibility that you might face problems that are beyond what we expect you to handle without our help. Please call your coordinator as soon as possible if you are:

- *the victim of sexual harassment or other abusive behavior from your co-workers, or supervisor, or company clients*
- *laid off from your job, regardless of the cause (i.e., budget cuts, buyouts)*
- *given a warning about being fired*
- *fired*
- *being paid less than promised*
- *having problems with your supervisor or co-workers that are difficult to discuss*

Additionally, call your coordinator if you have brought up any of the following problems with your supervisor, and the conversation has not produced a change:

- *you are given far too much or too little work to do on a regular basis*
- *your job is not what you were led to believe it would be, and you are not having a good learning experience*
- *you are stressed out due to the work, your co-workers, or your customers*

Sometimes a problem can be easily fixed if addressed quickly, while it can become a huge issue if ignored. When in doubt about the seriousness of a problem, contact your coordinator.

15. When faced with ethical dilemmas, make sure that you always act in a way that allows you to maintain your self-respect, integrity, and clean record.

We hope that you won't face too many ethical dilemmas during your practice-oriented work experience. However, any job can potentially present you with tough situations. For example, would you cheat on your timesheet: even if you were sure you could get away with it? Sadly, Scott has had students caught for falsifying their hours, and they were terminated immediately—all those potential references and resume-building experiences permanently ruined or severely damaged, just for the possibility of a little extra money. This kind of offense also may lead to suspension or expulsion from your college.

What would you do if you became aware that another employee was stealing money, supplies, or equipment from the organization? If you make a potentially

CO-OP JOB SUCCESS – A STUDENT'S PERSPECTIVE

by Gabriel Glasscock

Don't sit back and say to yourself "I'm just an intern." This is your job, and you have the ability to make the most of it. Some jobs will have downtime; it's just a fact. You can spend that time surfing espn.com, and boston.com, or you can go to your boss and say "Hey, I have some downtime, is there anything I can do?" In one such situation, I went to my boss, and she ended up shipping me off to a very expensive class on Web development in which I learned an immense amount, and thus had more responsibility at work.

If there is a problem at the job, don't be afraid to talk to your manager. If you're not doing anything stated on your job description, don't go silently. Remember: it's up to you to take charge. Your advisor or boss can't do anything unless they know about it.

***Gabriel Glasscock** was an MIS student at Northeastern University, Class of 2002* critical mistake and become aware of it later, should you tell your supervisor or simply hope that no one notices your error?

A few years ago, a student of Scott's faced a major dilemma. He had been asked to do the back-end work involving in getting antivirus software ready to go on the desktops of a big department. A full-time worker was supposed to take the final steps to get the software operational. When the student followed up with him to see if it was completed, his co-worker said to him, "I had trouble getting it to work, so I basically just decided to forget about it."

The student agonized about whether or not he should go to their mutual boss to report this. If he spoke up, he knew he would feel that he had "squealed" on a co-worker. But if he kept his mouth shut, and a new virus ended up causing significant problems, then he could be getting himself and others in trouble as well. What would you do?

The student ended up handling it very well. He went to his supervisor and told him about it, but he did so in a way that *assumed the best* of his co-worker. He told his boss that his co-worker had not completed the task, but he also said, "He might have been intending to get back to finishing up once he solved the problem." His boss was grateful, pointing out that the people in that group downloaded things all the time, and a major virus and worm problem would have reflected badly on the whole group.

Ultimately, every individual has to decide for himself or herself how to act in situations when no one—not your coordinator, your supervisor, or your parents—is looking over your shoulder. Basically, it's simple: Do the right thing, and you will save yourself a lot of guilt, fear, and worry about the consequences. If you're not sure about what the right thing is in a given situation, contact your coordinator.

16. Sit down with your manager during the first week of your job to set goals for your co-op work period.

If your program uses a standard work evaluation, you and your manager should review the entire evaluation upfront to know how you will be judged at the end of the work period. Additionally, though—whether or not your program requires it—you should write at least three goals for your work assignment, and you should do this in the first few weeks of your work experience.

What might your goals be for a given work assignment? They could vary dramatically depending on your major, the job, and your level of previous experience. For some first-time student employees, one goal may simply be to learn how a corporation works and how to perform effectively day-in, day-out in a professional environment. Some goals may relate to refining soft skills, such as improving presentation skills, proving to be a dependable employee by arriving at work early every day, or perhaps learning how to multitask or to prioritize in the face of deadlines or multiple responsibilities. Other goals may be more advanced and/or more geared to specific job skills: "I hope to find out if I'm comfortable working hands-on with patients of all backgrounds as an aspiring physical therapy assistant;" "I intend to learn how to use ASP to make database-linked dynamic websites," or "I want to be immersed in the activities of this cat hospital so I can learn if this veterinary environment is right for me."

Sharing your goals with your supervisor early in your internship may pay off in unexpected ways. One of Tamara's drafting students shared with her supervisor that she hoped to learn as much as she could about structures built with precast concrete, the product manufactured by her employer. After she had been on the job for several weeks, the supervisor made special arrangements for her to go with the field technicians on several occasions to watch the installation of their products, something never offered to prior students. By letting your supervisor know what you'd like to learn, you give him or her the opportunity to support your learning.

With goals in place, you and your manager will have a better mutual understanding of what you are supposed to be accomplishing in your role, and you can both do a better job of tracking your progress toward these objectives as the work period progresses.

SETTING GOALS – A CO-OP PROFESSIONAL'S PERSPECTIVE

by Jamie Kelsch

Creating written goals is important because it will help you determine what you will be learning while providing you with a way to gain your supervisors support toward reaching those goals. I recommend that you make an appointment with your supervisor early in your co-op to go over them. I also encourage you to work collaboratively with your supervisor on your goals because he or she may have ideas and offer opportunities for learning that you haven't considered.

There are two common mistakes students make when creating their goals. One mistake is making them too general. For example, "learning more about what it takes to be a professional" is quite vague. Consequently, students struggle to figure out if they have met that goal or not. Be as specific as you can about what you want to learn and how you hope to learn it.

The second most common mistake is setting goals that are not attainable within the term. While it's okay to have a "reach goal" that you may or may not attain, it's important to have several goals that are realistic with an honest effort. When students set goals that are way too ambitious, they generally can't meet their goals and end up feeling frustrated that they didn't accomplish enough. Yes, goals should be challenging but not so big that they can't be done.

I find that a best practice is for students to keep notes or a journal about their learning related to their goals all through the term. This simple process makes it easy for students to look back and then document their learning for midterm reports and end-of-term learning reflection assignments.

***Jamie Kelsch** is a faculty Cooperative Education Coordinator in Business at Lane Community College*

17. Do everything you can to become part of the work team and not "just a student."

To make the most of your job experience, make an effort to integrate yourself as fully as possible in the workplace. This is especially important if you work at a company that employs more than one student. Some students have the tendency to go to lunch with their fellow students, socialize outside of work only with fellow students, and generally avoid significant contact with full-time employees. This is understandable—in a new and strange situation, a person may be tempted to cling to something or someone who is familiar or similar. However, if you fail to make some connections with full-time employees, you're missing out on one of the great things that co-ops, internships, and other practice-oriented roles have to offer.

Initially, talking to full-time people at work will help you learn the "unwritten rules" of that particular workplace regarding what is and is not acceptable and appropriate. Ultimately, your experience can become a chance to rub elbows with people who work professionally in your field as well as other areas of possible future professional interest. As tempting as it may be, eating lunch at your desk while you work may not be the best way to be seen as a member of the team. You will need to go out of your way to connect with them. Simply joining these people in the lunch room or going out to lunch or for a bite to eat after work may be a good way to pick up invaluable information about:

BECOMING PART OF THE WORK TEAM

by Marie Sacino

Our computer information systems interns at the Queens Public Library work on the client side, providing 24/7 functionality, troubleshooting, changing hard drives, and ghosting as ongoing support tasks. Interns also work in the field on new PC rollout projects—2,000 new PC installations at branches throughout Queens this past summer.

What does it take to be a successful IT intern? Philip Darsan, Director of Information Technology at Queens Public Library, has some good thoughts. "An intern needs to begin to understand their working environment, to ask more questions, to utilize the department's organizational chart, to be cognizant of naming conventions—firewalls, deployment, DNS, IP," Darsan says. "We need serious students who really want to learn and don't watch the clock. Most IT personnel work 50 to 60 hours a week.

"I try to give the students an opportunity to open their eyes to the technology," adds Darsan. "Just how wide they choose to open them is up to the student. I'm interested in students who have a technician's perspective and who are customer-service oriented. I'll ask a student, 'How well do you communicate?' Without solid communication skills—interpersonal, reading, writing, speaking—there will be little growth for a technical support person."

***Marie Sacino** is an Associate Professor of Cooperative Education at LaGuardia Community College*

- how to succeed in your job
- whether or not you have much in common with people who work professionally in the career that interests you
- what kinds of coursework, job experiences, or self-study projects will help prepare you for a great career after graduation
- how people perceive the pros and cons of their own career choices

Another benefit of getting to know full-time employees is that once they begin to think of you as part of their group or team, the more likely they are to give you tasks to do that are appropriate to your interests, experiences, and skill levels.

18. However, be careful about mixing business and pleasure.

Sure, you want to be part of the work team. This can mean going out for lunch with co-workers or going out after work. It's great to fit in and be part of the gang, but you need to be careful when it comes to drinking with co-workers or getting romantically or sexually involved with people at work.

First, let's talk about alcohol. In some organizations, drinking is very much a part of the culture. You may be encouraged to drink at lunchtime before going back to work for the afternoon. In some offices, going out for beers after work is routine—or even having beer or wine brought into the office on a Friday afternoon by the organization itself! What should you do? You have to decide for yourself, but remember a few things. If you're underage to drink in your state, it's simply a bad idea to drink with co-workers—even if they urge you to do so. Scott had a student years ago who got fired from a prestigious firm because he drank at an office Christmas party. His boss had been proactive—telling him in advance that he could come but he could not drink. At the party itself, though, co-workers twisted his arm and got drinks for him: His boss found out, and he was fired.

Even if you are legal to drink and enjoy doing so, you should be discreet about doing so. We would never recommend that you take the initiative in ordering a drink if you're out with a colleague. If you're with several people who are drinking, it might not be a big deal to have a beer or a glass of wine—but be very moderate at most.

The same goes with getting romantically and/or sexually involved with people at work. In particular, it's never advisable to date a supervisor or someone who works for you. Even if someone is a fellow intern or a co-worker of similar age, you need to proceed with caution. What will you do if you break up with someone, and then you need to keep working closely together? Not a fun situation for either party. At the minimum, the best bet is to wait until after you complete your job before considering any relationship with a co-worker. Remember, also, that making unwanted advances can lead to embarrassing disciplinary and potentially legal issues as well.

One other reminder: When are student employees most likely to forget that it's not such a great idea to get involved with co-workers? You guessed it: When they've been out drinking with them! If you're not careful, this issue can be double trouble, and it can affect how people perceive your professionalism at work.

19. If you're on a full-time job, your job performance should be your highest priority.

When you're in classes full-time, that should be your top priority. But if you're on a full-time co-op or internship, you need to focus your energy on performing your co-op job to the best of your ability.

Two factors can interfere with your job performance if you're not careful: First, some students choose to take classes while on co-op or an internship with long hours. To do so, you may need the permission of your co-op employer and your co-op or internship coordinator. Before seeking their permission, however, be honest with yourself: Can you take on one or two classes without jeopardizing your job performance or your academic performance? If in doubt, it is best to avoid taking classes on co-op or to keep them at an absolute minimum.

20. If you're doing a part-time co-op while attending classes, you need to manage your time very effectively.

In many community college programs, students regularly juggle a co-op or internship with classes. You'll have to master the ability to be a student and worker at the same time without compromising your performance level in either role. This challenge may not end when your co-op is over—many co-ops opt to stay with their co-op employer on a part-time basis when their co-op experience officially ends. Either way, working part-time poses several challenges.

Here are a few tips to avoid this pitfall:

- *Don't over-commit.* Some students ambitiously promise to work 25-30 hours per week part-time. The employer counts on this resource, only to have the student start to realize that it's too much to balance—so he cuts back to 18 hours.... Then 15. This is all very annoying to the manager. Better to under-promise and over-deliver.

  Also, keep in mind the expectations that are set if you are in an arrangement for earning credit on your transcript. This agreement often determines the number of hours you'll work each week or the total hours you'll need to work during the term. Avoid over-committing by creating your weekly work schedule based on the number of hours your coordinator has indicated you need to work. If he or she says ten hours a week, work ten or eleven. If you're told you need to work 15 hours a week, schedule no less than that amount, making sure to build in an hour or two of "wiggle room" in case you are ill or cannot make it to work. This way you'll have "banked" some hours and won't need to make them up.

- *Set a regular schedule and stick to it as much as possible.* Committing to 15 hours a week generally doesn't mean that you go in whenever you feel like it in a given week. Look at your course schedule and block out some times that you can regularly do. Maybe three half-days; maybe two whole days—it doesn't really matter as long as your supervisor agrees to the arrangement and you regularly stick to it. If you have voice mail and e-mail at work, make sure to include a message that informs everyone about your hours and what to do in your absence. Likewise, if you have a desk, office, or cubicle of your own, prominently post your part-time schedule so people will know when you will be working next. In scheduling, also remember that coming in for just an hour or two here and there seldom works well, especially at first when you are just learning the job.

- *Plan ahead.* As soon as you get your syllabi, note the dates of exams and major due dates on your calendar. Since final exams are not typically on the same day or time as regular classes, many schools publish the final exam schedule at the beginning of the term to ensure students have the information early. In that case, you can approach your boss with plenty of notice to let her know that you'll need to alter your work schedule around your exam times. There is really no excuse for calling in the morning to say that you can't come in because you have an exam that day.

21. If you are relocating for a job, be careful about how your situation can affect your perceptions of the job.

If you take advantage of an opportunity elsewhere in the country, you may end up living with other students who work for the same employer or with a different employer. As a result, students sometimes end up comparing notes about jobs, employers, supervisors, co-workers, etc. If both students are having a good experience, this is fine. But if one student is having a bad experience, everyone in that living situation needs to make sure that they continue thinking for themselves. In other words, decide for yourself whether or not you are having a good experience: Don't let anyone tell you what you should or shouldn't be thinking about your unique situation. This is true of any roommates who live together while working, but the negative effects can be magnified when you're living a long way from home and perhaps eating, breathing, and sleeping your practice-oriented experience every minute of the day. It's a powerful experience, so you have to make sure you maintain some objectivity.

Working in a different part of the country can be an excellent idea. In a sense, you're guaranteed of having a "double learning experience"—you'll learn on the job, and you'll learn off the job about what it's like to live in a different region. At best, you may find a place you enjoy more than your home city. At worst, you'll appreciate your own region, campus, or home more when you return.

22. Learn to master "cubicle etiquette" if necessary.

Many work environments feature cubicles or other arrangements that blur the lines between what behavior is public and what is private. Basically, a somewhat contradictory but useful rule of thumb is to assume that all of your own behavior is on public display... but also that you need to respect the privacy of others despite the lack of doors.

First, here are some good reminders relating to the fact that your own behavior is quite visible and public:

- keep your phone ringer on a low volume and your speaking voice relatively low as well obviously, avoid speakerphones
- be aware that most phone conversations can be overheard
- turn off your phone ringer—or forward your calls appropriately—when not in your cubicle
- e-mail or even instant messaging can be useful in this context to communicate to co-workers without unnecessary noise
- keep computer sound levels low
- try to avoid eating hot or highly pungent foods like tuna at your desk—the aromas may distract those who are hungry or disgust those who are not hungry or who don't share your food preferences

When it comes to respecting the privacy of others in a cubicle environment, here are some more good tips:

- Act as if your co-workers' cubicles have doors. Don't just barge in and start talking: Knock on the cubicle's wall.
- Don't be a "prairie dog," peering over the tops of cubes to see if someone is in or to talk. And, don't shout across the "cubicle farm." Go to the other person's location.
- If you go to see someone in their cubicle, and they're on the phone, leave and come back later. Don't hang around where you can readily overhear their conversation.
- Here's a really challenging one: You may overhear a question or comment occasionally and be tempted to respond because you know the right answer. Unless the question is directed to everyone in the area, don't do it! It will bring attention to the fact that you've been eavesdropping, intentionally or not. Wait until someone asks you directly.
- If you have to share a cubicle or workspace with a colleague, you might want to suggest arranging different breaks or lunchtimes so each person gets at least some privacy regularly.

23. Return to school with a network of new contacts.

Lastly, don't miss the golden opportunity of co-ops and internships: When you're working in any position, make sure that you have acquired a network of new contacts before you complete the job! You have the opportunity to earn the respect of many people in your field during your work period. That's great, but make sure you capitalize on that by collecting business cards and/or contact information before you leave. Connecting with full-time colleagues on LinkedIn is advisable, too. You never know who might be in a position to help you out when you're networking for another job in the future. If you only know one or two people at your worksite, you might be out of luck if those people move on and can't be located.

Assuming you've done all you can to make a positive impression, having plenty of names can pay incredible dividends in the future when it comes time for another job search. Even if those individuals can't directly hire you, they may be in a position to recommend you for other jobs or to give you valuable career advice. Don't miss the boat!

E-MAIL AND IM ETIQUETTE

Tamara has been working with students since 1987 and Scott has been working with co-op students since 1995. Without question, the biggest change we have seen over the time is the degree to which e-mail has come to dominate business communication. Likewise, the average person is far more likely to be much more familiar with this form of communication. People love e-mail because of its speed, ease of use, and relative informality. However, all of these characteristics also can lead to blunders in the workplace. So let's review what every professional should know about e-mail.

The 'E' in E-Mail

Most people know that the "e" in e-mail literally stands for electronic. However, it's important to remember that 'e' stands for many other words as well: embarrassing, everlasting, eternal, evidence.

Because an e-mail seems to disappear into cyberspace, it's easy to imagine that it's less "real" than a hard copy. However, the opposite is true. E-mails have lives of their own, and there is always a chance that once they are sent that they will never go away. Maybe you only intended to send it to one person, but who's to say that they won't forward it on? Perhaps you sent something confidential to a friend… but what might happen if that relationship turns sour? You never know when e-mail you sent might reappear at the worst possible moment.

One terrific student that Scott had in class a few years ago had an experience that showed how 'e' can be embarrassing. While at work, she fired off a hasty e-mail to her boyfriend, basically implying that she was looking forward to spending a very passionate Sunday with him. But with a few unsent messages open, she accidentally e-mailed the steamy message to her supervisor!

What happened next was rather amazing. The supervisor thought it was funny and forwarded the message to six or seven colleagues in the Boston office, adding a little joke about how he seemed to be making quite an impression on his intern. Those six or seven colleagues passed it along to others in that office... and to colleagues at *another* office in another city. By the time Scott saw the message, it had been forward to over 60 employees in five cities!

To the student's credit, she owned responsibility for her part in this embarrassing fiasco. Interestingly, though, her manager was reprimanded for passing along the message instead of quietly confronting the co-op to make her aware of her mistake. Still, the co-op could not have enjoyed knowing that her private feelings were now known across the company.

Remember, anything you send as an e-mail is NOT private. Scott had an IT co-op whose job was "sniffing" e-mails. As a senior, he spoke to Scott's class of first-time co-op students, describing how part of his job was to look through e-mail messages. He often came across porn, illegally downloaded music and videos, and many other incriminating messages. Scott will always remember how horrified the class looked as he described what he found and how he reported it to his supervisor, who in turn went to Human Resources. The students were shocked to know that their electronic communications at work were fair game for scrutiny.

Basically, you should be careful about what you send from your home computer... and maybe even a little paranoid about what you e-mail from your work computer. Don't think you can beat the system by sending questionable e-mail from a Hotmail or GMail account: Any e-mail can be traced back to the computer from which it was sent!

If you stop to reflect that e-mail really is everlasting, embarrassing evidence, you'll go a long way toward avoiding problems.

Preparing To Send An E-Mail Or Instant Message

Before you send your first e-mail as a new employee of a professional organization, there are several factors to consider and steps to take:

1. *Become familiar with your organization's culture regarding e-mails.* Every organization is different when it comes to communication. We deal with employers who almost never use e-mails to communicate internally, favoring the telephone or face-to-face interaction. On the other end of the spectrum are companies like Microsoft, where employees may often e-mail individuals who are in the office next door!

   In your early weeks in a new job, pay attention to who e-mails who and for what reason. You may need to e-mail less or more frequently than you ordinarily would to fit in with the new culture. If you're not sure, ask your co-workers or manager how to proceed.

2. *Set up your e-mail account to ensure that your name is obvious to message recipients.* We routinely receive 50-75 e-mails daily during the busiest times of the year. As a result, we end up scrolling through dozens of messages all day long. One minor annoyance is when it's not possible to deduce the sender's name. It may say something like jg1967@hotmail.com, which gives no clue as to the sender's identity.

   Avoid inflicting this minor bit of inconvenience by setting your e-mail properties up so your name is readily obvious to the recipient. Then that message will appear as coming from Jill Gómez <jg1967@hotmail.com> in the message itself.

3. *Fill in the "To:" field LAST when sending any e-mail message.* Depending on the e-mail application you use, it can be surprisingly easy to send a message before you've finished writing or proofreading it. Therefore, it's a good practice to leave the recipient's e-mail address out until you're definitely ready to hit SEND. Because once you do, that message is not coming back!

4. *Always use a concise, descriptive subject for each e-mail message.* This is another problem area for many young professionals. It's not unusual for students to use problematic subjects when e-mailing us. Both of us have had students who seem to think it appropriate to use a complete sentence as a subject: "Mr. Weighart I have some things I need to discuss with you." Other students simply write "IMPORTANT" for almost every message... and, believe us, the subject matter rarely turns out to be all that important. That almost feels like a Spam e-mail tactic—using a vague subject that conveys some sense of urgency.

   Keep your subjects concise, but also be sure to give some sense of what the message concerns. Here are some good and bad examples:

Good e-mail subjects	**Bad e-mail subjects**
Question regarding Munze account	Call me ASAP!
Agenda item for Monday's meeting	Hi!
Quick update on JTC project	This is Henry.
Expense report – January 2008	Hey, how's it going?
Dentist appointment tomorrow	John can you answer these questions for me?
Following up on yesterday's meeting	<no subject>

5. *Don't abuse the "high priority" or "high importance" options.* This e-mail option can become like the story of the boy who cried wolf. If you abuse it in an attempt to get a quick answer to a less-than-urgent question, people will resent it. It leads people to question whether your judgment is good... and eventually they may not take it seriously when something really is high priority!

   If you're looking for a quick answer to a simple question, you might just indicate that with an e-mail subject that reads "Quick question." Save the high-priority option for situations that truly are emergencies. For example, Tamara uses it when a student is injured at the work site and must alert college staff for insurance purposes. You may never need to utilize this option at all, and consider it carefully. If the matter is all that important, you might want to just pick up the phone.

6. *Use an appropriate salutation.* Surprisingly, some of our best co-ops and interns have struggled with this one. Scott had a top student at Microsoft recently, and she had to e-mail a group of about 50 people with a project update. She knew that introducing the e-mail with something like "Hey guys" would be inappropriate, but a better alternative didn't come to mind immediately.

   First, though, let's consider the easier situation. When writing an e-mail to an individual, there are several options that may be appropriate:

   Dear Charlie, — This is a little more formal but fine.

   Hi Charlie, — This is a bit more informal but also acceptable.

   Hello Charlie — Another less formal but acceptable salutation.

   Charlie, — Perhaps a bit more of a down-to-business salutation, but it's fine, too.

   If you're writing to someone you don't know as well, go a little more formal, avoiding the assumption of being on a first-name basis:

   Dear Mr. Bognanni,

   Hi Ms. Bacher,

   Ms. David,

   In limited situations it is acceptable to not include any salutation at all—just launch into the body of the message. This is usually acceptable after several emails have been exchanged rather quickly between two individuals over a specific topic and repeating "Hi Steve" one more time is superfluous.

   Above all, avoid the salutations that you might see in e-mails from a friend:

   Hey Charlie!

   Hey, how's it going?

   Hey there,

   When writing to a group, we recommend something like one of these:

   Hi everyone,

   Hello _____ (fill in name) Team (or Group),

There are other things that would work there—including no salutation at all—but no salutation can be viewed as very abrupt. And some research shows that people are less likely to respond when there is no personal salutation. Since one of your goals is to develop good relations with your co-workers and demonstrate good communication skills, the simple act of using a salutation is the simplest and most effective.

7. *Be wary of the cc and bcc options.* There are times when it's appropriate to use the cc function, which sends an extra copy of your e-mail to another person. Maybe you're updating a colleague on some issue but feel that your supervisor also should hear about it—but more as an FYI rather than as an action item. That's a good time to use the cc function. It can be a good way to keep people informed while also implying that you don't necessarily expect a reply from them.

   Unfortunately, though, people get carried away with sending a cc of their e-mails. There are those who overestimate the importance or interest level that their news will generate, and—even worse—there are those who send a cc to show a third party how dumb the original message was and/or to escalate the intensity of the problem. As we'll see when we consider "flaming" e-mails, this can get out of hand in a hurry.

   Then there is the bcc, which technically stands for "blind carbon copy." In this case, you're letting a third party see the e-mail without the primary recipient being able to see who else is allowed to see it. There are times when this makes a great deal of sense. We use the bcc when we write to groups of people but want to make sure that others don't see the individual e-mail addresses, which may be considered private. For example, if ten students are late in getting some task done for Tamara, she will e-mail them all at once to save time... but she will bcc them all, as it would be potentially embarrassing for each student to know who else is not getting things done on time. It's also no one else's business.

   But both of us try to avoid bcc in most cases. Some feel that it's rather unethical—Scott heard of a bcc recipient being referred to as a "blind co-conspirator." However, the biggest risk is that the bcc recipient will accidentally hit REPLY TO ALL, and then the primary recipient will become aware that others saw the initial message. If you want others to see an e-mail that is somewhat sensitive, just forward a copy from your Sent folder AFTER sending that initial message.

8. *Beware of REPLY TO ALL.* This connects to the previous point. It's all too easy to click "reply to all" instead of simply "reply" when you receive a group message. What is the impact? At best, you end up sending information to a group that has no need whatsoever to read your response. For example, sometimes invitations to events go out on work e-mails, and recipients are told to reply to the sender to RSVP. Instead, the person hits REPLY TO ALL, and the whole group gets

a message indicating that, say, that person will not attend the event because of a dentist appointment. Not a horrible thing to share with a group, but it's basically just another message that needs to be deleted.

However, there are other situations which can lead to serious embarrassment, bad feelings, or even disciplinary action. A few years ago, Scott received an e-mail on a nationally distributed listserv that reached thousands of individuals. One person sent a perfectly fine message to the group. But then a colleague at her own organization hit REPLY TO ALL and informed the e-mail sender that the toilet in their building was clogged yet again! The exchange went back and forth a few times before a recipient finally wrote to say "Do we all really need to read about your bathroom issues?" A mortified apology followed.

Even worse, though, is another possibility. Let's say that Tom sends an e-mail to his entire work group, noting that there will be a farewell party for Jane, a co-worker who is leaving the company. Then Jack—a very close friend of Tom—intends to send a message back to Tom that is for his eyes only. But he accidentally hits REPLY TO ALL. There are any number of things that he might say that could have terrible consequences. He could ask Tom if he thinks the boss will make another of his stupid speeches at the event, or he could express delight that Jane is leaving the company at last. He could talk about a "hot" co-worker who he plans to ask out after the event. The possibilities are almost infinite.

The moral of the story is to think twice before you put anything in an e-mail which will reflect poorly on you if others see it—either due to it being forwarded, intercepted by someone in IT, or accidentally shared through REPLY TO ALL.

9. *Don't open file attachments unless you're very sure that they can be trusted.* File attachments often contain viruses. Even if a friend or co-worker sends a file attachment, look out for vague messages with file attachments. They may be the result of a virus, worm, or Trojan horse that's infected their machines. More obviously, don't open files from people you don't know.

10. *Don't forward virus threats, offensive content, or chain letter e-mails.* Sometimes e-mails claiming to warn people of virus threats actually contain viruses or worms. Let your IT department stay current on such threats.

    Offensive content is very much in the eye of the beholder. What's funny to one person might offend someone else. In general, stay away from forwarding jokes—especially when you're new at an organization and probably not clear about what people will find humorous or even how they might feel about you spending time at work forwarding jokes. If you're just there temporarily for a co-op or internship, I would say that you never should send e-mails to co-workers that have nothing to do with work.

    Many people get sucked in by chain letter e-mails. Periodically you may receive emotional pleas in which, say, a warning of a terrorist act is passed along or a child dying of cancer wants to see how many e-mails he can receive from around the world before he or she dies. Sometimes there is a claim that the American Cancer Society will donate a few cents to cancer research for everyone who receives the e-mail.

While such appeals may bring out your humanitarian nature, don't be fooled. More often than not, these e-mails are hoaxes. You can go to www.snopes.com to see if e-mails are true or not, as this site reports diligently on "urban legends." Most of them are hoaxes, so you're often just wasting your time and that of your friends and co-workers by passing along such nonsense.

11. *Don't reply to spam e-mail messages.* You may receive quite a few annoying spam messages, offering everything from discount drugs and loans to elaborate scams promising you massive amounts of money for helping some overseas widow get access to a massive inheritance. Unless your organization has a spam-reporting mechanism to follow, the best thing to do is to simply delete such messages. Responding to them or clicking on a link—even when doing so supposedly removes you from a mailing list—actually can help a spammer confirm your e-mail address and may lead to getting even more spam or viruses.

12. *Strike when the iron is cold.* Never reply to an e-mail when you are angry, frustrated, or otherwise not prepared to write a professional, businesslike message that you can live with forever. We call this "striking when the iron is cold"—exactly the opposite of the expression "strike when the iron is hot." As a professional, you want to respond with a rational, constructive response—even when you are agitated.

    It's very easy to blast someone when you are angry, saying things that you never would say face to face. Sometimes it's best to resist the urge to fire off a response when you first receive an emotionally charged e-mail. Take a walk, talk about it with someone, maybe sleep on it if you can. Ask yourself what kind of response will reflect you best as an aspiring professional. Then write back when your frame of mind is more positive. Otherwise you'll have a long time to regret responding in the heat of the moment.

The E-Mail Message Itself

Now that we have considered everything that should go into preparing to e-mail, let's go through the writing of the actual message itself. Here are several pointers that will help you write effective e-mails:

1. *Be concise.* Limit your professional e-mails to "need to know" information. Be quick to describe why you are writing, what you need to tell or ask, and what steps, if any, the respondent needs to take in response. Then thank them and end it.

    It's also a good idea to take a moment to reflect on whether an e-mail really is the best way to convey your message. If you can't convey the information in a few short paragraphs—or if the information is complicated and requires additional input—it may be best to use the phone or have a brief meeting.

2. *Create templates if you find yourself writing identical or highly similar e-mails on a regular basis.* Depending on your job, you may need to write highly similar messages repeatedly. Why waste time rewriting them from scratch every time? We both keep a Word file of messages that come up constantly. If we get a request for information about the co-op program or about how to set up an appointment among other things, we can paste in the appropriate response and add the appropriate salutation on top. That saves hours and hours each year.

3. *Use blank lines to separate paragraphs as opposed to indenting.* Just as in any piece of writing, you want to avoid massive paragraphs with no visual or conceptual break. Getting a 25-line e-mail with no spacing just makes the recipient groan. Try to limit each paragraph to no more than 5-6 sentences or lines, and hit ENTER twice at the end to go to the next paragraph without indenting.

4. *Understand that e-mails are one-way communication.* When you have a face-to-face conversation with a co-worker, you can infer a great deal from the speaker's tone of voice and body language. You also can adjust your message based on how the listener reacts to what you say as the conversation progresses.

   Naturally, all of these helpful cues go out the window in an e-mail message. It can be very difficult to grasp the writer's tone. Sometimes it's hard to tell if someone is angry or just in a hurry as well as whether they're joking, serious, or sarcastic. As a result, it's good to be cautious in drawing conclusions. Ask clarifying questions if need be, and avoid emotional topics.

5. *Use "smilies" or "emoticons" sparingly in professional e-mails.* Smilies and emoticons are small symbols that are sometimes used to compensate for the one-way nature of e-mail and IM communication. There are literally dozens of them out there, but here are some common examples:

:)	Happy
☺	Happy
;)	Winking
:(	Sad
:-o	Surprised

Experts differ as to whether such symbols have any place in professional e-mails. Some believe that it can be helpful to add an emoticon in order to make sure that there is no misunderstanding about whether you're joking. For example, an intern who receives an e-mail informing her that she is going to have much more responsibility going forward might write the following text in response:

Looks like I'll have my hands full for the next month.

If the message is left like that, we're not sure whether her reaction is an expression of complaint, anxiety, or enthusiasm. So writing it this way makes that very clear:

Looks like I'll have my hands full for the next month. :)

The best advice is to use these emoticons sparingly. There are quite a few that will baffle e-mail recipients who don't use them at all. For example, can you even guess what these represent?

:C

*

{}

:\'-)

Respectively, they are supposed to indicate astonishment, a kiss, no comment, and tears of happiness! But you'll baffle most co-workers by using these or other less common emoticons, so stick with the common ones if you use them at all.

6. *Capitalize appropriately and avoid IM slang.* Many young professionals are experienced e-mail writers and users of AOL's Instant Messenger (IM) or similar instant message applications. As a result, they bring their highly informal e-mail and IM habits into the workplace. We cringe when we get a professional message in which someone writes something like this:

can i meet with u l8ter 2day? maybe 4 lunch?

Occasionally, we'll get e-mails using other abbreviations, such as LOL (laughing out loud), FWIW (for what it's worth), or IMHO (in my humble opinion). These are fine for personal e-mail but not in professional e-mail. We think it's fine to use FYI (For Your Information) and maybe BTW (by the way), but generally these acronyms should be avoided.

This issue can be confusing. You may receive e-mails or IMs at work from very senior people who opt for punctuation-free e-mails with plenty of IM slang and not a single capitalization. However, even though it's obviously faster to ignore capitalization and use "shorthand slang," it can come across as unprofessional.

Also understand that it's not just IM slang that is a problem. Scott had a student who made a serious mistake at work. When Scott encouraged him to apologize, he wrote an e-mail that included this sentence: "That definitely was my bad." Scott was irritated. You might say "my bad" when you make a bad pass in a pick-up basketball or football game, but you would never use such an expression in any form of professional communication. Basically, if it's not the kind of word or expression that you would use in a term paper, don't use it in an e-mail.

7. *Avoid attaching large files unless absolutely necessary.* You may need to forward a Word or Excel document at work. That's fine. However,

EMAIL ETIQUETTE—A PROFESSIONAL'S PERSPECTIVE

By Dr. Sarah David

"What if you receive an inappropriate email that has been copied to many other people? How would you handle it? I remember when I just started a new job in my professional career as a career counselor I received an email from someone who did not quite understand proper e-mail "netiquette." I was being questioned about an issue in the e-mail and the tone was rather abrasive. The e-mail was not only sent to me but was copied to a number of other administrators including the president.

My first reaction was that of embarrassment, frustration, and anger. This individual was making statements about issues in which she was misinformed. She did not understand my role and was making requests that I had already professionally addressed with her. My first knee-jerk reaction was to shoot her back an email with an immediate response to clear up any misunderstanding and perceptions she may have put in the mind of others about me. It turns out that she dropped the ball on an issue that she had informed me she would take care of on the project.

Instead of responding "emotionally" right away, I decided to open a word document and type my heart out regarding how I was feeling at that moment. After I finished typing out the emotional part of the word document, I then explained the situation without coming across as defensive in the word document. My goal was to turn this rude, unprofessional and misguided e-mail that I received into a very productive, professional, and informative response that showcased me in a positive light. I then saved my word document, went home and slept on my response. The next day I responded un-emotionally to the e-mail and informed the sender in a way that did not leave her embarrassed about how she had come across in her original e-mail. I took the high road by sending a professional communication that merely informed the sender with proper information without causing her embarrassment. I replied to all to make sure there were no misunderstandings by the others that she copied on the original e-mail. By taking the high road and not responding emotionally, I was able to bring a conflict to a successful resolution. Always be professional!"

***Dr. Sarah David** is a Certified Personal Branding Strategist, National Certified Counselor and Certified Career Management Coach. She teaches a Career Exploration class in Human Development where she serves as a Counselor and Professor at Lone Star College – Tomball*

many organizations have size restrictions for attachments and large files will not open. Receiving massive audio or video files in one's e-mail account can get annoying—especially if they have no relevance to work. Generally, avoid sending large files. They can be especially annoying for those accessing their e-mail accounts from slower home computers.

8. *Use threads and quotes sensibly.* Many e-mail applications give you the option of simply hitting "reply," or "reply with history," or "Include message received from sender." So what should you do? It depends, but including at least some of that history may be very helpful to your e-mail recipient. Not infrequently we get a response to an e-mail without that history. Sometimes we know what the writer is talking about, sometimes not. If the message says, "Yes, it would be great if you could do that for me" and nothing more, we may have to dig through our Sent folders to figure out what the heck the person wants us to do—especially when we have looked at 50 or 100 e-mails in between the new message and the previous one!

   Keeping the "thread" of previous responses allows the recipient the luxury of scrolling down to remind himself of what had been said previously. That can be very helpful... and it also can get a little out of control. If you've exchanged many previous messages—including some with file attachments—the e-mail can get to be quite large. A simple way to manage lengthy email threads is to select the reply that includes the message from the sender and then edit out everything except the last one or two exchanges (This is typically referred to as 'editing down'). Another solution is to cut and paste the last two or three exchanges into a new message. Another option would be to just cut and paste small bits of text so the person can see what you're talking about. This can be indicated with a > sign as follows:

   > When can you meet on Tuesday?
   Any time from 9:30-11:30 works for me.

   > Do I need to bring anything?
   Just bring your hard copy of that report.

9. *Don't write "flaming" e-mails or respond in kind if you receive one.* A flaming e-mail is a message that is intended to provoke with inflammatory comments. An example might be the following:

   I CANNOT BELIEVE THAT YOU FAILED TO INCLUDE THE COST OF GOODS SOLD ON THAT SPREADSHEET. WHAT WERE YOU THINKING???

   Writing an all-uppercase message is something to avoid in general, as is the emotionally charged tone of the e-mail. Faced with such a communication, it may be tempting to get defensive or to go on the warpath in response. Don't engage in the same behavior, though, or you'll regret it. As a rule, it's best to not respond at all via e-mail but to call or see the individual to deflate the tension. Bashing the person in reply may be momentarily satisfying but will not win any points for you in the long run.

10. *Prepare an automatic electronic signature for the end of your e-mail.* It's relatively easy to set up an electronic signature that automatically appears whenever you compose a new e-mail or reply to an existing one. The signature should include your name, title, organization name, phone number, and e-mail address, which may not be obvious from the e-mail itself. Your mailing address at work may be included as well if that will be helpful to your recipients. If you are often not at your desk due to the nature of your job, you might include a cellphone number too. It's a professional courtesy to include this data when e-mailing, so someone can have ready access to your contact information.

    Some people include brief quotes with their signatures. These can be nice but also could create problems, especially if your quote is a religious one or controversial in any way. They certainly aren't something you need to include in an e-mail signature.

11. *Proofread and spellcheck.* Many e-mail applications can be set up to proofread messages automatically before they are sent. While this can be useful, remember that spellcheckers are far from foolproof. They often fail to find missing words or words that really are words… but that are not the correct word for that context. So use your spellchecker, but also proofread messages carefully before sending them. This is especially true for those who are prone to spelling errors and typos.

Scott had an employer who hired a terrific interviewee, only to be horrified at the quality of her e-mails. Now the employer always includes a writing component in the interviewing process. After having his department embarrassed by unprofessional e-mails, he came to realize how important it was to avoid them. We hope that this section will help you do the same.

After You Send An E-Mail

After the e-mail goes out, there are just a couple of things to bear in mind:

1. *Don't "recall" a message.* What if you do send a message that includes a mistake—whether a factual error or a bad typo? Many systems now have the option of allowing you to "recall" an e-mail. This may give you the impression that you can "take back" an e-mail that you now regret for whatever reason. Instead, what happens is that the recipient finds both the original e-mail message in his or her inbox along with another e-mail notifying him or her that the message has been recalled. Being human, most of us will be immediately curious about what dumb error is in the first e-mail. In other words, it effectively draws more attention to it.

If you do make a factual error, it's best to send out a correction. In some cases—when you have incorrectly named a time or place for a meeting—you might have an e-mail with an explanatory subjection: CORRECTION on meeting location. Don't profusely apologize—just explain the mistake and clarify what the message should have said.

If a small typo or other stylistic error is made, it's probably best to just let it go. Drawing more attention to it might make it worse.

2. *Be responsive to any e-mail messages that require a reply.* At work, you will receive many group messages that require no reply at all. However, when a message is sent to you individually, it's good to acknowledge receipt of it, briefly. For most professionals, the rule of thumb is to reply to any personal e-mail message within 24 hours (or one business day) if it's a message that requires any sort of response. Responding faster is better if possible and potentially critical if it's a more urgent question.

   Failing to respond quickly to e-mails may start to create unfortunate negative perceptions. Your manager or co-workers may believe that you lack attention to detail, organizational skills, or the ability to manage your time effectively. Responding efficiently and effectively will reinforce the notion that you do have these qualities.

THE EMPLOYER'S PERSPECTIVE

All of the recommendations listed in this chapter generally reflect the expectations of most managers and organizations. HOWEVER, remember: *Every manager and organization is different.* One of the most important survival and success skills in any job for the rest of your career is to pay close attention to the written and unwritten rules of each workplace. Don't make assumptions about what is or is not okay!

Find out what drives your supervisor crazy and what makes her happy, then make any adjustments accordingly. Some bosses really don't care what time you arrive as long as you do a great job—others are upset if their employees don't arrive early every day! In some environments, wearing jeans and a t-shirt is acceptable; in others, wearing anything other than business formalwear is a major mistake. In some organizations, how you dress, speak, and act may have very different rules depending on the department. Scott visited a small software company a few years ago: The software developers wore ripped jeans and t-shirts and were playing chess at 2:00 in the afternoon. Meanwhile, the marketing personnel were wearing suits and working hard from 9-5 with a brief lunch break, while the accounting personnel were wearing business casual clothes and working fairly flexible hours. All of this was happening in a company of about 40 people. Any co-op student entering that environment would have to be very careful in figuring out what was and was not appropriate behavior. Regardless of your position, you must begin to think and act like a professional.

Figuring out what is and is not okay with a given employer can be much trickier than you might imagine. Just because you see a couple of co-workers take a two-hour lunch, you can't assume that it's okay for you to do the same. If you see someone wearing shorts at work, that doesn't mean that this should be your dress code as well. On the whole, you need to keep your eyes open: Don't make the "lowest common denominator" at work become your standard. We have many co-op students who prove to be more motivated and productive than their full-time counterparts. Make sure that you're doing whatever you can to exceed expectations, whether the issue is attire, breaks, effort, or anything else.

Don't worry whether you are being compensated or not for extra work. A marketing manager recently calculated what his salary worked out to be on an hourly rate, only to discover that he was making just a few more dollars per hour than his co-op students!

ON-THE-JOB PERFORMANCE – AN EMPLOYER'S PERSPECTIVE

by Mike Naclerio

Students can get the most out of their jobs by taking the initiative. Many co-op positions in the business field have heavy administrative functions built into them. Do the administrative part thoroughly and without resentment and find additional opportunities to contribute in the organization. Do not get stuck in the gossip and pity trap of how bad my co-op and/or supervisor is. It is all what you make of it. Ask for more work and if your supervisor doesn't have anything, come back to them with a proposal to fix a major problem they may be facing or overlooking. Do not wait for the company to provide you with the opportunity because many organizations are just too busy to focus. If you come to them with a well thought out plan that addresses a key problem, you are sure to stand out.

As far as dealing with conflict, just deal with it. If you are having a problem with a supervisor or co-worker, ask them if they have a few minutes to talk, go somewhere private and clear the air. There is no time for drama in the workplace and most people should respect the directness.

***Mike Naclerio** is the Director of Relationship Management at the workplace HELPLINE*

SPECIAL CONSIDERATIONS FOR HEALTH SCIENCE PROFESSIONALS

If you're majoring in one of the health sciences—nursing, physical therapy, occupational therapy, pharmacy, athletic training, cardiopulmonary science are some examples—you may do clinical assignments as well as co-op jobs. In both cases, you're working in the world of practice as opposed to the classroom. However, there are some key differences between the two experiences. The sidebar box on page 176 addresses them. As you'll see, the contrast can be ironic—some behaviors that are extremely appropriate for a health sciences co-op can be quite out of place on a clinical!

FINAL THOUGHTS REGARDING ON-THE-JOB SUCCESS

Getting on top of the many details in this chapter obviously has an enormous impact on the job experience. Perhaps the biggest key is owning the responsibility for your own success. Sooner or later in your career, you'll have to contend with a poor manager, a difficult co-worker, or a problematic or uninspiring work environment. Some high-level managers at Microsoft like to say, "It's not the situation: It's how you handle it."

One senior manager at Microsoft told Scott the following: "When I interview people now, I mainly try to weed out the whiners, complainers, and moaners," he said. "Years ago, I sometimes interviewed people who told me that they were held back in their old jobs because of poor managers, a negative work environment, or a lack of resources. I hired some of these people, because I believed that once they got to Microsoft—where we have great managers, a very achievement-oriented work environment, and plentiful resources—they would shine. It didn't happen. Instead they found new excuses. I've learned that good people just learn to overcome obstacles."

By adhering to the principles discussed in this chapter, you will learn to be solution oriented, preventing problems from arising and building a foundation of success in the workplace that will help you get your next job and excel in it. Above all, if in doubt about what to do and how to do it, ask someone. Then you'll find out how to live up to your interview.

CLINICAL VERSUS CO-OP – A HEALTH PROFESSIONS CO-OP PERSPECTIVE

by Jean Harcleroad

Clinical experiences for nursing students occur in a variety of agencies and sites including hospitals, outpatient clinics, nursing homes, physician offices, and simulated laboratory situations. A college nursing faculty member is generally on site with nursing students, and there are specific course competencies that students must meet each term in order to progress through the program. At our college, and in most collegiate nursing programs, clinical practice learning situations are required for all nursing students, students are assigned to their learning sites, and students usually participate in clinicals 12-16 hours per week during each term of the Associate Degree curriculum.

Different from the generic program, cooperative education (co-op) for nursing students is an elective course beyond the requirements of the Associate Degree Nursing Program. Enrollment in co-op allows students to choose from a variety of work site options to seek an enrichment experience. At the site, students typically work one-on-one with an approved facility staff nurse. One advantage of the co-op program is that students can go to sites that are not part of the regular nursing curriculum. Prospective students are sometimes interviewed prior to acceptance at a particular site, especially in the high-risk areas such as Intensive Care and the Emergency Department. Another difference from the generic nursing program is that co-op students establish their own learning objectives in collaboration with their nursing co-op faculty supervisor. These objectives are specific to the unit in which they are completing their co-op experience. For students to be eligible for co-op at Lane, they must meet a GPA requirement and have a letter of recommendation from their most current nursing faculty documenting that they have achieved a level of skill and motivation. This ensures that the student will represent our nursing program safely and professionally while in the field.

As I explain to students, every day of work at their co-op site should be viewed as a job interview. Clinical sites view co-op as a way to screen potential employees, so your co-op job performance may be scrutinized with an eye toward your long-term employability. I had a student this summer who came late to work, had a poor attitude, and was not engaged in the tasks at hand. Her supervisor said to me, "Thanks, but we would never hire her." I had another student who gave too much personal information at work about her friends and lifestyle. Her preceptor reported to me that she would "never hire this person" based on what she had learned. In contrast, another student was exceptionally well motivated, enthusiastic, professional, and responsible. She was promised a job immediately upon graduation.

In our tight job market for nurses locally, students who have successfully completed cooperative education gain the advantage of additional skill development and the opportunity to integrate theory into practice. In addition, these students have been interviewed and observed while on the job and identified as prospective full-time employees. Last year, all nursing students who were hired immediately after graduation and successful completion of Board Exams were students who had completed at least one term of cooperative education in addition to clinicals.

__Jean Harcleroad__ is a Nursing faculty and former faculty nursing Cooperative Education Coordinator in Nursing at Lane Community College

CHAPTER 4 REVIEW QUESTIONS

1. List three different ways in which performing well on your job or internship will benefit you.

2. Give three examples of specific goals that you would like to be able to set for your internship or co-op job.

3. Name four on-the-job situations in which it would be highly advisable to contact your internship or co-op coordinator.

4. Describe three common mistakes students make when trying to juggle a part-time job or internship with full-time coursework.

5. Name at least three things that the 'e' in an e-mail can stand for besides 'electronic.'

CHAPTER FIVE

Making Sense of Your Experience

Eventually, your co-op, internship, or practicum will end. At this point, you may return to the classroom full time, continue working in your field part time as you continue to take classes to finish your degree (and possibly earning more credit). Alternatively, you may have completed your degree and are about to begin working as a regular employee in your new career. Whether your experience was terrific, terrible, or anywhere in between, you need to take the final steps toward getting credit for your work experience as well as figuring out what comes next in your career. At most colleges, this process includes a) having your site supervisor complete and return an evaluation of your work performance, and b) completing a reflection requirement. At some schools, you may also need to provide documentation of your work hours. Make sure you find out what's required in your program.

Receiving a performance evaluation and fulfilling reflection requirements offer you a chance to make sense of what happened while you were on your work term. Because the primary goal of co-ops or internships is to learn from anything you experienced at work—whether positive or negative—the evaluation and reflection processes will help you gain some perspective on how you did and what you can take away from the experience. This will help build self-awareness—including a sense of what you need to do to keep growing and improving as a professional in the future. It's not uncommon for a student to emerge from a co-op or internship with a greater sense of self-confidence as well as an urgency about the classroom. For that matter, it's not unusual for students to improve dramatically in their coursework after co-op. In addition to seeing the practical relevance of the material in the "real world," taking classes sometimes feels relatively easy after a demanding work experience!

As the sidebar box on the next page indicates, internships and co-op jobs don't only answer some career questions that you may have—they also may raise new questions regarding what comes next.

YOUR EVALUATION

As your co-op job comes to a close, you generally will be evaluated. Most programs have a standard form that employers complete and return to the program coordinator. Often you will be asked to summarize the job and your sense of how it was as an experience, while your supervisor will write up her or his thoughts on your responsibilities, strengths, areas for further professional development, and on your soft skills: interpersonal relationships, dependability, judgment, etc. You also may be given an overall rating, such as outstanding, very good, average, marginal, or unsatisfactory.

Some employers will prepare an evaluation form that is typically used for all employees in their organization. These forms can be several pages long and are quite detailed. At some organizations, the format involves asking you and your manager to reflect briefly in writing on how successful you were in reaching your job-related tasks and objectives.

Whatever your evaluation looks like, keep a few things in mind when receiving your first performance evaluation:

1. *Don't take it too personally.* You and your manager may not see eye to eye on how you did in your job—and it won't always be because your supervisor has a higher opinion of your performance than you do! You may receive criticism that you believe to be inaccurate or unfair. Regardless, you want to end your relationship with any employer in a gracious, classy manner—don't blow it because of an impulsive, emotional reaction to evaluation comments. Even in large communities, professionals in related businesses often know each other, and you will need this person as a job reference.

2. *View the evaluation experience as a learning opportunity.* If you have communicated consistently with your manager throughout your co-op, you should not be too surprised by your evaluation. In any event, your evaluation gives you things to think about and talk about with your co-op coordinator—it can lead to specific goals for personal improvement and success in your next co-op. No one is perfect, and no one is perfectly aware of all of her or his strengths and areas requiring further development. Use the evaluation as a tool in your professional development.

3. *If you feel your evaluation is unjust or unfair, take the initiative to discuss it with your supervisor as well as your co-op/internship coordinator.* Getting evaluated on co-op is hardly an exact science. Some employers may rate students higher than they deserve because they fear that a negative or neutral review will cause undesirable conflict or impair your academic progress. Other employers may have impossibly high standards or

RETURNING TO THE CLASSROOM – A CO-OP PROFESSIONAL'S PERSPECTIVE

by Ronnie Porter

In my program, students sometimes realize what the theories really meant when they were put into the practice—or sometimes the other way around: They've done things on co-op and then studied the theory and figured out why things were done a certain way. Either way, it just naturally flows into the academics and into thinking about how they want to do things next time around on their co-op.

Through their co-op experience, they may know that they need to take courses to enhance their expertise in a certain area. In Arts and Sciences, the question should not be, say, "Can you give me a list of all the philosophy jobs?" We say, "That's not the right question." We're interested in "Why are you interested in philosophy and what do you want to do with it?" So it's a different approach. There's no list of jobs, rather there are a lot of conversations around what the person wants to do and what their hopes and expectations are about how they're going to use this information that they're learning.

***Ronnie Porter** is a cooperative education faculty coordinator in Biology at Northeastern University* just believe that most employees should receive average reviews unless something really astonishing was accomplished. In other situations, you may have a change of manager midway through your co-op, or perhaps you reported to numerous people or maybe even to no one at all. Obviously, any of these developments will affect the fairness or accuracy of your review.

In an ideal situation, you will meet with your supervisor to discuss your evaluation. He or she will privately explain the evaluation to you before it has been returned to the college. If this doesn't happen, it is completely appropriate to request such a meeting, especially if you aren't thrilled with your supervisor's written remarks about your performance. Begin a meeting like this by asking for a general explanation of your evaluation. Stay calm and professional, even if you are told things you believe to be inaccurate or unfair. At the end of the meeting, thank your supervisor and ask what you would need to do to significantly improve your performance evaluation in the future. It doesn't matter if you will no longer be working at this co-op site. The information you will receive will be invaluable for your future work performance.

Once of Tamara's students made the effort to meet with her supervisor after receiving a less than outstanding evaluation and had a surprising outcome. As the supervisor talked to the student about her evaluation, he pulled out a red pen and started changing it to be more favorable. He went on to explain to her that he had filled it out in a hurry. Upon closer consideration, he didn't think his original marks really reflected the quality of her work. He apologized and offered to write her a letter of recommendation. The student earned a full grade better because of the supervisor's revised evaluation!

You'll also want to discuss concerns about your evaluation with your coordinator. We know that evaluations can be an issue, and it also can be quite challenging for us to figure out the truth amidst many different perceptions. Your coordinator should be able to provide you with a more objective and balanced view of how you did if you're not sure what to think about your review.

4. *After a few months have gone by, review your evaluation again.* It's easy to lose your objectivity when you're immersed in a job. After you have been out of that specific work environment for a good while, you may find that it's easier for you to consider the positives and negatives of your review more openly and less emotionally. It's also good to reconsider your performance before you begin your next job search, so that you are ready to discuss how your job went with a future employer. This is a good opportunity to show self-awareness and graciousness. Even if you have lingering bad feelings about a previous job or supervisor, you need to move on and take the high road when discussing past events with a potential new boss.

INTEGRATING PRACTICE WITH COURSEWORK – A CO-OP PROFESSIONAL'S PERSPECTIVE
by Rose Dimarco

I find that as an undergrad student in health care, you learn quickly when to do something and how to do it. The why you are doing it—why you are doing that range of motion or stretching exercise or providing certain pharmaceutical drugs—comes in the classroom. So it's up to you to take the where and when and connect it with the why. Now you're slowly going to evolve from studying nursing to becoming a nurse—that's going to come from that interchange.

***Rose Dimarco** is a cooperative education faculty coordinator in Physical Therapy at Northeastern University*

While most co-op students get anxious about their initial performance evaluation, the great majority of our students do very well in the eyes of employers. Over 80 percent receive very good or outstanding evaluations. Still, everyone always has ways in which they can improve, and it's generally very helpful to get feedback from an experienced manager in the professional world.

PURPOSES OF REFLECTION

Quality cooperative education programs have always required some form of reflection assignment for co-op students. Why do co-op programs require reflection? There are numerous reasons:

1. *Making connections between classroom and the world of practice.* One purpose of co-ops and internships is to give students a practice-oriented element to their educations, making learning "hands-on" instead of just learning about theories. Reflection often requires you to think about how a work experience brought classroom concepts to life, or how practical work experience changed an understanding of something you thought you understood in a course. In return, your job experience gives you raw material that you bring with you to class to help you understand new concepts and theories in your field.

   Curiously, research shows that most individuals—regardless of age and experience—do not automatically make connections between knowledge learned in different settings. It's not that people are not capable of such "knowledge transfer;" it's just that it does not occur to people to do so. However, research also shows that forcing people to "think about their thinking"—a process called metacognition—can be very successful in helping individuals connect what they learn and use it in new situations.

   Another purpose of field experience, particularly in career technical areas, is to give students exposure to equipment, products and processes not available in the classroom. Through reflection you have the opportunity to document your unique experiences, often with cutting-edge technology, and consider them in light of what you are learning about the future of your career field. Many a student has discovered that a manufacturing job is pretty amazing when you get to use multimillion dollar equipment.

2. *Having an opportunity to compare your experience with those of others.* Going to reflection seminars gives you a chance to hear about where your classmates worked, what they did, and how it all went. It can be useful to hear about how others dealt with challenges that they faced and to hear the thoughts of fellow students who may be in their second or third term of participating in internships. At best, you may be able to learn from the successes and mistakes of others.

3. *Learning about future job options.* Hearing about other students' experiences may give you some added perspective about where you

might want to work in the future as well as jobs or organizations that you may wish to avoid. HOWEVER—Be careful about drawing conclusions from the experiences of others! Just because one industrial engineering student complains bitterly about her internship at Amalgamated Suitcases, does that mean that YOU wouldn't like the same job? Maybe, maybe not. In the same reflection seminar, you may hear another student praising his electronic technician job at an organization called advancedlogistics.com—does that mean this job is great for everyone? Of course not.

Whenever Scott starts his reflection seminars, he usually tells the tale of two students who did the exact same job at the same time with the same employer. In one reflection seminar, the first student said, "My PC support job was fantastic—I'd recommend it to anyone. The day goes by really quickly because there's always something new to handle—you're not stuck behind a desk; you're going all over the company to troubleshoot problems. When you go to see end users, they're usually upset about their computer problems, but when you fix the problem, they are SO grateful! What a great job!"

At the next reflection seminar, that student's co-worker complained bitterly about his job: "Don't ever work in PC support! What a bunch of headaches—you come in and try to get a project done, and you keep getting interrupted constantly by end users. They're generally pretty clueless about computers, and they're in a foul mood when you go to see them. Every day I went home with a headache."

Which student is "right?" Both… and neither. The quality of a job experience is very much in the eye of the beholder. When students describe their previous jobs, listen more carefully to their descriptions of the job duties and the reasons why they liked or disliked their jobs. Make up your own mind as to whether that job would be good for you.

4. *Having the opportunity for more detached and objective appraisal of one's experience, after the fact.* Working at an organization is kind of like being in a relationship. Whether you're in a romantic relationship, living with a roommate, or working in a job, it can be easy to lose your perspective when you're immersed in the situation. Positively or negatively, you might do things you wouldn't ordinarily do—and then wonder why that happened, after the fact.

Reflection gives you an opportunity to make sense of your experience in a more detached, open way, toward the end or after you are no longer in the situation. This may lead to new insights and a new appreciation of what it all meant.

Reflection also can be quite surprising for both students and coordinators. One time Scott was running a reflection seminar for entrepreneurship/small business management students. One student reported that he had worked at a small restaurant but found it frustrating because the entrepreneur was highly secretive about the financial affairs of the business. "My guess is that he didn't want to show me the books because he was cheating on his taxes," the student said. "But I guess that's what you have to do to make it as an entrepreneur."

Scott managed to hold his tongue and asked if anyone else in the room had another perspective on the situation. A second student raised his hand. "My family has run a business for several generations, and my grandfather went to jail for basically thinking the same thing as your boss." It was a powerful moment and a great chance for the group to reflect on the challenges and ethical dilemmas that entrepreneurs face—as well as considering the potential consequences of running a business that is engaged in illegal activity.

FORMS OF REFLECTION

Generally, there are many ways in which you can fulfill your reflection requirement. Which one will you end up doing? It all depends. Many colleges have a standard set of activities or assignments that all co-ops or interns complete. In other colleges, your coordinator determines your assignments. All reflection methods have pros and cons, so let's consider briefly the different forms of reflection.

1. *Small-group seminars:* Some students participate in a reflection seminar in a small group—usually no more than 15 students. At Northeastern, business students are required to go to one 60-minute session with their coordinator and a group of students in their field. On the positive side, this method is fairly quick and painless for most students and coordinators. It also gives students a chance to exchange ideas and experiences with classmates. On the negative side, it's hard to go into serious issues in great depth in a one-time, one-hour session. Also, some students may feel awkward or uncomfortable sharing their job experiences—especially if something unpleasant happened at work. For these students, another reflection method may be preferable.

2. *Writing a reflection paper:* This is another common form of reflection. Your coordinator may provide you with some questions or topics that can be addressed in a paper that is written at the end of the work experience. Often the focus is not so much on a plot summary of your work experience: instead, the idea usually is to try to make connections between the real world and the classroom and to get across what you learned about yourself and the organizational world while on an internship or co-op—even if that included getting fired from your job! Here are some questions that might be considered for a paper:

- How has this job experience helped you understand concepts that you previously learned when taking classes in your major? Has this experience changed your attitude toward being in classes and your ability to perform since returning to campus after completing your job? How have liberal arts classes helped you build useful transferable skills for the professional world?
- What was the purpose of your job? How did your job fit into the overall organizational mission?
- How did you learn how to do your job? Formal training? Personal instruction by your supervisor? "Peer-to-peer" learning—did you pick things up from co-workers? Figuring things out for yourself? Break down the various ways you learned about appropriate behaviors as well as work tasks or products.
- From this experience as well as prior work experiences, describe what differentiates an excellent manager or supervisor from a poor or average one.
- How and why did your job confirm or change your career direction?
- Describe the organizational culture of where you worked and whether or not this culture is the best for you as a worker.
- What were the norms or "unwritten rules" regarding what was and was not acceptable where you worked? Was it difficult to learn these norms and adjust to them?
- How would you rate the quality of your job as a learning experience?
- What did you learn in this job that had nothing to do with your technical skills or your major/concentration?
- How would you rate your performance in the job, regardless of the job's quality?
- Now that you have had this experience, what are your plans for your next job, whether co-op, internship, clinical, or post-graduate?

Papers are advantageous in that they provide a chance to really go into depth about what you learned, and they also are a more private form of reflection. The downside is that they may be more time consuming and don't allow you the chance to hear the perspectives of fellow students.

3. *Keeping a journal:* Some students write weekly journals reflecting upon their development throughout the job experience. At the end

of your co-op, it can be quite remarkable to look back at your anxieties and concerns and see how you have changed. Some coordinators may set up electronic systems to journal including e-mail, blogs, message boards, and web-based tools. You may have questions

e-mailed to you for your consideration and response. Sometimes programs like Blackboard, Moodle, online message boards, or the Web are used in order to create places where students write journal entries as well as connect with other students and their coordinator. The best thing about these methods is that they help you have opportunities to reflect when there is still time to make changes in your performance or address problem areas at work. The negative is primarily the time involved, although technology is a hurdle for some co-op programs.

4. *Taking a work-related seminar or class DURING your co-op.* In a number of colleges, students are required to attend a co-op seminar or take a course for credit during their co-op. The frequency of these meetings and the assignments students must complete for them varies widely from three one-hour seminars during the term to weekly hour-long sessions for an entire term. Many students have found this to be a great opportunity to discuss ethical issues or concerns while they were in the midst of them in the workplace. Students who attend weekly meetings report that they like having a regular opportunity to share and don't feel so alone when things go wrong at their co-op. Fellow students can be a good source of ideas for ways to deal with difficult workplace situations and issues.

5. *Having a one-on-one meeting with your coordinator.* Many co-op coordinators would love the time to meet with each student one-on-one but find it is impossible given their heavy student loads. However, in some institutions, the practice is common. At Tamara's college, all co-op students in Health and PE programs engage in a half-hour "exit interview" as part of the reflection requirement. Do not hesitate to ask your coordinator for a one-on-one meeting if something particularly difficult happened on the job. This may be an important and useful option in order to confront problems, learn from mistakes, or to determine if there are issues the coordinator must address with the employer.

GETTING CREDIT FOR YOUR WORK EXPERIENCE

For most students, getting an at least average performance evaluation and completing a reflection requirement means that they will get a passing grade for their

MAKING SENSE OF YOUR CO-OP – A STUDENT'S PERSPECTIVE

by McKenzie Baldwin

My internship as a production assistant for a media production company was very important to me and my career. I had gone through school in multimedia and jumped through all the hoops associated with earning that degree, but I didn't have very much real world experience. That all changed after interning with Chambers Productions.

From day one at Chambers, I was thrust into the "real world." I was able to see how a real production worked from start to finish. This in turn showed me that I could do something like this, it wasn't impossible because I was seeing it with my own eyes. If I had gone straight from school to a working situation, I think I would have been lost, looking around in awe. Instead, with the experience I received at my internship, I can walk onto any set and feel prepared for what will come my way.

The internship also allowed me to make mistakes in a safe environment. If I did something wrong, my supervisor, Leonard Henderson, would take me aside and explain what I did, and how I could do it differently next time. That isn't always the case on a real set; if you mess up, someone will let you know about it, and they probably won't be as nice as Leonard was.

Most importantly, my internship led to a job. I have been working with Chambers Productions since completing my internship and have been gaining more onsite experience ever since. I have worked on local commercials, national commercials, and even a big budget movie since completing my internship. I've even used my knowledge to help my own personal projects.

I can say, without a doubt, that if I had not taken the internship I would not be where I am today. I would probably still be sitting on my couch waiting to get in the game. Instead I am working in an industry I love.

***McKenzie Baldwin** graduated with an associates degree in Multimedia Design from Lane Community College in 2009*

work experience. Sometimes, though, the outcome is in doubt. Any of the following can jeopardize your ability to get a passing grade for your work experience:

- failing to get approval to earn credit for your job from your coordinator before it begins
- accepting an offer from one employer, only to renege on your agreement to accept an offer with another employer
- quitting a job without getting your coordinator's permission first
- getting fired (or getting a poor evaluation)
- failing to turn in required forms in a timely manner, including your supervisor's evaluation of your performance

- failing to complete assignments including the reflection requirement

In the end, *your coordinator* will determine the grade you receive for your work experience, not your worksite supervisor. Make sure you understand the grading criteria. Make sure that you're never in a borderline category by doing a

MAKING SENSE OF YOUR CO-OP – A STUDENT'S PERSPECTIVE

by Katie Van Meter

When I arrived for my internship as a computer game development assistant with Mad Otter Games, I was unsure of what I'd be doing but I was enthused. Although I assumed that I'd be stuck in a low-risk, mind-numbing task that no other employee wanted, in the back of my mind I had grand visions of doing a little bit of everything. Above all, I wanted to be useful.

I was quickly swept into experiences I had only dreamed being a part of, getting a flavor of each unique role the game industry offers. I handled every task they offered me and ended up publicizing the company's products through social media, communicating with their fans, writing in-game dialogue, and doing documentation. My creative mind flourished under the freedom and feedback my supervisors gave me, and I was graciously included in discussions and meetings. I soaked up every bit of information I could, relishing the ability to talk with legendary game developers and find out more about our local industry.

The best and worst part of the internship was the thrill of the NDA (non-disclosure agreement). It's always fun to have a company announcement that begins with, "You can't tell anyone this, but...." All of the exciting and interesting things I learned I can't share. I was delighted to discover that the tools that I had learned in school were actually used by the company at which I interned. It's all too easy as a student to assume you will never use a school-learned skill in the workplace, but I was encouraged to find out that the majority of what I had learned was actually useful!

After my final internship meeting had completed, I felt a sense of loss. The company president called me into a meeting that day and I thought he would say his farewells and this grand chapter in my life would come to an end. When he instead asked if I would like a job, I literally was bursting at the seams with joy.

Co-op experiences are what you make them. If you go in unexcited, unenthused, and thinking it's a waste of time, you probably won't get much from the experience. If you go in looking to work hard, improve yourself, and help the company thrive, you and your employer will have a more rewarding experience. I challenge you to go in not with the mindset of "What can they do for me?" but "What can I do for them?" Make yourself a valued contributor, and you might be surprised at the outcome.

***Katie Van Meter** earned an associates degree in Computer Simulation and Game Development from Lane Community College in 2009*

MAKING SENSE OF CO-OP – A STUDENT'S PERSPECTIVE

by Gabriel Glasscock

When I began my co-op career, my expectations weren't high. I expected to be exposed to the corporate climate and have minimal responsibilities at a few companies, graduating with my foot in the door at a few places. Before I knew it, I was in Tampa, Florida, standing in a classroom in front of 80 over-analytical recent college graduates, giving them lectures on the Java programming language. The most surprising thing I've learned is that you can ride this co-op roller coaster as fast as you want to if you're not afraid to take on challenges.

Co-op has humbled me but also made me aware of my capabilities. It tests your resilience, and helps you realize what you really want to do with the rest of your life. It has helped me mature and exposed me to many things. I now know what it's like to have 12 friends laid off on the same day!

Co-op prepares you mentally for the reality of working and dealing with life after college. I truly consider myself lucky to have had these opportunities. In some areas, I consider myself 100% different, and for the better. Typical four-year programs? Heck no! CO-OP!

***Gabriel Glasscock** was an MIS student at Northeastern University, Class of 2002*

great job and completing all steps with your coordinator! After all, failing your work experience doesn't look so great to future employers who may be reviewing your transcript.

FINAL THOUGHTS ON CO-OP SURVIVAL AND SUCCESS

After reading this much of the guidebook, you should have a good foundation when it comes to understanding workplace survival and success. If you can apply the concepts that we've covered in these pages, you will emerge with greater self-awareness, a sense of accomplishment, and a set of experiences that will entice employers looking to hire new graduates. You also will have a new appreciation for how, why, and where learning happens as you go from one job to the next as well as from the classroom to the world of experience.

For a co-op coordinator, internship director, or career services professional, the most satisfying part of the job is seeing students accomplish their career exploration and learning goals and become professionals with a keen sense of who they are, what they want, and what they are capable of accomplishing through hard work. We have seen students who were barely employable who ultimately graduated with incredible experience and a very attractive job offer. Scott often tells students that internships and co-op jobs are not sprints: They are marathons that reward those who display persistence and consistent effort over the months of a co-op position.

The rest of the book features appendices that may be useful to you now or in the future.

- **Appendix A** covers the job search process through the Co-op Learning Model.
- **Appendix B** is a Skills Identification Worksheet that you can complete and tally up. We've found that this is a real confidence builder when used shortly before beginning work on your first resume. Many fledgling co-ops believe that they have nothing to offer a prospective employer. This exercise will help you realize that you probably have at least 20-30 soft skills that are going to be attractive to employers.
- **Appendix C** details how to write cover letters—whether for obtaining an internship, a co-op job, or your first job after graduation. Generally, you won't need to write a cover letter if you're applying for a job through a co-op or internship program, but sooner or later you will want to learn how to write a cover letter that is every bit as strategic as the interviewing approach described earlier in the book.
- **Appendix D** features other typical interview questions you can use when practicing interviews.
- **Appendix E** includes a "bridging" exercise that will help you make connections between your resume and a specific job description. Doing this activity will help you realize how you need to change gears and emphasize different strengths and skills based on the job description at hand.
- **Appendix F** has more in-depth information on behavioral-based interviewing, including several excellent student examples. Being able to rehearse specific, vivid stories that can be used to prove that you really do have a given skill is a great way to prepare for any kind of interview, not just a behavioral-based one.
- **Appendix G** is a resume rubric that Tamara uses with students to help them prepare outstanding resumes.

Good luck with your co-op career, and remember: The goal is to shine and not simply survive!

CHAPTER 5 REVIEW QUESTIONS

1. Explain why many students start getting better grades in classes after completing a co-op or internship?

2. What are three benefits of attending reflection seminars?

3. Think about the last job that you held. What was the purpose of that job? How did it fit into the goals of the organization that employed you?

4. Name three situations that could result in a student not getting credit for a co-op or internship.

5. Of the student sidebar boxes on the benefits of co-op, which one resonated the most with you? Why?

APPENDICES

APPENDIX A

The Co-op/Internship Process

In this book we have covered a great deal of information about co-op. Nonetheless, you may very well be wondering "what do I do next?" Every program has its own rules, regulations, and idiosyncrasies, causing difficulty in making generalizations about the job search process across colleges. However, there are enough commonalities to make it worth our while to review them here.

More than anything, though, we want to make sure to preface this information with a warning: *The job search process is always evolving and changing over time. Colleges are continually revising their co-op and internship processes, making changes to computer systems and student requirements such as deadlines for turning in resumes, creating e-portfolios, and changing ways to get referred to employers. As such, ALWAYS stay in touch with your coordinator to be sure of the requirements and deadlines for your specific program!* If in doubt about when you need to get started, make contact and find out sooner rather than later. Failing to do so could make all the difference between success and failure in your job search.

CO-OP LEARNING MODEL

The Co-op Learning Model is a simple but useful way to understand the three primary phases of the co-op process: preparation; activity; and reflection.

The Preparation Phase

The preparation phase includes all of the activities that you undertake to get ready for your co-op or internship. Contrary to the opinion of a few misinformed students, most programs are not job placement services. In other words, you can't just waltz into your coordinator's office a few weeks before your scheduled work period begins and—just like that—get "assigned" to a job. The system doesn't work that way. Why not? The most important reason is that we want you to own much of the responsibility of your job search, so you will understand how to do everything you need to do to get a job for the rest of your professional career! To put it another way, we'd rather teach you to fish for the rest of your life than simply feed you for a day. Therefore, most co-op professionals won't write your resume for you, don't tell companies who to hire, and require an employer evaluation to help determine if you should get a passing grade for your work experience.

Because of all of this, preparation takes time! Generally, you will be asked to revise your resume more than once, and some students may go on more than a dozen interviews before getting and accepting an offer.

The Activity Phase

After you get a job, you'll start working regularly with your employer; the work period is the activity phase. During this phase, your focus should be on understanding and meeting your supervisor's expectations regarding everything from work hours to job responsibilities, setting goals together to ensure that you have a mutual understanding about your level of job performance.

During this phase, it also may be advisable to check in with your coordinator back at school—especially if any concerns or problems arise. The objective is to earn the best possible performance evaluation and reference.

The Reflection Phase

Typically you need to complete the reflection phase to get credit for your co-op. You will want to make sure that your coordinator receives your supervisor's performance evaluation of your work and find out about reflection requirements. It's also advisable to update your resume, while the job is still fresh in your mind.

Now that you have an overview of the co-op process, let's take a closer look at the details that may be involved in each step.

WORKING WITH YOUR INTERNSHIP/CO-OP COORDINATOR

As mentioned briefly in Chapter 1, it's critical to build a good working relationship with your co-op coordinator—and with other co-op faculty if necessary. Here are some key pointers:

Stay On Your Coordinator's Radar Screen.

Given that your co-op or internship coordinator may work with hundreds of students each year, you can't expect him or her to hold your hand through the process. It's absolutely critical that you own the responsibility for finding out and remembering how early and often you need to come in and what you need to accomplish each step along the way. If you're not sure, call or send an e-mail. "I just didn't have time to get in touch" doesn't cut it with us—not when it takes all of one or two minutes to update us with an e-mail or voice mail at whatever hour of the day or night. If you're not in touch with us regularly—especially during the months before you're scheduled to start your job—we have to assume that you're really not that interested in working.

Know How To Determine Your Co-op Coordinator's Availability.

Find out if your co-op/internship coordinator can be seen individually either by appointment or by going to walk-in hours. But how can you find out when a given co-op coordinator is available? See if your coordinator has a calendar—either online or just outside the door of their offices.

If you have trouble finding a time to meet with your coordinator, you should drop an e-mail or call your coordinator to see if additional times are available. If we don't know that you're trying to meet us, we can't help to accommodate you!

Here are a few other helpful hints about working with co-op and internship coordinators as well as career services professionals. With a little thought and communication, you can avoid considerable frustration.

1. *If you are on a tight schedule in general, try to schedule appointments.* Some students have limited free time available due to classes, part-time jobs, clubs, and varsity sports. If you fit this description, be proactive, schedule appointments ahead of time and ask your coordinator for ways to ensure regular meetings. Most coordinators and career professionals will schedule meetings at irregular times if a student has legitimate conflicts and is proactive and polite about addressing the situation.

2. *If you prefer to come to walk-in hours, try to come right when the walk in hours begin and/or bring homework or reading material if you must come when it's busy.* During the months leading up to the beginning of a work period, coordinators can be very busy seeing students. Some students end up frustrated because they haven't really thought about how to avoid the walk-in logjam. There are many ways to minimize your waiting time. First, come in early—early in the day and early in the process. Many college students are not early risers, so most coordinators tend to have shorter walk-in lines during the morning hours. Anytime after 11:30 tends to get really busy during the peak times of year. Likewise, if you come in several months before your co-op for that first resume review, you will beat the rush and be in good shape the rest of the way.

   Sometimes, though, you can't avoid a long wait—especially during peak months. With this in mind, bring some homework or reading material. That way you won't sit around feeling impatient if you do need to wait a while.

3. *If you really can't come in every week or so during referral period, you need to stay in contact via e-mail or voice mail.* Some students keep popping by during a busy afternoon walk-in hour time… only to find that there is a long line. If they get discouraged and leave, the coordinator has no idea that the student has made any effort to get in touch. Thus, you really need to stay in touch by voice mail or e-mail—even if it's just to give a quick update regarding your job search or to let your coordinator know that you're having difficulty coming in during the available times. If you fail to let us know that you're having a problem, then we won't know!

4. *Be reasonable about what you expect your coordinator to be able to do for you in person, on the phone, or by e-mail.* In person, don't expect your coordinator to write or rewrite your resume for you or to describe numerous available jobs to you. You will be expected to do many things for yourself. As for e-mails, bear in mind that they should not replace

individual meetings. One of Scott's frustrations is when students e-mail their resume to him and ask him to critique it or correct it. It's incredibly time-consuming to edit a resume this way, as it results in extremely long e-mail replies: "On the fourth line of your second job description, three-quarters of the way across the line, add a comma before the word 'demonstrated.'" Ugh! There may be situations in which long e-mails are unavoidable—for example, when you are facing a major problem at work and can't openly talk about it on the phone or come into the office because you're on the job full-time—but resume reviews are generally not one of those situations. Many situations just require a personal meeting. One good rule for e-mails: Unless you're in an unusual situation—such as facing an immediate crisis at work and unable to speak on the phone—e-mail is best reserved for questions that can be answered in a few short sentences.

5. *When faced with frustration or uncertainty, assume the best of your coordinator.* If your coordinator doesn't reply to your call or e-mail as quickly as you like, assume the best in this situation. It may be because you wrote your e-mail on Monday night, and the coordinator was out visiting companies on Tuesday. Then that coordinator may be welcomed back to the office with a few dozen e-mails, 15-20 voice mails, and a long line of students filling up the whole morning of walk-in hours. It doesn't mean that you have been forgotten or that your coordinator doesn't care. If more than three days go by without hearing back—or sooner if you are facing a real emergency—follow up politely and professionally: "I'm sure you're very busy right now.... I just wanted to follow up to make sure you got my message and to see if there was anything else I should be doing right now. It would be great to hear from you when you get a moment. Thanks!"

   This is good practice for when similar situations arise with managers and co-workers on co-op. In either situation, this kind of message goes a long way in terms of getting a quick and professional response.

THE STEP-BY-STEP PROCESS

Preparation Phase

STEP 1 – *Become Aware of ALL Deadlines and Requirements As Soon As Possible.*

If you're a first-time student—and especially if you are a transfer student—meet with your coordinator as soon as possible to learn about your options regarding when to start co-op. *Don't assume that you can start your co-op or internship whenever you feel like it!* Co-ops and internships are not guaranteed for all students—if you blow off meeting with your coordinator, the consequences generally will be severe. If you miss deadlines, you may not be allowed to use the resources of the co-op department in finding a job. The student who does this will end up seeking his or her own job and risks getting a failing grade for co-op.

Step 2 – *Have a One-on-One Meeting with your Co-op Coordinator.*

This is a mandatory step in most programs. You will identify and discuss your short-term and long-term co-op and career objectives with your coordinator. Unless your coordinator has previously approved your resume for use, you will bring a hard copy of your resume to your co-op coordinator, so he or she can critique and edit it. Save these edits, and use them to revise your resume accordingly. Bring a hard copy of your revised resume to your coordinator along with the edits, so your resume can be proofread quickly and effectively. It may take a few rounds of corrections, but eventually your coordinator may ask for an electronic copy of the finalized resume to e-mail to employers.

Step 3 – *Review Co-op Job Descriptions and Rank Them.*

Once your finalized resume has been approved by your co-op coordinator, you generally will be allowed to start pursuing jobs. Make sure you understand your school's system—including how to work with computerized job listings.

Study the description and requirements and try to determine which jobs represent good learning experiences for you as well as being within your reach. If you're not sure, ask your coordinator. Many coordinators will require you to print out job descriptions that are of great interest to you and rank them—this will help you and your coordinator to determine if the job is a good fit and if you meet the qualifications. Keep the job descriptions in a folder.

Step 4 – *Meet with your Co-op Coordinator to Review your Job Rankings.*

The next step generally is to review your job rankings in an individual meeting with your co-op coordinator. Find out how early you can do this, and also if there is a deadline for making this happen. Bring your folder of printed job descriptions to your co-op coordinator.

Your co-op coordinator will review your rankings. In all probability, he or she will have additional suggestions and also may determine that a given job might be too much of a reach for you. Don't be discouraged—it's part of the process, and sometimes seeing your "reach" jobs can help your co-op coordinator suggest other jobs that are steps in the direction of your "reach" jobs. In many but not all programs, coordinators will limit how many jobs you can pursue simultaneously. Coordinators definitely do not want students to just fling dozens of resumes at employers—they want you to be more selective. This also means that you should really know each job description when you come in: Don't just look at a company name or job title and print out the job description without really thinking about how you match up with the job duties and requirements.

We can tell you that students vary *dramatically* in how they interact with a coordinator. We have had students interrupt a meeting with another student—or a phone call—by walking into our offices regardless and saying "Send this to Gillette for me for the such-and-such job." Such behavior says a great deal about a student's professionalism—it's never a good idea to treat a coordinator as if she or he is your servant or administrative assistant.

On the other hand, there have been any number of times when we have been absolutely wowed by a student. If someone comes in and is upbeat, professional, and polite, we're going to try that much harder to help them. There have been many occasions when such a student came in asking about a job that was already filled—and we were so impressed by them that we encouraged them to apply for other good jobs... and even recommended them to an employer! Basically, our assumption is that how you treat us will be a good predictor as to whether you will impress a prospective employer or not.

Step 5 – *Stay in Touch with your Coordinator Regularly throughout the Process.*

After your rankings and referrals have been completed, your resume will start going out to employers. Most coordinators e-mail resumes out at least once per week. At this point, there are many different possibilities. Some students get a few interviews out of their first batch of resumes to go out to employers; others don't get any—especially less experienced students.

If you get an interview, let your coordinator know—even if only by e-mail or voice mail. Ask your coordinator how often you should check in. At some point, your coordinator may be able to fill you in a little. You may be told that a company has not contacted any candidates yet, or you may learn that you are not one of the candidates chosen for an interview. In any case, your coordinator will suggest sooner or later that you select some more jobs and then come in again to discuss the new selections.

The worst thing you can do is to get discouraged by not getting interviews or by getting interviews and no offers. These developments don't always come easily! Some students start on time and do everything right—but then disappear completely after they send a batch of resumes and get no reply! Other students definitely intend to stay on top of things, but then they get distracted by mid-terms or other academic responsibilities. *You have to stay in touch*—even if it's just to say that you haven't received any calls and aren't sure what to do next.

Repeat the process of ranking jobs, getting referrals, and going on interviews as many times as you need to in order to get a job. In a job search, you never know if you're ten percent of the way to getting a job or whether you're incredibly close. But you always have to assume that you're really close and that with another push of effort it will happen for you.

Step 6 – *Responding to a Job Offer.*

Remember these key points:

- Money should not be the deciding factor in which job you accept for your co-op. Here's why. First of all money is NOT a motivator! That's been proven in many studies. Secondly, the purpose of this experience is to gain skills, prove yourself in your new career, and build your resume so you'll be attractive to an employer who is offering wages and benefits that better fit your needs. Your co-op job is your opportunity to learn and develop; choose it for how it will help you in the long run. You are not doing yourself any favors by taking the higher paying co-op job where you'll be bored or miserable. The small amount of extra money will not make up for a lousy co-op experience. And remember, you are only committing to the job for the length of the co-op, not for the rest of your life.

What WILL motivate you? A job with the following characteristics:

—you like the work itself

—you have opportunities for personal and professional growth

—you have opportunities for achievement and recognition

If you're choosing between a great learning experience that is an unpaid internship, or a mediocre experience that pays minimum wage, which will you choose? Depending on your field and other alternatives, you very well may be better off taking the unpaid position. On the other hand, there's nothing wrong with taking a great job that pays $14/hour over a comparable job that pays $10/hour.

For most students, our advice is to go after the best learning experience at this point in your career. That may mean getting out of your comfort zone and stretching yourself by accepting a job that you know will be difficult for you. If you focus on your career development now, the financial rewards will come sooner or later—and you'll be happier going to work every day in the meantime.

- If you are offered a job that is not your first choice, you can ask the employer for a short time to consider the offer—usually no more than three business days. Chapter 3 details how to put an offer on hold gracefully.

- Once you have accepted a job, meet with your coordinator to do an agreement form and any other paperwork. If you are an international student (here on F-1 and J-1 visas), it is absolutely critical that you receive work authorization BEFORE starting ANY job in the United States. After 9/11, the government has become incredibly strict about international students who are working without formal authorization. Deportation is becoming much more common. For all students, though, meeting with your coordinator is a good opportunity to discuss success factors for your co-op job, including how to avoid problems and get the best possible evaluation and reference.

- REMEMBER—do NOT accept a job unless you are prepared to honor your commitment no matter what else happens. It is completely unacceptable to renege on your acceptance if you get another offer later—even if the other offer is a much better offer for significantly more money. Students who don't honor their agreements risk getting a failing grade for co-op. If in doubt, ALWAYS talk to your coordinator before you accept a job offer.

- That said, be careful about being too fickle when it comes to job offers. Increasingly, we have had students waffling about accepting a perfectly good offer—merely because "I really hoped to have several offers to choose from." Applying for a job is not like applying to college, where you might apply to eight or ten schools and then have weeks or months to choose between three or four who accept you. You need to make a prompt decision in fairness to other candidates who might accept if you decline.

- Re-read Chapter 4 of this guidebook before starting your job, as this chapter has many good ideas about on-the-job success.

Developing Your Own Job

Chapter 1 goes over the guidelines for developing your own job, so you should re-read them if you have any questions about how the process works. Most importantly, remember that students developing their own jobs still need to be in regular contact with their coordinators. You can't go off and do a job without getting it approved beforehand by your coordinator.

Activity Phase. You are expected to complete the entire work period once you have accepted a job. In other words, you can't do a job for a few weeks and then decide you don't like it and just quit. There may be rare occurrences in which a student may be released from their commitment—for example, if the employer misled the student about the nature of the job, or if harassment is going on. HOWEVER, it is the student's responsibility to bring any problems or concerns to the attention of the co-op coordinator instead of just quitting as soon as a problem arises. Send an e-mail, make a call—anything—just let the co-op or internship coordinator know what's going on and get her or his advice before taking action.

Note that most co-ops and interns rarely get vacation days during their co-op work period: There may not be a "Spring Break" for students working winter and spring, for example. Likewise, students can't end a full-time co-op job in early December to get an extra long Christmas break: At best, your co-op will end a few days before Christmas. Likewise, students who work may end their co-op on a Friday and start classes by the following Wednesday!

You are expected to work on any days that the organization is open—meaning that some students will get a day off on Columbus Day, while others will not. Organizations have different policies regarding paying students for holidays, but most often employers simply pay you for whatever hours you work.

Contact your coordinator with any problems that arise on the job.

Reflection Phase. Most of the whys and wherefores regarding reflection can be reviewed in Chapter 5. To get credit for co-op or an internship, most programs require that you:

- complete your co-op job successfully
- turn in a relatively good performance evaluation form that has been prepared by your supervisor
- complete a reflection requirement or some other follow-up activity

APPENDIX B

Skills Identification Worksheet

Instructions: This worksheet is designed to help make you aware of how many skills you already have—probably more than you realize! Put a check mark in every box that reflects a skill that you have as well as WHERE you have demonstrated that skill. Then add up the total number of skills in each column and answer the questions on page 205.

COMMUNICATION	JOB EXPERIENCE?	SCHOOL EXPERIENCE?	OTHER EXPERIENCE?
Sales/Marketing			
Teaching/Training			
Explaining/Listening			
Public speaking			
Total # of Skills			

INTERPERSONAL	JOB EXPERIENCE?	SCHOOL EXPERIENCE?	OTHER EXPERIENCE?
Working in a team			
Advising			
Resolving conflict			
Negotiating			
Total # of Skills			

CREATIVE	JOB EXPERIENCE?	SCHOOL EXPERIENCE?	OTHER EXPERIENCE?
Designing/Inventing			
Developing solutions			
Out of box thinking			
Conceptualizing			
Total # of Skills			

LEADERSHIP	JOB EXPERIENCE?	SCHOOL EXPERIENCE?	OTHER EXPERIENCE?
Owning responsibility			
Setting/Reaching goals			
Delegating			
Managing/Supervising			
Total # of Skills			

QUANTITATIVE	JOB EXPERIENCE?	SCHOOL EXPERIENCE?	OTHER EXPERIENCE?
Bookkeeping			
Budgeting			
Calculating			
Collecting			
Estimating			
Recording			
Total # of Skills			

COMPUTER	JOB EXPERIENCE?	SCHOOL EXPERIENCE?	OTHER EXPERIENCE?
Data Entry			
MS Word			
MS Excel			
Databases			
Programming			
Web Design			
Total # of Skills			

SOFT SKILLS	JOB EXPERIENCE?	SCHOOL EXPERIENCE?	OTHER EXPERIENCE?
Ability to learn quickly			
Positive attitude			
Work ethic			
Dependability / Reliability			
Flexibility			
Good judgment			
Total # of Skills			

SKILLS IDENTIFICATION SUMMARY

SKILL	TOTAL NUMBER OF SKILLS
COMMUNICATION	
ORGANIZATION	
INTERPERSONAL	
CREATIVE	
LEADERSHIP	
QUANTITATIVE	
COMPUTER	
SOFT SKILLS	
Grand Total:	

QUESTIONS

1. What area would you most like to improve before starting co-op?
2. Name two ways in which you could improve some of these skills before starting your first co-op:

APPENDIX C

Writing Effective Cover Letters

If you're looking for a co-op job with the assistance of a co-op program, you may not need to write any cover letters. It may be enough to submit your resume through a co-op coordinator in order to obtain a job interview. Sooner or later, though, you will need to write an effective cover letter in response to a job listing. We have read thousands of cover letters over the years, and it never fails to amaze us how bad they can be—and how good they can be.

The most common mistake made by job applicants is to write a cover letter that really doesn't say anything useful... or not to write one at all. The bad cover letter will be extremely short, often saying no more than this:

> "In response to your listing (in The Boston Globe, on monster.com, etc.) I am writing to be considered for the position of Accounts Payable Coordinator (or Financial Analyst or Desktop Support Manager). As you can see on the enclosed resume, I have a degree in business. I am a hard-working individual who would be a good fit for a company in any number of different accounting and finance roles.
>
> "I am excited about the possibility of working for your organization. If you wish to arrange an interview, please contact me at...".

What's wrong with this approach? It breaks the cardinal rule of cover letters: You need to think of the cover letter as a bridge connecting your resume to a specific job description. For the letter to be an effective connection between your resume and the job, it needs to do more than explain you're interested in the job and to refer to your resume. An effective letter "sells" the employer on the idea of hiring you. It allows your personality to come through while also painting a picture of how you can help the employer meet his or her goals.

The Digital Age also has greatly changed the process of applying for jobs. In many ways, it is now too easy to apply for jobs. Years ago, submitting an application required reading through tons of job descriptions in the newspaper, then producing hard copies of a resume and cover letter on good paper, and then getting to a post office to mail the whole thing.

Today, job seekers can set up search agents on various job boards to automate the process of trawling through jobs, and it's possible to see many more than those that were listed in the local newspaper. Applying is much easier, too. It's all too easy to just copy and paste a cover letter into an e-mail or attach it as a step on an applicant tracking system.

We say "all too easy" because job seekers often take the easy way out: They write a simple cover letter that is so general that it can be modified quickly to send to another employer. While this has the advantages of being efficient and convenient, there is no question that this is a short-sighted perspective. As it's so easy to apply for a job these days, a recruiter or manager may receive 100-300 applications. Inevitably he or she sees quite a few cover letters that are completely generic. Fairly or unfairly, the reader of the quick and general cover letter will make several assumptions about the candidate. It's easy to conclude that the applicant is probably flinging his resume at dozens of jobs—maybe even sending out a hundred cover letters and resumes in the hopes of getting a small handful of interviews. The potential interviewer has to question whether the applicant has even given any serious consideration to whether he really wants the job in question. It's certainly hard to believe that the candidate really wants this specific job, and why would you ever want to hire someone who doesn't really want the job at hand—even if they have a terrific resume?

THE SEVEN DEADLY SINS OF COVER LETTERS

After leaving his job at Northeastern at the end of the 2009-2010 academic year, Scott became a consultant. One of his first jobs was to handle all of the recruiting steps from A to Z for a start-up company. He needed to fill four positions and ended up reading hundreds of cover letters as a result. He was amazed at how few of them were tailored to the jobs for which he was screening candidates. Most remarkably, he noticed several candidates who apparently had copied and pasted their generic cover letter from their application to another job. In other cases, there was no question that this is exactly what had happened, as the candidate even left in the name of the other company and its job title in their cover letter. Here is one of his e-mail responses to such a candidate:

> Joe,
>
> Your resume came to me through the LinkedIn job application process, but I believe that this represented some sort of error on your part. Your cover letter refers repeatedly to the fact that you are an ideal candidate for "Student Advisor." That may be the case, but you submitted your resume and cover letter to an organization seeking a Director of Marketing.
>
> I thought I should let you know, so you could be sure to submit your application materials to that position if you have not done so already.

The candidate responded to apologize for his mistake, adding "Geez, what a way to make a first impression!" He said that he would resubmit his application but never did, obviously recognizing that the damage had been done.

After reviewing hundreds of cover letters with a great variety of mistakes, Scott devised these Seven Deadly Sins of Cover Letters:

- *The first date analogy:* If you went on a first date and your date became furious with a waitress over some minor issue, would your assumption be that your date is just having a bad day? We doubt it. You'd probably run screaming in the opposite direction, figuring that an individual is probably on their best behavior during a first date… so why wait to see the *rest* of their behavior! With a cover letter, the equivalent is submitting a cover letter that is fraught with typos, spelling errors, and incomplete sentences.
- *The copy and paste nightmare:* This was described above with poor Joe, the "ideal candidate" for the Student Advisor job. Scott saw others make the identical mistake, most notably someone who submitted her resume for a job with a bra manufacturer, touting her expertise in marketing a physical product. That was a problem, given that Scott was trying to fill a marketing job that didn't involve a physical product at all!
- *It's all about me:* Some candidates go into extensive detail about why the job is great for them without describing why they are good for the job. *"This job would really build my understanding of marketing and give me exposure to working with MS-Access, a skill that I very much want to learn."* Sure, we want to hire people who are excited about the job, but we don't want to pay someone purely to fulfill their professional development needs.
- *Right person, wrong job:* In some cover letters, the candidate does a terrific job of touting their strengths, experiences, and competencies. The problem is when these qualities bear little or no relationship to the job at hand. Scott literally has seen someone talk about their skill, experience, and preference in working for a team for a job description that strongly emphasized that the individual would be working very independently. Not too smart a position to take.
- *The cliché fits like a glove:* If Scott had a dollar for every time someone referred to themselves as the "ideal candidate" for the job, he could fly from Massachusetts to Oregon to visit Tamara! Likewise, so many people provide a list of admirable qualities that they possess: hard-working, eager to learn, motivated, etc. While soft skills are important, the cover letter needs to talk about experiences and qualities that *differentiate* you from the many other candidates.
- *Instruction Manual needed:* When posting his first job description on LinkedIn and craigslist.com in July 2010, Scott noted that candidates should send a resume and cover letter. Many couldn't manage to follow that instruction, sending only a resume. Others did send a cover letter, but it was completely generic. So when he posted another job a few weeks later, he made sure to note "Be sure to submit a resume and a cover letter *that specifically describes why you would be a good match for this particular position."* The results? A higher percentage of people

wrote customized cover letters, but most did not. We guess it just seemed like too much work. Whatever the reason, Scott reached the conclusion that a) the candidate wasn't all that interested in the job, and/or b) couldn't follow a simple instruction. Those are not qualities that an employer is seeking.

- *Let's see what sticks:* Some cover letters definitely give the resume reviewer the impression of someone who is throwing a handful of spaghetti against the wall to see what sticks. In other words, they send a very abrupt cover letter that doesn't mention the company or the job at all. Maybe they don't even send a cover letter. Without even looking at the resume, the recruiter figures that there is an 80% chance that the candidate's experience does not remotely align with the job qualifications. It's very easy to ignore these applicants.

So a cover letter can result in ruling yourself out of a job almost immediately. On the other hand, a great cover letter will not get you a job—but it can get you in the door for an interview, even if you're not a perfect candidate on paper. At best, the cover letter can make the interview much easier by covering the fundamental, strategic reasons why you are a good match for the job. So let's take a look at what comprises an effective cover letter before walking through some specific examples.

ELEMENTS OF AN EFFECTIVE COVER LETTER

Yes, writing a cover letter is more time consuming than you might like because of the need to tailor each letter individually for each job that you're pursuing. The good news is that there are numerous elements that can be applied to all cover letters. While you can never reduce cover letter writing to a formula, you'll find that they become easier to write because the style issues are quite consistent. Here they are:

Start off flush-left with the date you are sending the letter. Create a flush-left heading two lines underneath the date that gives the appropriate name, job title, and address of the cover letter's recipient. Usually this would look something like this:

Nov. 15, 2010

Ms. Lenora Fritillary, Human Resources Manager
Schlobotnick Products
123 American Way
Roanoke, VA 33547

You then would begin your cover letter with "Dear Ms. Fritillary,".

At other times, you may not have a name and may have to use a job title:

Network Administrator
Byte Size Products
1200 Easy Street
Walla Walla, WA 94239

If the job is one that you are pursuing without any contact name, call up the main number of the organization and ask for the name of the person who is doing the hiring for the position. If you're told it is the human resources department, ask to speak to the office staff there and see if you can get the name of the individual responsible for hiring for the position. It can be very effective to tell the office staff person you just need the name because you are sending them something in the mail. It's always better to have a real live person listed as the cover letter's recipient unless the ad obviously indicates that the employer prefers to avoid a personal contact.

If you are simply unable to get the name of a person, use a greeting that omits a person's name. Some experts suggest using the company name in the greeting as in "Dear Oregon Detailers." Here are some additional suggestions for greetings: "Dear Hiring Manager," "Greetings," "Hello," "Good Day," "Good Morning," or "Good Afternoon." All of these greetings are effective however they are less formal and may not be considered appropriate in your area of the country or in your career field. On the west coast, the use of "To whom it may concern" is considered very formal and somewhat old fashioned and therefore not typically recommended. On the east coast, the greeting "To whom it may concern" is more acceptable. Check with your co-op coordinator for his or her recommendations. Briefly state how you learned of the job opportunity (if there is one) or simply express your interest in potential employment. Just as you always want to target a specific individual when you write your cover letter, you definitely want to write a cover letter with a specific job description in mind whenever possible. Otherwise, you face the challenge of writing a cover letter that implies that you're equally excited about any of a wide range of possible jobs. That's a much tougher sell.

This first paragraph should communicate your enthusiasm and convey energy with the language you use. Just flatly stating the name of the job and where you learned of it is boring to read and will not entice the receiver to read further. Demonstrating that you've done your research about the company and indicating how you fit into the organization can also contribute to the opening paragraph. Here are a few ways in which you might describe how you learned about the job at hand and will create interest in you as a candidate:

Example 1:

> I am writing to express my interest in the Accounts Payable Assistant position, which was advertised in last Sunday's Boston Globe and to offer my talents to your company. I understand XYZ Company is dedicated to manufacturing quality widgets. If you seek a dependable employee who has well developed accounting skills and who is willing to work hard to contribute to the success of your organization, than I am the person you want to hire.

Example 2:

> Speaking to my friend Patti O'Furnichoor, who works in accounting at your organization, I learned that your organization is looking for a GIS Technician,

> especially one who brings solid GIS software skills, a positive attitude, and who can be an effective liaison between departments. From my research, I have learned that XYZ Company provides services to planners in both government and industry, and I am confident that my recent GIS education coupled with my solid work history have prepared me to effectively fill this position.

Example 3:

> Having completed the majority of an intensive two-year drafting program, I believe I am well qualified to fill the CAD operator position advertised on craigslist.com. My strengths include solid AutoCAD skills and an extensive mechanical background; these skills should prove valuable to help your company manufacture cutting-edge material handling equipment.

If you have no choice but to submit a cover letter without knowing what jobs might be available, you are forced to write something more general.

Example 1:

> If your organization would benefit from a trained office assistant with exceptional interpersonal and organizational skills, please consider bringing me in for an interview. My recent course work in Office Administration has prepared me for a range of positions in your corporate office. I am confident that my well-developed facility with all Microsoft Office products as well as my familiarity with a variety of other office software has prepared me to contribute to your organization's success.

Example 2:

> After doing extensive research on the Internet, I know that your company has 600 employees at your Eugene office. With this in mind, I was wondering if there might be opportunities available in PC/LAN support, database administration, or web development. Through my recent computer information technology course work at Lane Community College, I have demonstrated that I learn computers quickly, and I have the flexibility to be effective in any number of IT functions.

In the body of your letter make several strong connections between your resume and the job description at hand whenever possible. At this point, you need to put your resume next to the job description and read the two side by side. Are there specific job requirements that you definitely have? Why would this employer hire you instead of someone else for this job? Why wouldn't this employer hire you? Making these assessments will help you figure out what your strategy should be—for the cover letter as well as for a potential interview. You need to come up with three or four concrete reasons as to why you are an excellent candidate to interview.

REMEMBER—the goal is to do more than justify why you thought it was okay to submit your resume! Some cover letters come off as a little defensive or apologetic in this way: "Your job description said that you were looking for someone with an accounting degree who also has strong knowledge of advanced functions in Excel. I hope to receive my accounting degree by the end of 2004. While my knowledge of Excel is not advanced, I am certainly very willing to learn…" If you're writing many sentences like these, you probably just aren't a good enough match to merit consideration.

As noted in the Seven Deadly Sins, another common mistake—both in cover letters and interviews—is to talk too much about why the job would be great for you, rather than why you would be great for the job! This ill-fated applicant might write something like this: "Working for your organization would give me a great opportunity to build my knowledge of hotel management. I would be very excited about enhancing my computer skills in this position as well…." Showing enthusiasm about the job is always a good idea, but not if you're only excited about what the job will do for you. You have to imagine yourself as the person reading a big pile of cover letters and resumes—your goal is to find the person who can best help in your organization in this role: not to find the candidate who most needs your help! As such, the hiring manager is going to pick out some number (probably somewhere between three and ten) of candidates who appear to be the most plausible for the job, based on the cover letter and resume.

There are no hard and fast rules about how many paragraphs you should have in your cover letter. Students who move right from high school to college may be fine with three paragraphs—the opening paragraph which we just described, a paragraph describing how you meet the employer's needs and then a closing paragraph describing your availability and asking for the interview.

On the other hand, students who are career changers and those of you who worked for a period of time between high school and college should consider four or more paragraphs—the opening paragraph, a paragraph that describes the skills you gained in school that meet the employer's needs, another paragraph or two that identifies what you bring from prior work experience, and then the closing paragraph where you ask for the interview.

One of the most effective ways to create a letter that sells you is to include testimonials from instructors and employers. Testimonials are a way to "prove" you have skills in a more believable way than just asserting it yourself. Anyone can say "I'm detail oriented" or "I'm a hard worker" but when someone says it about you, and that person can be contacted to verify it, then it is believable. Here are a couple of examples of testimonials:

Testimonial Example #1

> "My drafting instructor, Margaret Robertson, is one of my references and would tell you that my drawing assignments in her courses are always error free and turned in on time."

Testimonial Example #2

> "If you spoke to my supervisor at ASI, he would tell you that I am a very dedicated and conscientious worker who is willing to lend a hand at a moment's notice in order to get the job done on time."

Like everything else you include in your letter, testimonials must be true—you can't make them up or exaggerate. And, we also recommend no more than one testimonial per letter.

We'll consider some full-fledged job descriptions and resumes shortly. In the meantime, here are a few examples of ways in which a good cover letter might "sell" you by making connections between a resume and a job description:

Example 1:

> Your job description details the need for candidates to have a strong background in marketing as well as excellent communication skills. I received a grade of A- in my Introduction to Marketing class; in particular, I earned a top grade on an analysis of market segmentation in the automobile industry. Additionally, I have worked in numerous retail positions, honing my customer-service skills and refining my knowledge of merchandising. As for my communication skills, I have obtained considerable presentation experience in my business classes and have augmented this by taking an elective in Public Speaking—a course in which I performed extremely well.

Example 2:

> From your ad on monster.com, I know that you are seeking a highly trustworthy individual with a solid understanding of accounting principles and Excel for your Accounts Receivable Associate position. Both in the classroom and on the job, I have shown that I possess these qualities. My overall GPA at Laneone Star Community College is 3.0 —but my GPA in accounting classes is 3.6. Many of my classmates struggled mightily with Intermediate Accounting in particular, while I received an A- in this rigorous course. While in school I also became proficient with Excel: I am extremely confident and comfortable when creating formulas, charts, and graphs—even pivot tables.
>
> As far as being trustworthy, I would encourage you to contact any or all of my previous employers, whose contact information is available on the enclosed reference page. I am confident that each supervisor will indicate that I was entrusted with depositing considerable amounts of cash after closing for the night and locking up the place of business. Additionally, they will tell you I have developed effective working relationships with team members that resulted in increased sales.

Notice that the education-related information is grouped in one paragraph and work-related information is grouped in another paragraph. This is an effective way to create a smooth flow of information. Also notice the use of a testimonial to make the skills assertion more believable while adding team skills to the content. When discussing previous or current employment, it can also be effective to comment on how you contributed to helping the company make money, save money or save time, as these interests are common to most employers.

Close the cover letter by reaffirming your interest and noting how you prefer to be contacted.

This is fairly straightforward. And, one other note here: for graphic design students, drafting students, and others in career fields where it is best practice to bring examples of your work to an interview, the closing paragraph is the right place to indicate you'll bring a portfolio or course assignment samples to demonstrate your talent and skills.

Example:

> I would welcome the opportunity to interview for the bookkeeping position. To arrange an interview, please feel free to contact me via e-mail at m.brooke@yahoo.netcom or by phone at 617-555-0000. I look forward to hearing from you soon.

Revise, edit, and proofread your cover letter and resume with extreme care—then find some other competent people to double-check your work. We can hardly overstate the importance of this point. As noted earlier, remember that "first date analogy." When reading cover letters and resumes, managers assume that they are seeing the very best that you have to offer. Intentionally or unintentionally—fairly or unfairly—an employer will infer a great deal from your cover letter. The potential employer will develop perceptions regarding your communication skills, attention to detail, level of interest in the job, self-awareness, and selling skills based on the quality of your cover letter. Accordingly, your cover letter needs to be perfect grammatically and completely free of any typos. Scott knew of one employer who would simply circle typos with red pen and return the cover letters to applicants, noting that "you clearly lack the attention to detail that we seek in all potential recruits." Most employers won't be that harsh—they simply won't bring you in for an interview.

From his experience as a recruiting consultant in the summer of 2010, Scott saw some amazing typos and errors on cover letters and resumes. The worst was from an individual who was applying for an executive position. This is how he wrote the last sentence of his cover letter's first paragraph:

> "I recently sold my start-up in May and looking to work in a"

The cover letter then went on to the next paragraph and a new sentence. The rest of the cover letter had three blatant typos. Regardless, he not only submitted that cover letter online, he also submitted the identical message to three other people at the company in his zeal to get an interview. Obviously, he would've been better off putting more energy into proofreading his submission instead of sending in this error-fraught message repeatedly.

A COMPLETE EXAMPLE OF CREATING A COVER LETTER

Remember the resume of Meghan Brooke from the sample resumes at the end of Chapter 2 of this book? Because we always must try to match a specific individual to a specific job description, let's use her resume in writing a sample cover letter. As for the job description, let's say Meghan is applying for the following job:

GLAMTONE PUBLISHING

Glamtone Publishing — a leader in the publishing and distribution of medical textbooks and other health-related media products — seeks a PC/LAN Support Associate to assist our 400+ end users with computer-related issues ranging from simple MS-Office issues to Intranet updates and ultimately more technical troubleshooting issues, including assistance with our Windows NT network.

Qualifications: All applicants must have familiarity with MS-Office, strong communication skills, and the ability to learn to use new technology quickly. Exposure to the following technologies is a plus but not required: HTML, Symantec Ghost, Windows NT Server, and TCP/IP. Looking for a team player with a great attitude who can handle a high-pressure environment!

Compensation: This position pays $42,000-$48,000 depending on experience.

To submit a resume, please write to Louise Guardado at Glamtone Publishing, 145 West North Street, Southborough, MA 01234. No phone calls please.

It would appear that Meghan has some chance of getting this position: She believes she has all the required skills and at least one of the "plus" skills. She decides to write a cover letter.

The first step in writing this cover letter would be for Meghan to try to be honest with herself regarding her strengths and weaknesses for this position. Here is a quick checklist of some questions for a candidate to ask herself at this point:

1. *Why would this company hire me rather than someone else?* You want to focus on attributes that might make you stand out from other applicants if at all possible. Lots of students have familiarity with MS-Office, for example, so that might not be the best primary selling point. For Meghan, her best bet might be to concentrate on her high GPA as a reflection of the "ability to learn quickly"—not everyone can say that they have a high GPA. Her customer service experience at two jobs—including the ability to learn quickly at Kohl's—would be worth citing as well.

2. *Why WOULDN'T this employer hire me, and can I do anything about that?* When looking at job descriptions, you can't just consider what jobs are attractive to you—you have to ask yourself how you can make yourself most attractive to the employer. You have to be honest with yourself—for example, could Meghan be beaten out by someone who has more of the preferred skills listed in this job description? Absolutely. Can she do anything about that? Maybe. If she really wants this job and has the time to do some additional research, she could take a few days to try to ramp up on the skills she lacks. She certainly could learn enough about Symantec Ghost to be able to mention it briefly in the cover letter and discuss it intelligently in the interview. But isn't that

a lot of extra work in light of the fact that she doesn't even have an interview yet? Of course it is. You have to be judicious about how much time you are willing and able to invest in each cover letter. However, if Meghan is completely sure that she wants a PC/LAN Support job, then doing some extra research on software applications is bound to pay off sooner or later. Doing research on the company also can help—though that would definitely be the kind of extra effort that is more of a one-shot deal.

3. *Is there anything I can reasonably do that will help get me inside information about the job?* If you were referred to the job by someone, you definitely should pump that person for information about the organization. It's also worthwhile to go to LinkedIn to see if someone in your network of contacts has a connection to the hiring organization. With some luck and effort, you may be able to find someone who will be able to tell you some useful facts about the organization's culture, the supervisor and/or interviewer, and the job itself. What do people really like and dislike about this job, this department, this organization? If you know some of these things, you may able to tailor your cover letter accordingly. At the very least, you could check out the company website or maybe drop by the company and tell the receptionist that you intend to apply for a job—is there any general information available about the company. Taking any of these steps can reflect your willingness to go the extra mile as well as your sincere interest in the job.

Once you have made this kind of self-assessment and done what you can do regarding your "fatal flaws," you can write the cover letter itself. On the following page, you can see what Meghan's finished cover letter might look like.

Ms. Louise Guardado
Glamtone Publishing
145 West North Street
Southborough, MA 01234

Dear Ms. Guardado,

I am writing to express my interest in the PC/LAN Support Associate position, which your organization posted with the job listings made available on LinkedIn. From my research on Glamtone Publishing, I know that you are a young, fast-growing publisher with a reputation for producing highly professional medical materials. After talking to Louise Shawerma in your Human Resources Department, I am confident I can perform this job effectively and would especially enjoy working in Glamtone's fast-paced environment.

As you can see on the enclosed resume, I have numerous skills and qualities that make me a great fit for this position. Despite challenging myself with a double concentration in MIS and Marketing, I have managed to maintain a 3.6 GPA at Northeastern University. I believe that my excellent academic record reflects my ability to learn quickly—a critical skill for any new hire in a technology-oriented position. In my previous job experience, I have an outstanding record of providing patient and effective customer service. This experience should prove invaluable when providing PC support to Glamtone's end users.

While I have not had the opportunity to work with Symantec Ghost or with Local Area Networks, I have done extensive reading on these areas since reviewing your job description. As a result, I have a good but basic sense of how to re-image a computer as well as an understanding of networking fundamentals.

I would be delighted to come in for an interview at your earliest convenience. Please feel free to contact me via e-mail or by phone to arrange an interview. For your convenience, I am also enclosing my references—I urge you to contact them to verify anything on my resume or to ask any questions about my work and academic history. I look forward to hearing from you soon.

Sincerely,

Meghan Brooke
617.555.0000
m.brooke@yahoo.com

WRITING A COVER LETTER AS A CO-OP STUDENT OR INTERN

In some instances, students also may write cover letters when attempting to find a co-op job—most often with a co-op employer who is not currently involved with a co-op program. When writing this kind of cover letter, you will need to provide a brief explanation of what you are seeking as well as why hiring a co-op student would be a good move for the employer.

With this in mind, let's revise the previous letter. In this case, let's assume that Meghan is a co-op student seeking an IT position for six months. We also will use this example to show how to write a more general cover letter. As noted earlier, you also want to write the cover letter with a specific job description in mind. If that is not possible, however, this might be a good approach. When writing a letter to investigate the possibility of a co-op position, always research the company and find a person to send your letter to, just as you would for regular employment.

Look at the following page to see this co-op job search cover letter in its entirety.

March 24, 2011

Sylvia Smith
Human Resources Manager, Glamtone Publishing
145 West North Street
Southborough, MA 01234

Dear Ms. Smith,

As a current student at Northeastern University, I am writing to express my interest in a computer-related co-op position (like an internship) with your company. In my academic program, I developed a variety of computer skills that would be put to good use in your organization. I am willing to consider any position that involves computers—some examples would include PC/LAN support, database design/development maintenance, Web page design and maintenance, QA testing, or positions that use computers to help other functional areas such as marketing and finance.

At Northeastern, co-op students are expected to attend classes full-time for the first half of the calendar year and then work full-time during the next six full months. I am available to begin working for you Monday, July 5 and would continue through December. As a co-op student, I will be earning academic credit, which means I have an additional reason to perform to the best of my abilities.

From your perspective as an employer, there are many benefits to hiring a co-op student. In these economically uncertain times, co-op student workers represent a relatively short-term commitment. Co-ops are cost-effective and benefit-free. Co-op students are trying to build great resumes and references for future employment, so they are highly motivated workers as well. Lastly, co-op hires are a good way to keep a recruiting pipeline active in anticipation of brighter economic times in the future.

As you can see on the enclosed resume, I have numerous skills and qualities that make me a great fit for a computer-related position. Despite challenging myself with a double concentration in MIS and Marketing, I have managed to maintain a 3.6 GPA at Northeastern University. I believe that my excellent academic record reflects my ability to learn quickly—a critical soft skill for any new hire in a technology-oriented position. In my previous job experience, I have an outstanding record of providing patient and effective customer service. This experience would prove invaluable if your Network Administrator needs assistance in providing PC support to Glamtone's end users.

I would be delighted to come in for an interview at your earliest convenience. From my research on Glamtone Publishing, I know that you are a young, fast-growing publisher with a reputation for producing highly professional medical materials. After talking to Louise Shawerma in your Human Resources Department, I would say that I especially would enjoy working in the fast-paced environment at Glamtone.

Please feel free to contact me via e-mail or by phone to arrange an interview. For your convenience, I am also enclosing my references—I urge you to contact them to verify anything on my resume or to ask any questions about my work and academic history. I look forward to hearing from you soon.

Sincerely,

Meghan Brooke

617.555.0000
m.brooke@yahoo.com

FINAL THOUGHTS ON WRITING A COVER LETTER

You may never have to write a cover letter during your undergraduate career, but sooner or later you will have to know how to write one effectively. Even when you learn about job opportunities through friends, family, fellow students, or former employers, you frequently will be asked to write a cover letter when submitting your resume.

Given that cover letters are time consuming, there is nothing inherently wrong with having a few cover letters that you re-use to some degree—certain elements might remain the same across quite a few letters. Scott has created cover letters geared toward jobs in recruiting, training, writing, career services, and consulting that he uses as a foundation before modifying to meet the specifics of a given position. However, as alluded to earlier in this section, don't EVER send out a cover letter without making sure that you have changed ANY customized references! Imagine how well it would go over if Meghan took her Glamtone cover letter and reworked it for another position—but accidentally left in the reference to Glamtone in the final paragraph!! All of a sudden, the first impression that the other employer has of Meghan is of someone who lacks attention to detail and who may indeed be flinging dozens of cover letters at jobs with only slight modifications.

Because organizations listing jobs may get tons of replies—especially in a tough economy—a little persistence can't hurt. If you hear nothing from an employer within a few weeks, you might try writing a brief, upbeat note to reaffirm your interest—particularly if you think the job is a great fit.

Several years ago, Scott replied to a *Boston Globe* ad listing a position that appeared to be an unusually good match for him at that time. Two weeks passed, and he heard nothing. Scott wrote a follow-up letter and politely acknowledged that he was sure that the company was very busy—particularly given that they were a small company listing a position emphasizing their need for a medical writer/project manager. In the letter, he reaffirmed his interest in the position and briefly recapitulated why he was a great match. Then Scott just said the honest truth— he was only a few weeks away from needing to make a commitment regarding a teaching position that was available to him. If the position was filled or if they were uninterested, he understood completely. If not, he urged them to arrange an interview as soon as possible.

Within three days of mailing the letter, Scott received a call to arrange the interview. Three interviews later, he got the offer and accepted it. Scott often wondered if that would have happened if he had simply waited however long it might have taken for them to acknowledge his first attempt. After the second letter, they definitely knew that he was seriously interested. We don't know any organization that wants to hire someone who only wants the job a little!

APPENDIX D

OTHER TYPICAL INTERVIEW QUESTIONS

by Linnea Basu

1. Why did you decide to attend *[name of college]?*

2. How did you decide to major in [*name of major]?*

3. What's your favorite class? Least favorite?

4. Why do you want this job? Why do you want to work for our organization?

5. What sets you apart from other candidates?

6. Rate your computer skills on a scale of 1-10.

7. Tell me about a time you had to meet a specific deadline and how you met that deadline.

8. How do you organize your time?

9. How would your friends describe you?

10. How would your boss or professors describe you?

11. What kind of a person do you like to work for?

12. Give me an example of a task or project you had to do which required attention to detail.

13. What motivates you to work hard?

14. What's your greatest accomplishment?

15. Tell me about a time when you had to work with a difficult team or group member and how you resolved the situation.

16. What has been your most rewarding college experience?

17. What has been the most difficult part of college life?

18. What's your dream job?

19. Give me an example of a time when you had to learn a skill or information very quickly and how you learned that skill.

20. If you could change one thing about yourself, what would it be?

21. If you could have dinner with any famous person, dead or alive, who would it be and why? What would you ask them?

APPENDIX E

Bridging Exercise: Practice Connecting your Qualifications to a Specific Job

Many individuals are strong job candidates, but they are hurt by failing to tailor their answers to the job for which they are applying. When they get asked general questions such as "Tell me about yourself," they always give the same generic response. This exercise attempts to counter that tendency, forcing individuals to see how different their answers might be to open-ended questions in one interview versus another.

This is useful as a prep class assignment or for students who want extra practice in connecting their qualifications to a specific job description. For instructors, Tamara and Scott recommend running through several resume/job description combinations in front of the class, so students can begin to see how different responses can be when job candidates are devising customized, strategic answers. For example, it can be a great exercise to take a marketing student's resume and first show how to connect it to a market research job and then demonstrate how different the result will be if we attempt to marry that candidate's background to, say, a sales job. In the first case, we might end up with a strategic answer that emphasizes analytical skills and data management, while the second job would require the candidate to change gears and focus more on assertiveness, customer focus, and the ability to stay positive.

If you really absorb the concepts here, you will develop a deeper understanding of how to adjust your personal marketing message for every cover letter or interview. This is a crucial and underrated skill.

DIRECTIONS FOR BRIDGING EXERCISE

Step 1 – Print out a copy of your resume.

Step 2 - From your school's job listings—or from any other source of job descriptions—print out a job description that interests you. Try to pick out a job that lists many qualifications, including some soft skills (e.g., ability to multitask).

Step 3 - Referring to your resume to some degree, write out a detailed answer to the question "TELL ME ABOUT YOURSELF." Your answer should include the three or four top reasons why YOU are good match for THIS job description, making sure to emphasize your most important reason. One good trick that will help you ensure that you have a *strategic* answer to "tell me about yourself" is to start off your answer by saying "I'm excited to be here at [*name of company*] today because I know you're looking for someone who…" Then proceed to list three or four specific soft skills, technical skills, job experiences, or classroom credentials that make you a great candidate for the job at hand. Refer to chapter 3 of the guidebook if you need assistance in determining what an EXCELLENT answer to this question would be.

Step 4 - Write out TWO specific stories about yourself that support two different strategic elements that you presented in your answer to "Tell Me About Yourself." For example, if you touted your ability to work in a fast-paced environment as one trait that makes you a good fit for the job, describe a specific story that shows you at your best in demonstrating that quality. Or, if you answered your "Tell Me About Yourself" question by highlighting your customer-service skills, your organizational skills, and your ability to learn quickly, you would need to come up with two specific stories that show two of those skills "in action." The stories could come from a job, a specific academic situation, or another part of your life such as an extracurricular or volunteer experience.

Choose two stories in which you were responsible, or a least had a role, in the positive outcome or resolution of the situation. Write the stories with enough details to be vivid and believable. Usually, they start out with a specific situation, challenge, problem, or conflict. Walk through the situation explaining step-by-step what happened, especially what you said or did, and ending with your contribution to the positive outcome. Do that with two different elements of your "Tell me about yourself" answer. Be sure to label your story to indicate which trait or skill you're intending to showcase with that story.

EXAMPLE OF A GOOD STORY

Here's a story Scott might use to back up his claim that he's a self-starter:

Story #1 – Self-Starter

"One summer I was doing temp jobs in offices, and I ended up in a state government agency, covering for an employee who was on a two-week vacation. Within a couple of days, I was surprised to find that I could complete her whole day's worth of work in under two hours.

"My co-workers encouraged me to take it easy—no one seemed to work hard in that office, goofing off was a part of the culture. For me, though, the day dragged if I wasn't doing much, and I wanted to feel like I was earning my pay. I started asking people if they had work for me to do.

"Soon the word got around: 'Hey, there's a guy on the fifth floor who will do your work for you! And he does it really well, too!' People from as far as three floors

> away brought me tons of work with spreadsheets and reports. It was maybe a little bit of a ridiculous situation from an organizational standpoint, but the bottom line was that I learned a great deal about a variety of jobs; I kept busy and had a much better time. By the end of my two weeks, my supervisor urged me to take the civil service exam so he could keep me there full time. I declined—not my kind of work culture—but I was flattered."

The great thing about using stories like this is as follows: You use a story to prove that you have one quality—in this case, being a self-starter—but you end up proving that you have many other good qualities. In this example, Scott could use this story to show that he is efficient, a quick learner, and a strong enough person to not be influenced by unmotivated co-workers. See Appendix F, Behavioral Based Interviewing for help with writing your stories and good story examples.

Step 5 - Assemble your finalized resume, the job description that you picked for this exercise, your typed answer to "tell me about yourself," and your two typed stories—each of which should be labeled to indicate what soft skill, trait, or quality that you're trying to demonstrate through each story. If your instructor wants you to do this as an assignment, turn it in per her or his instructions. If not, hang on to the final product and consider trying to repeat the exercise with a very different job description that is of interest to you.

APPENDIX F

Behavioral-Based Interviewing

In Chapter 3, we touched on Behavioral-Based Interviewing (BBI). For a number of years both of us have taught BBI to our preparation classes and have come to believe that interviewees should devote much more time to preparing BBI stories for interviews. The good news is that this has come to be the favorite part of the class. Putting some energy into planning what stories you will use and writing them out is incredibly valuable. Once you have a handful of BBI stories, believe me, you'll find opportunities to work them into ANY type of interview!

Behavioral-based interviewing is an increasingly common interviewing method. Many large companies use it, including Microsoft and many consulting firms. Just recently, Johnson & Johnson had a new interviewer come to Scott's campus and ask students for stories as a major component of the interview—stories about making the transition from high school to college; stories about previous jobs, and so forth. While some interviewers almost exclusively use this approach, others may ask one or two BBI questions as part of an otherwise conventional interview. Although all interview methods are far from perfect in predicting future job performance, behavioral-based interviews generally are considered the most valid tool available. Why would that be? Probably because BBI questions require that you use true stories instead of scripted answers that sound good. Unless you're a pathological liar, it's quite difficult to make up a vivid, believable story with considerable detail.

But what if your interviews prove to be entirely conventional? Well, we've come to believe that ALL interview candidates should be prepared for BBI questions. Even when interviewers use the conventional approach to questioning, it's always helpful to be able to tell a couple of specific and vivid stories. After all, anyone can start off an interview by touting their excellent interpersonal skills or ability to juggle multiple tasks: But just saying that is not proving that you really have those traits. You need to show what you really mean, and it needs to be a true story for it to be credible and believable. In any interview, your strategy is your foundation, and BBI stories are a great way to build on that foundation.

Characteristics of Behavioral-Based Interview Questions

BBI questions are pretty easy to spot. The interviewer will often start questions by saying "Tell me about a time when….," before going on to ask you about a specific instance in which you demonstrated one of any number of qualities: customer service skills; ability to multitask; organizational skills; ability to be a good team player; willingness to go the extra mile; ability to overcome adversity; passion for technology; etc. Here are some examples of BBI questions:

- Tell me about a specific time when you encountered adversity working in a group. Describe the group's goals, the nature of the adversity, what your role was in the group, and how the situation turned out.
- What would you say has been the greatest achievement of your life thus far? Walk me through how you accomplished it.
- Please give me an example of a time when you failed at something and how you handled that.
- Tell me about a time when you went above and beyond expectations in a school or work situation.
- Describe a specific situation in which you took an unpopular stand.

From these questions, you might imagine that the interviewee ends up doing most of the talking in these interviews. If so, you would be correct. After setting the stage with the question, the interviewer probably will listen and take notes, occasionally stepping in with a clarifying question.

When faced with a behavioral-based interview, most candidates find it difficult to come up with a great and relevant story off the top of their heads. Sometimes the first answer that comes to mind may not be the best one to illustrate a given quality. You need to think in advance about the situations that truly show you at your very best.

Answering Behavioral-Based Interviewing Questions

Many career professionals favor an approach called STAR (Situation, Task, Actions, Results) in answering these questions. While this is a memorable acronym, we think that it perhaps oversimplifies the approach to answering these questions. With that in mind, here are the principles:

1. *Think STORY, not EXAMPLE.* What's the difference between a story and an example? When asked to give an example, many interviewees fall into the trap of responding too generally: "When I worked at Papa Gino's, we always had to juggle multiple tasks. We usually had many tables to handle at once, and more often than not we had a packed restaurant...."

   Right away, this answer is off to a bad start. If you find yourself saying things like "always" or "usually" or similar words, you're being much too general. If you're asked a BBI question in an interview, and you respond with a general overview of a job or classroom experience, the interviewer often will follow up by saying, "Okay, but can you tell me about a specific time when you [had to handle conflict, overcome adversity in a team, etc.]?" Often the interviewer will keep pushing until you do.

Here are some good questions to ask yourself when attempting to come up with the best possible stories:

- What was my very best day in that job? What was the hardest day or week?
- What was my most challenging task or customer or problem I had to overcome? What was the biggest crisis I faced?

Unlike an example, a story starts at one moment in time—maybe it's Tuesday, July 19 at about 10:30 a.m. Think in terms of a good book or movie. Usually any good story starts a moment of conflict or crisis or challenge. Sure, we may get a very quick overview, but make sure to get to that moment of truth very soon. Next, remember that you are the protagonist. Therefore, we are most interested in YOUR actions, thoughts, and emotions—be sure to convey them. Lastly, many a good story has been spoiled by a dissatisfying end. Be sure to RESOLVE the conflict by briefly describing the outcome, impact, or aftermath of the story.

2. *When you use a really good story to prove you have one particular soft skill, you will end up proving that you have three or four other soft skills.* BBI stories are usually rich in material. You usually have to convey so much detail to prove that you have a given quality that you end up showcasing other positive traits as well. Therefore, it's always great to use BBI stories—even when you're not in a BBI interview.

   Here's a terrific example of this phenomenon. Scott did a practice interview many years ago with one student, and used a mostly conventional style. Her interview was absolutely mediocre: She wasn't providing any sense of what made her unique or why she might be a good potential employee. So in an attempt to see if he could pull more out of her, Scott asked her a BBI question: "What, specifically, would you say has been the greatest achievement of your life?"

   She thought about it for several seconds, and then she blew him away with her reply. "When I was very young, there were some sudden deaths in my immediate family. As a result, I grew up feeling very terrified of death and of any possible medical emergency. But one day when I was in high school, I just got fed up with being that way. I decided to get CPR training, and then I joined a Rescue Squad in my hometown. Now I know that if anything were to happen to a loved one, I wouldn't be powerless to help."

   Wow! All of a sudden this woman's many admirable qualities were evident. Here was someone who had self-awareness and who had the courage to tackle a weakness head-on. Here was someone who certainly was able and willing to learn and who had training in handling high-pressure situations. More than anything, though, she became a multidimensional, sympathetic human by telling this very specific and revealing story. At the end of the interview, Scott told her that he wanted her to push that story to the beginning of her interview—using it as soon as she was given any open-ended question, such as "Tell me about yourself" or "What are your strengths?" He also reminded her that she could tap into these experiences for any number of other BBI or "specific example" types of questions. It didn't take long for her to have a dynamic interview.

3. *Make sure to walk us through the story step-by-step.* After you've identified a pretty specific day or week or job task, then walk us through it step-by-step:

   A. Give us a quick, brief overview of the job or situation. Ideally, use the overview to help us understand what is really "at stake" in the story.

   B. Pick a specific moment in time when something caused a problem or conflict.

   C. Walk us through the situation step-by-step: What did you do in response? What were you thinking as you dealt with it? What were you feeling? What was the final outcome?

   That's a good rule of thumb if you feel like your stories lack depth or meat: Dig deeper into your actions, thoughts, and feelings to help us understand HOW you got through this situation. Some interviewers will pull your thoughts and feelings and specific actions out of you, but it's much easier if you can just lay them out without being asked.

4. *Focus on YOUR role in the situation.* There's an old cliché that "There is no 'I' in TEAM." Well, that's not true in behavioral-based interviewing. In fact, there are FOUR "I"s in BEHAVIORAL-BASED INTERVIEWING! When you're telling a story about a work or school team, make sure to describe YOUR individual role on the team—not just the team as a collective. There are many ways to contribute to a team: describe what KIND of team player you are by spelling out roles in a team situation.

5. *Don't "use up" a job in just one story!* Another problem with the more general stories is that you can use up a job in just one story… and you may need more stories later in the interview. If it's a job you've done well, there should be MANY stories from various days, customers, tasks, projects, and so forth. Odds are that these stories can be used to highlight many, many transferable skills.

6. *Be sure to pick a high-stakes story if you have one.* Stories about doing something simple to turn around a slightly disgruntled customer or solving a fairly minor problem at work or school aren't terrible, but they do make one wonder if this is really the individual's best achievement. If it isn't, the person made an error in judgment in picking that story. If

it is, maybe the person just isn't all that impressive. Start off by thinking about some of the proudest moments in your life—overcoming a major weakness or fear or failure, or maybe just something where you blew away people's expectations in a situation. Dig deep and give this some thought in coming up with more great stories.

A few years ago Microsoft asked this question during interviews: "Tell me about a specific time when you failed at something and how you responded to that failure." A couple of students talked about getting a D or F on a first paper and then responding by working harder and getting, say, a C+ in the course. That's not too inspiring. Maybe it was the best story they had, but we have to think that with more planning they could have come up with something that would be more impressive. In contrast, another candidate talked about failing accounting despite going to office hours, getting tutoring, working harder, and so on. The interviewers were impressed because he was able to convey his emotions about all of this—what stood out was how much this failure upset him. They were even more impressed when he talked about taking his accounting textbook to work every day the following summer so he could study during breaks. He wrapped up by telling them that he finally retook the class and got a B+. That was a great story: He showed that he DID care about his grades, and he also showed the soft skills of persistence, initiative, and overcoming adversity. By the way, this student just graduated and has accepted a job at Microsoft.

7. *Vivid details make the stories come alive.* One good mnemonic device is ABC, as it helps remind you to inject *affective, behavioral, and cognitive* elements—emotions, actions, and thoughts—into your stories. Just like in a good novel, the interviewer wants to get inside your head—especially when you get to that "moment of truth" in your story. For every major plot twist in your story, try telling what was going through your mind at those critical moments. Quantitative details also make the story come alive. In other words, explain how much, how often, or percent to help bring the story to life.

8. *Be careful about too little information—or too much!* When there was a problem with story length, often the stories were too short. If it's something you can tell in three or four sentences and less than 30 seconds, the story probably lacks depth. Microsoft talks about interviewees failing to "drill down into the details."

   One analogy that may be helpful is to think of your stories the way a novelist or film director would think of them. There are times in movies or novels where we skip over the action quickly... and there are times when we have that extreme close-up, that tight focus when we really see and hear everything that the protagonist is doing. Give us a quick overview, but be sure to have that extreme close-up too.

   Conversely, some stories are too long. Avoid any information that is not "need to know." Some details may be entertaining, but if they aren't really showcasing your skills or traits, they aren't helping you. Even in BBI, a good story can be told in about 60 seconds, maybe 90 at most... and remember that you don't want to speak too fast in an interview! If you're not sure if you've gone on too long, try timing yourself while speaking at a reasonable pace.

9. *Life lesson stories also can work.* In Scott's days in fiction-writing workshops, he learned that there are rules... but sometimes they can be broken. This came home to him again just this semester. As you'll see with one of the following stories, it is indeed possible to have a story in which you learned something not so much from something you did but from something that happened to you. You have to be careful with this kind of story, as you don't want to come off as a passive person as opposed to a change agent in life. But if you can frame the life lesson in a way that shows how that experience helped you learn, grow, and change as an individual, it CAN work!

10. *What have you done for me lately?* When one prominent interviewer came to Scott's class he reported afterwards that his BBI questions yielded some good answers... but that some candidates only told stories from a long time ago. For those of you with a work history, choose stories from your most recent work experiences, especially those that show that you have qualities that are important for success in your new career. It is also good to have a story or two that reflect accomplishments in the last year or two. If you don't believe that you have any great successes from your college years, you need to think harder... or to start working toward the kind of performances in the classroom or in jobs that will result in some great success stories!

Your prior work experience should be a rich source of stories for you even it your jobs were in fast food, store clerking or in a completely different field from what you are now studying to become. In fact, past behavior is considered a good indicator of future behavior so stories about how your good behavior on any job will be seriously considered by an interviewer. The key is to pick stories from previous jobs that demonstrate traits, skills and qualities that fit your new career.

Tamara had a student not long ago who worked as a pretzel maker while studying to become an engineering technician. During an interview she was asked "What did she find interesting or challenging about her last job?" Now many of us might have said that there isn't anything very challenging about making hundreds of pretzels by hand however this is what she told them: "It can be rather repetitive making pretzels over and over so what I do to make it fun and interesting is to see if I can make each pretzel as perfect as I can in the shortest time. I create a game of making identical pretzels and try to beat the number I do each shift." The two engineers who interviewed her told Tamara they where wowed by this answer because engineering is a very exacting field that requires lots of repetition as well as extreme accuracy, two qualities beautifully exemplified in her answer. The engineers felt that this particular answer, coupled with her other solid skills, tipped the interview in this student's favor and she was hired within the week.

So even if you don't have high stakes stories, find out about the characteristics of successful entry level professionals in the job for which you are applying and then carefully choose stories from recent experiences that demonstrate you have what it takes to do that job.

11. *Link your story to the job for which you are interviewing.* At the end of your story make the connection between your experience and issues employers care about such as increasing profit, improving productivity, solving problems or improved morale. This is actually a lot easier than it may seem. Make a statement at the end of your story like this one:

> "This is an example from my past that shows that I am a person who ___ (looks for ways to improve, finds ways to make things more efficient, contributes to team effort, can find creative solutions, etc)."
>
> Tamara's pretzel making student might have said at the end of her story "As you can see I am very good at doing repetitive tasks in a way that keeps me interested in the job while also improving my skill and speed. I bring these qualities to my work with your company. "

Here's an assignment that we recommend: Write up three stories that show you at your best. Then, for each story, write up at least three soft skills or marketable qualities that each story could be used to illustrate.

Each story should incorporate the following steps: What challenge or problem or situation did you face? What did you think, say, and do in addressing that problem, step-by-step? What were the positive outcomes and results of your actions?

To give you some excellent examples of how to do this, here are some of the best stories that students submitted in response to the bridging assignment in Appendix E. Each story has been taken a step further by mentioning three additional soft skills that the story could be used to show.

GREAT STORIES – STUDENT EXAMPLES

1. Ali Ciccariello wrote up this story to prove that she has analytical and multitasking skills:

> "During the time I worked at the Fruit Center Marketplace, I was eventually promoted to a managerial position in the front-end department. Being in a supervising position was a great experience for me, allowing me to recognize store priorities and multitask different problems. I consider myself to be very analytical, so when I came across a particular store problem I enjoyed finding solutions to it.
>
> "I can remember one particular Saturday when everything in the store seemed to be going wrong. The Fruit Center had just received new cash registers, and my fellow bosses and I were still trying to figure out all the new "kinks" in the

system. The registers had been working normally all day, until suddenly one register froze and wouldn't turn on. Believe it or not, it is a huge problem when even one register stops working on a high-volume day.

"Immediately, I tried to prioritize the problems I had to deal with. I knew customer satisfaction was the main goal of the Fruit Center, so I calmly and politely explained to the customers in that particular line what was occurring and suggested moving to another line for business. Because I had clearly explained the situation to the customers and apologized for it, they were willing to move to another line without incident. I then dealt with the cash register malfunction. I called the computer company that serviced the register, and their support staff walked me through the steps necessary to deal with the register problem. Although it was a stressful situation, I was able to work well under pressure and still manage to prioritize what needed to be done."

~ Alexandra Ciccariello, Northeastern University Class of 2008

Did Ali prove that she had strong multitasking and analytical skills? Absolutely! But there are several other skills that are displayed here: customer-service skills; problem-solving skills; ability to stay calm under pressure; and ability to prioritize. That's a pretty amazing assortment of skills!

The power of this story is that it pinpoints the focus on one specific day while still giving a little background for that day. The more you tighten your focus on "one moment in time," the more likely you are to make the situation really come alive. When that happens, the interviewer can see all kinds of great qualities that you have—even ones that you're not trying to display!

The other bonus from a rich story is that Ali not only has a powerful story up her sleeve; she also has a story that can be used to showcase different qualities in different interviews. Our students find that once they have done the heavy lifting of writing the story, they manage to find opportunities to work it into conventional interviews—not just BBIs.

2. For her job description, Aimee Stupak needed to show dedication:

"Last summer, I took a new position in the West Hartford Building Department as a temporary Office Assistant. I was eager to experience a new position with more responsibility. I quickly learned to dress in more businesslike attire and to wake up two hours earlier than I used to for my previous job. I learned to appreciate the office setting very quickly as well, and given the fact that initiative is the number one thing my boss was looking for, I excelled immediately.

"From the first day, I took the initiative to understand the filing system and to help organize the files in a new way, so as to simplify the process of finding files for anyone in the office who needed to. I set up new labels for the cabinets and was instantly shown appreciation from the secretaries that I was working for.

"After only a week, the head supervisor and main building inspector asked me if I'd be interested in attempting a job they had been trying to find someone to do for a while. He brought me in to "the Vault" which is full of barrels that contain building plans for single-family homes, stores, and apartment complexes all over the Town of West Hartford. Unfortunately, the barrels were dated back so far that "the Vault" was becoming overfilled and impossible to work with. No one, however, was willing to do the "dirty work." My supervisor explained that I would need to search through each barrel, and weed out only the plans that applied to single-family homes. After collecting these plans, he asked me to send them back to the home to which they applied.

"I started the job immediately, completing my daily responsibilities and entering "the Vault" at any point in the day that there was some downtime. I made a lot of progress and ended up cleaning out a very large portion of the space. When my last day came at the job because of the upcoming semester, I was thanked by all and told that my motivation and intense dedication to the job would be greatly missed."

~ Aimee Stupak, Northeastern University Class of 2008

This story shows dedication but many other qualities as well: willingness to do whatever asked without complaint; positive attitude; persistence; and organizational skills. Scott is fond of this story because it's a good reminder that most students have had high-school jobs that included a good amount of "gruntwork." As a result, many students believe that they don't have interesting experiences to use for a BBI, as they haven't done anything "important" enough. Yet a story about taking on the task that nobody else wanted is a great way to show off some very attractive qualities in an entry-level professional.

3. Here's a story that Nat Stevens used in an attempt to prove that he has strong organizational skills:

"As the day lagged on at TextHELP Systems, I thought about how it was already 3:30 p.m., and that I only had an hour and a half left to finish up the logs. Just then the phone rang. I picked it up to hear the lovely voice of one of our sales reps on the west coast. She started off by saying, 'You're going to hate me,' so I knew that something challenging was coming. She added, 'I need you to get a mailing out to about five counties in Texas, by tonight. I didn't realize it until now.' I thought to myself about how difficult this would be, but I told her it wouldn't be a problem and I would gladly get it done.

"I started my work. First, I had to pull the names of all the directors from these counties that she wanted me to mail information to. The final list came to about 441 people. Next I had to print all the labels. In the meantime, I used two copy machines to make sure the first page of two of the press releases for the mailing were on letterhead. Then I had to make sure that the following pages were correlated appropriately. Finally, I had to fill each envelope, stamp them, and label them. Needless to say, although I had intended to leave at 5:00 pm, I did not step out of the office until 8:00 pm. The sense of accomplishment for completing the job provided me with much more satisfaction than I had originally anticipated."

~ Nat Stevens, Northeastern University Class of 2008

Here Nat attempts to prove that he has strong organizational skills, and he succeeds. However, a good story always ends up showing much more than one skill or quality! Nat could use this story to show many other valued traits: positive attitude, dedication, willingness to go above and beyond... maybe even customer-service skills if we think of the salesperson as an internal customer.

4. Jared Yee's story below proves a useful point: Many job seekers take their early work experiences for granted. If you reflect on them, you're bound to come up with an impressive incident. Note how he jumps right in the phrase "One time... "—a good hint that we're about to get a story of one especially challenging or interesting day or incident.

"One time at BJ's Wholesale Club where I worked, it was incredibly busy. All the lines at the registers were filled almost to the middle of the store. My supervisors were busy helping customers and the managers were too busy to assist customers. My supervisor told me to take over some of her responsibilities. She told me one of the freezers with dairy products was broken and that I needed to find one of the managers to fix the problem. She told me afterwards to help a customer with a problem she was having. I went to the produce section but the manager was busy. He told me to get another manager to handle the situation. This manager however, was unavailable to fix the freezer.

"I realized that the freezer would not get fixed for possibly hours. I took matters in to my own hands. I got three carriages from the parking lot, filled them with all the dairy products from the broken freezer, and brought them into the storage section of a nearby freezer. After that was resolved, I found the very frustrated customer who was trying to buy a computer and was in a rush because she had to pick up her daughter. The computer she wanted was not on the shelf but she wanted the one on display. I had dealt with a situation like this before but with a supervisor's help.

"However, due to the chaos within the store I was told to handle the situation on my own. I wrote down the codes of the computer she wanted, being unable to look it up on the system's computer because it was being used. I then went to the storage room and looked for the empty display box with the same code. I found it, went back down to the display shelf, and packed it along with all its parts in the box. I then assisted the customer bringing the computer to my register line, since all the others were filled and she was in a rush. The manager said this was alright to do because she had been waiting for a long time. After ringing up the customer's computer, she thanked me and said that I had 'saved her from a terrible day.'"

~ Jared Yee, Northeastern University Class of 2009

Jared picked this story because he wanted to show the ability to handle multiple projects at one time—a qualification for a job with Deloitte and Touche. However, Deloitte also seeks an excellent team player who is highly organized—two other qualities that this story captures. It also could be used to show an ability to work independently, persevere, and customer service—to name just a few qualities!

5. The next story is by Rebecca Harkess. As you read it, remember that the ultimate goal is to be able to write a story FIRST, and then to list at least THREE soft skills that the story could be used to prove about yourself. So as you read this story, try to think of all the different soft skills or qualities that Rebecca could use this story to prove during an interview:

> "At my high school they take their yearbook very seriously. The book is over 400 pages long, has an annual budget of over $200,000, and has won numerous national awards. There is typically an editorial staff of 2 editors-in-chief and 8 section editors, along with a staff of 30. My senior year our advisor asked if I would be willing to take on the position of editor in chief by myself as she did not feel anyone else was qualified for the job. I agreed and spent the summer before preparing the layout of the book, setting up our office and buying new equipment.
>
> "Our first deadline of around 80 pages was due in mid-October. I decided to tell the staff the deadline was at the end of September so we would have adequate editing time. The due date I set came and I went to collect layouts from my staff and found that only half had completed their layouts and even those were only mediocre. I went home that night feeling that I had already failed. I had nothing to work with and yet in a few weeks I was responsible for turning in 80 pages. No one had listened to the revisions I had made and I felt powerless.
>
> "I decided that I couldn't give up; I was going to get this book done and done right because I had been given the responsibility to do so. I stayed up almost the whole night and wrote a two-page speech to deliver to my staff the next morning. I knew I had to be careful to balance coming off as angry to get my point across that I was serious, but at the same time I did not want everyone to think that I was on a power trip, especially because a lot of these students were in my same grade and people I considered friends. On the way to class that day I stopped at the grocery store to buy some doughnuts for the staff as I knew this was a way to show that I really cared about them and that I wanted this to be an enjoyable experience.
>
> "I then sat everyone down and explained to them how I was very disappointed with the results I had seen and that they were unacceptable. I outlined a plan of how I wanted the layouts to get done including showing them new forms that I had created so that each student could review his or her own work before turning it in to me. I stressed the fact that I believed in the ability of each one of them and that I truly believed we could have a lot of fun and produce a

book that we would all be really proud of. I could tell when I was done that everyone seemed much more motivated; they really wanted to work hard as a team and get this done.

"Every deadline after that I almost always received layouts on time and in near perfect form. In addition, our staff really bonded throughout the year and we had a really great time. When the book came out at the end of the year we heard from countless students that of all the years this was their favorite yearbook. I felt so proud of the book and my staff."

~ Rebecca Harkess, Northeastern University Class of 2010

Rebecca's story is one of the best BBI stories that I've seen in a long time. Consider some of the elements: Even when she is giving background/overview to set up the critical moment of the story, we learn some things that are impressive about her. Due to the quantitative and qualitative details, we see that her editorial position was a high-stakes role.

The next great thing about this story is how well it conveys her thoughts, emotions, and actions as she encounters a major obstacle. We really know what it was like to be her in this role, and we have an appreciation for how seriously she took the failure that she faced. She proceeds to walk us through her thought process and actions in addressing the problem and carries it right through to the outcome. Just wonderful.

Better still, the story is one that Rebecca will have up her sleeve in case she needs to prove any number of qualities or soft skills: leadership, responsibility, conflict management, results orientation, interpersonal skills to name just a few!

6. The next story is from Cheyenne Olinde. This story is an almost fiendishly clever story for a Supply Chain Management (SCM) major to use in an interview. Cheyenne has never worked in corporate SCM... but this story absolutely will resonate with SCM professionals: After all, it entails meeting a logistical challenge—one that required consideration of manpower, equipment capabilities, delivery time, and so forth. So while the story illustrates many soft skills—see if you can spy them as you read—it is particularly smart in showing that he has an appreciation for what a SCM interviewer may want to know.

"As a combat photographer, I have been fortunate enough to document every aspect the Marine Corps has to offer. I have documented everything from aerial reconnaissance to autopsies. I have been deployed to Cuba, Spain, Seychelles, Malta, Greece, Italy, Puerto Rico, Djibouti Africa, and Wisconsin. The one thing that all my missions had in common was that I was serving a customer. Whether it was a Captain for a routine passport photo, or aerial photographs of a military base's security weakness for a General, I have always interacted with clients. Many times my customers would want certain photographs that were impractical and I would have to tactfully explain why their request would not work and offer a solution to solve their problem. Other times, I would get a call from an important client who needs an exceptional amount of work done in a very short window of time.

"When our Marines were preparing to go to Afghanistan, we had to provide them with the tools to help teach their Marines basic Arabic. Their request was for over 1000 instructional Arabic CDs, needed in less than seven days on top of the other 30 jobs we currently had. My shop had neither the manpower nor the equipment to handle the request, and the customer did not have the funds to go elsewhere. I had to make it work.

"The original CDs were provided; we just needed to make the copies. We only had the capability to copy 20 CDs an hour, plus the work could not interfere with our other jobs requested by my other customers.

"I implemented a split schedule of three eight and half hour shifts, operating non-stop. This allowed for the constant copying of CDs, and the continuous work on other current productions. Not only did we meet the goal in less than three days, we made an extra 500 for future operations and completed all the current productions in house.

"I approached my commanding officer and requested time off for the team after the hard work and dedication my Marines showed. I then had them all come over to my house and treated them to a BBQ to thank them. After that, there was nothing my Marines would not do for me, and superiors knew that there was no challenge too large I couldn't handle."

~ Cheyenne Olinde, Northeastern University Class of 2010

If I remember correctly, Cheyenne used this story to prove that he had good customer-service skills. While it does so, it also could be rolled out to illustrate problem-solving skills, leadership, and time management skills.

7. This story is from Matt Ray. Pay special attention to how his story reveals what kind of worker he is even though he is doing something that does not require much skill. Notice that a story does not need to long to demonstrate skills and attitude. In the last two sentences of this story, notice how Matt effectively identifies his soft skills and indicates how he will use them to benefit his new employer!

"Let me tell you about one of my final days working at TJT, a modular home trailer and axle trading company that picked up and delivered items all over Oregon. Unfortunately the tire and axle business was deteriorating and the location was closing. To complete the site closure my boss and I needed to load up roughly 5,000 tires onto truck-trailers for shipment. So, every day for two weeks, we worked together loading thousands of tires onto trucks, a tedious and repetitive task. When we were down to the last three rows of tires on the heap it turned out that they had no air in them and the bands that held them together were very loose. We didn't think this would be an issue and loaded the last of them onto the trailer. Not long after we left for the day I received a horrible phone call —the tires on the truck were still on it but they had swayed half way off the truck and were about to slide onto the road creating a serious road hazard. The truck was able to drive slowly back to our site and for the next 5 hours, after I had already worked a full 10-hour day, my boss and I re-banded every 1,200 of those tires and reloaded them onto the trailer. During that time I used my sense of humor to keep us motivated and help the time pass while making sure that the tires were properly banded so we would not need to do it again."

"As you can see I have a very strong work ethic, can be relied upon to go that extra mile to solve problems and I am one of those guys who is calm in the eye of the storm. Be assured, when I work for you I will contribute to your organization's success in a productive and collegial way."

~ Matt Ray, Lane Community College Class of 2011

Remember the rule: Use a specific, vivid story to prove that you have one great quality, and you'll wind up proving you have at least three other great qualities!

As described earlier in this appendix, write three stories showing you at your best. Then, read over your stories, and list three different transferable skills that each story could be used to prove.

As you look at a job description's qualifications, think of stories you might use to prove that you have those qualities. However, it's also worth your while to come up with situations that show you at your best, and THEN figure out various ways in which you could apply them in job interview situations. It's always smart to find opportunities to tell your best stories.

Once you have done this successfully, you should have a good collection of stories to bring your interview to life!

Appendix G

Resume Evaluation Rubric: Taking your Resume from Good to Great

Instructions: This is a simple tool designed to help you see if your resume is as good as it can be. The columns on the next pages are detailed lists for each level of resume from 'Beginning' to 'Exemplary.' To evaluate your own resume read all content in the boxes *across* each row and circle the bullet points that most closely match your resume. After you have done this on every page, scan all the pages to see which column has the most bullet points circled.

If most of your circled bullet points are primarily in the 'Beginning' and/or 'Developing' columns, you have work to do! If your circles are mostly in the 'Exemplary' column, you can have confidence your resume is a good one. On the other hand, if your circles are fairly evenly split between 'Accomplished' and 'Exemplary,' your resume is professional and useable but could be even better. Use the bullet points in the 'Exemplary' column as a guide for revising your resume to make it a great one.

USE BY FACULTY AND INSTRUCTORS

You can effectively use this rubric in two ways. First, as students are developing their resumes, have them refer to the 'Exemplary' column as a guide for best practice. After students have developed their resumes and turned them in for review, you can then use the rubric to provide individualized feedback—just copy a set for each student, put their name on the first page, circle the bullet points that reflect your evaluation of the resume and return to the student—quick, easy, and effective.

	EXEMPLARY	ACCOMPLISHED	DEVELOPING	BEGINNING
IMMEDIATE IMPRESSION	* Pleasing layout with not too much or too little blank space * Important points stand out	* Balanced use of text and white space.	* Somewhat poor balance of white space and text; may have too much or too little white space * Important information is somewhat difficult to find	* Very poor layout with highly unbalanced use of white space and text * Important information is very hard to find
HEADING	* Information is complete: name, mailing address, phone and e-mail * Name, phone # and e-mail are emphasized using larger font size & spacing * E-mail address is professional	* Information is complete: name, mailing address, phone and e-mail * Name, phone # and e-mail are evident in same or slightly larger type than text * E-mail address is professional	* Information is incomplete; may be missing mailing address, phone &/or e-mail * Font size is too small * E-mail address is cute, macho or a nickname	* Information is incomplete; may be missing mailing address, phone and/or e-mail * Font size is too small * E-mail address is silly provocative, cute, macho or a nickname
OBJECTIVE *Optional section of a resume*	* Features skills offered to employer specifically related to a position or job category * Free of clichés such as "benefit your organization" or "will be an asset"	* Clearly related to the type of job applying for * Position or job category applying for may be referred to * Free of clichés such as "benefit your organization" or "will be an asset"	* Vague, too general, lacks reference to job specific skills and/ or focuses on what you want rather than what you have to offer the employer * Includes clichés such as "I will benefit your organization" or "I will be an asset"	* Focuses only on what you want from a job. Includes language such as "challenging job that will use my skills and abilities with room for advancement"
SKILLS	* Three to five core skills essential for job are listed * Up-to-date computer skills including hardware/ software are included * Written in active voice using action verbs	* Skills list has three to eight items and some are not directly related to job * Skills are written with some variety of language	* Skills listed are good general skills however job specific skills are missing * Word usage is repetitive such as "able to..."	* No skills are listed

	EXEMPLARY	ACCOMPLISHED	DEVELOPING	BEGINNING
FORMAT & STYLE	* Headings utilize language appropriate to industry/career * Type size is 11pt or larger * Like items are written the same using current standards (two letter state abbreviations) * Employment information is formatted consistently for all jobs efficiently using space * Created originally as a regular Word document and is not from a template * Bullets, when used, are consistent, professional and businesslike * If a second page is used it includes a heading with "name and page 2" on it * Information that belongs on a Reference sheet is not on the resume (no employer addresses, phone #'s or supervisor names) * Appropriate use of capitals * Margins create an attractive, professional framing for content	* Headings are clear and are in appropriate order for job * Type size is 11pt or larger * Like items are written the same (all states are either written out or abbreviated) * Employment information is formatted consistently for all jobs * Is a regular Word document, and is not from a template * Bullets, when used, are consistent and appropriate * If a second page is used it includes a heading with "name and page 2" on it * Information that belongs on a Reference sheet is not on the resume (no employer addresses, phone #'s or supervisor names) * The phrase "References available upon request" is not used anywhere on the resume * Appropriate use of capitals * Margins are appropriate for content	* Some headings are used * Type is smaller than 11pt or too large * Like items are inconsistently written (for example state is written both as OR and Oregon) * Employment information is inconsistently formatted * A template has been used to created resume * Bullets are of inconsistent size and spacing * Resume may have dense paragraphs with lengthy job descriptions * Full sentences may have been used in job descriptions and/or objective * Margins are a poor choice; may be somewhat too large or too small * Some information that belongs on a reference sheet is listed such as employer address, zip code, and/or phone number	* Headings are repeated (such as Experience & Work History) or are missing * Type for content (not headings) is too small or too large * Like items are inconsistently written (for example the name of the state is not written the same each time) * Employment information is inconsistently formatted, disorganized and in no particular order * Resume has been created using a template * Full sentences may have been used in job descriptions and/or objective * Words are capitalized inappropriately * Margins are very large or much too small * Complete employer information has been listed such as address, zip code, and/or phone number

	EXEMPLARY	ACCOMPLISHED	DEVELOPING	BEGINNING
CONTENT	* Details within each section are focused and highly appropriate to the job being sought * Numeration of details is evident and appropriate * The sequence of information in the job descriptions start with 1) most related to position seeking and 2) most complex/ highest level of skills * GPA of 3.O or higher is listed * Job history does not go back farther than 10 years unless there is a compelling reason to do so (includes a job 15 years ago in a related field) * College information is complete and prominently featured especially if changing careers; expected graduation date may be included * High school graduation date only listed if it won't contribute to age discrimination * Within job descriptions, very low skilled duties such as sweeping floors or cleaning are not listed * Accomplishments are clearly identified showing how you made $, saved $ or saved time for company	* Details within each section are adequate and appropriate * GPA of 3.O or higher may be included * Job history does not go back farther than 10 years unless there is a compelling reason to do so (includes a job 15 years ago in a related field) * Some college information is included and is complete * High school graduation date only listed if it won't contribute to age discrimination * Job information in job description includes reasonable amount of detail * Within job descriptions, very low skilled duties such as sweeping floors or cleaning are not listed * Interests and volunteer work may be listed – job related items are emphasized and/or activities of common interest such as hiking/ biking/camping	* Some detail is listed in each section * Job history is only a list of employers/ dates with no information about skills and abilities used on the job * Job history may have incomplete entries; city & state for employers may be missing * College information is incomplete or inaccurate (name of degree is incorrect, missing information) * The phrase "References available upon request" is used * Reasons for loss of job are indicated such as "fired" or "conflict with supervisor/co-workers" *Includes content such as dates or affiliation that might contribute to hiring discrimination	* Details are listed in no particular order * Job history is missing or very general * No job descriptions or job titles are indicated; only employers are listed, often with incomplete information * There is no reference to current college enrollment or course work * The phrase "References available upon request" is used * Reasons for loss of job are indicated such as "fired" or "conflict with supervisor/co-workers" *Includes content such as dates or affiliations that might contribute to hiring discrimination *Includes negative information such as 'did not graduate from high school'

	EXEMPLARY	ACCOMPLISHED	DEVELOPING	BEGINNING
CONTENT (Continued)	* Additional information is included such as foreign languages skills, memberships, or that you financially supported yourself through school * Interests and volunteer work is listed – job related items are emphasized and/or activities of common interest such as hiking/ biking/camping			
WORD CHOICE	* There is clarity, variety and consistent parallel phrasing (nouns, present or past tense verbs within a section); gerunds (ing's) are avoided or limited * Job descriptions begin with action verbs * There are no pronouns or complete sentences * Content is positively phrased * The tone of the narrative reflects confidence, seriousness, truthfulness and professionalism * Free of jargon unless appropriate	* There is clarity, variety and consistent parallel phrasing (ing's, nouns, present or past tense verbs within a section) * Job descriptions begin with action verbs * There is no use of "I" or "my" in any part of the resume with no complete sentences. * All content is positively phrased * Free of most jargon unless appropriate	* All job descriptions are written in present tense or mixed tense within one job description * The words "I" and/ or "my" are used * Some inappropriate abbreviations and jargon are used * Poor grammar is used * Repeated use of words such as "duties included…" or "responsibilities included…"	* The words "I" and/ or "my" are used * Extensive use of abbreviations and jargon * Poor grammar is used * One or more job descriptions are written identically
SPELLING & PUNCTUATION	* Free of spelling errors * Punctuation is consistent * Appropriate use of capitals	* Free of spelling errors * Punctuation is consistent * Appropriate use of capitals	* One or two spelling and/or punctuation errors are in document * Words are capitalized inappropriately	* Document contains multiple spelling and punctuation errors * Words are capitalized inappropriately